One Less H‹

101

Internationale Forschungen zur
Allgemeinen und
Vergleichenden Literaturwissenschaft

In Verbindung mit

Norbert Bachleitner (Universität Wien), Dietrich Briesemeister (Friedrich Schiller-Universität Jena), Francis Claudon (Université Paris XII), Joachim Knape (Universität Tübingen), Klaus Ley (Johannes Gutenberg-Universität Mainz), John A. McCarthy (Vanderbilt University), Alfred Noe (Universität Wien), Manfred Pfister (Freie Universität Berlin), Sven H. Rossel (Universität Wien)

herausgegeben von

Alberto Martino
(Universität Wien)

Redaktion: Ernst Grabovszki

Anschrift der Redaktion:
Institut für Vergleichende Literaturwissenschaft, Berggasse 11/5, A-1090 Wien

One Less Hope

Essays on Twentieth-Century Russian Poets

Constantin V. Ponomareff

Amsterdam - New York, NY 2006

Le papier sur lequel le présent ouvrage est imprimé remplit les prescriptions de "ISO 9706:1994, Information et documentation - Papier pour documents - Prescriptions pour la permanence".

The paper on which this book is printed meets the requirements of " ISO 9706:1994, Information and documentation - Paper for documents - Requirements for permanence".

Die Reihe „Internationale Forschungen zur Allgemeinen und Vergleichenden Literaturwissenschaft" wird ab dem Jahr 2005 gemeinsam von Editions Rodopi, Amsterdam – New York und dem Weidler Buchverlag, Berlin herausgegeben. Die Veröffentlichungen in deutscher Sprache erscheinen im Weidler Buchverlag, alle anderen bei Editions Rodopi.

From 2005 onward, the series „Internationale Forschungen zur Allgemeinen und Vergleichenden Literaturwissenschaft" will appear as a joint publication by Editions Rodopi, Amsterdam – New York and Weidler Buchverlag, Berlin. The German editions will be published by Weidler Buchverlag, all other publications by Editions Rodopi.

Cover art: Alexa Ponomareff

ISBN: 90-420-1979-4
©Editions Rodopi B.V., Amsterdam - New York, NY 2006
Printed in The Netherlands

Contents

Introduction

1

The lives of too many of the major Russian poets of the twentieth century were tragic. One common cause of their tragedy was political, in that the Russian revolution of 1917 and the totalitarian order that it brought into power, put political demands on their poetry which interfered with the natural flow of their creative development.

This collection of essays concerns itself with twelve major Russian poets who were not willing – some earlier, some later – to let political ideology dictate their poetic work. In so doing, they left a significant mark on the history of twentieth-century Russian poetry.

The political impact of Soviet Russian totalitarianism on these poets forced them into internal or external exile which, more often than not, brought persecution, death or suicide in its wake, and homelessness, poverty and misery, coupled with a profound sense of isolation and loneliness. Though they belonged to the most important poetic modernist movements of their time – to symbolism, acmeism, futurism and imagism – they were, one and all, exemplary of Osip Mandelshtam's definition of poetry as expressing each poet's "consciousness of his or her own rightness"[1] to follow their own individual creative paths.

They paid a heavy price for this sense of poetic rightness and its consequences in a merciless totalitarian world at home, or in other exclusive social environments abroad. Vladimir Mayakovsky, Segey Esenin and Marina Tsvetaeva committed suicide. Nikolay Gumilev died in front of a Bolshevik firing squad. Mandelshtam perished in a Soviet concentration camp. Alexander Blok, mentally and spiritually distraught, died, in his own words, from the lack of creative freedom. And though Anna Akhmatova and Boris Pasternak survived Stalin's reign of terror which ended with his death in 1953, they remained inner émigrés in their own country. Pasternak was literally hounded to death by the communist regime after being awarded the Nobel Prize in 1958 for his novel *Doctor Zhivago*. Akhmatova too, though she was honoured with the Taormina Prize for Poetry in Italy in 1964, and with an honorary degree from Oxford in 1965, just before her death in 1966,

---

1 Osip Mandelshtam, *Sobranie sochineniy,* edited by G. P. Struve and B. A. Filippov (3 vols.; Washington, 1967-71), II, 236. Further references to this edition will be given in the text as Ma. The translations are mine.

did not escape the ever watchful censorship of her work by a hostile regime. Vyacheslav Ivanov, Marina Tsvetaeva, Vladislav Khodasevich and Boris Poplavsky chose exile in the West after the Revolution of 1917, an exile which brought them renewed isolation in the politicized and polarized atmosphere of Russian émigré life, and Joseph Brodsky, much later, was officially exiled to the West in 1972 for his poetic "dissidence". He was, after Pasternak, the only exile poet to receive world-wide recognition when he became the recipient of the Nobel Prize in 1987.[2]

2

The essays in this collection represent a close metaphorical reading of the poets concerned, and were written with a view to exploring the poetic and psychological meaning of their texts. This metaphorical approach has at times harvested interesting shifts in focus away from established critical interpretations of these poets' works.

The poets before us were all caught between cultures and were at the mercy of, or out of tune with their political and/or social environments be they in or outside of the Soviet Union. Still, what united them was a common artistic and cultural heritage which we might identify as European modernist.

In the Russian cultural context they remind us most of all of Russian pre-revolutionary modernism, and especially symbolism, of which the symbolist Blok is a poetic touchstone. Whether they were in Russia or abroad in Western Europe, each of these poets in their own way became estranged and alienated from their social environment, sought refuge in their poetry which functioned as a mirror of their inner selves. Their idealization of poetry or – as in Khodasevich's, Esenin's or even in Brodsky's case – their poetic *disillusionment,* and their intense poetic consciousness, had much in common with the acute romantic sensibility and poetic experience of the Russian symbolists. Even their *thirst* for God (to use Rimbaud's word) or for a transcendental realm, or for another compensatory moral, spiritual or aesthetic reality, connected them to Russia's far-reaching symbolist adventure.

But the poets under consideration here were not only the spiritual offspring of Russian symbolism. They were also highly gifted original poets, and they used the remarkable power of their poetry to witness and to counter the descent into human nightmare and desolation. They have much to tell us about totalitarianism in the 20th century and its tragic spiritual consequences

---

2   See Roman Jakobson, "On a Generation That Squandered Its Poets," (1931) in *Major Soviet Writers. Essays in Criticism,* Edited by Edward J. Brown (London/Oxford/New York, 1973), pp. 7-32.

as reflected in their poetry. Indeed, because poetry, in Edith Hamilton's words, can help us sometimes to overcome tragedy and survive, – "For tragedy is nothing less than the pain transmuted into exaltation by the alchemy of poetry,"[3] – their poems are truly a special gift to us, holding perhaps the power to heal.

The essays end with a cultural perspective that provides a wider context for twentieth-century Russian poetry.

I would like to express my gratitude to professors Dr. Alberto Martino, the series editor of IFAVL, and to Dr. Norbert Bachleitner of the University of Vienna for their unflagging support of my work over the past few years. I would also like to thank Ernst Grabovszki for his fine work in formatting my manuscript. As always, I owe much to my wife Barbara for her loving, patient and critical eye.

---

3   Edith Hamilton, *The Greek Way to Western Civilization* (New York, 1960), p. 165.

Conscience in Anna Akhmatova's Poetic Work

> Thus conscience does make cowards of us all;
>
> Shakespeare: *Hamlet, Prince of Denmark*

> Odnoy nadezhdoy men'she stalo,
> Odnoyu pesney bol'she budet.
>
> (April, 1915)
>
> One less hope becomes
> One more song.[4]
>
> Anna Akhmatova: *White Flock*

Introduction

In the year that Akhmatova was born, Anton Chekhov published a story he called *Pripadok* (Paroxism) which, in an autobiographical sense, recreated in the central character Vasil'ev, Chekhov's own agonized sense of the pain of human existence.

Akhmatova's poetic work with its affinity for human pain connects her to Chekhov's writing. Perhaps this is not surprising if one remembers that her close friend Osip Mandelshtam – and with him the critic Viktor Zhirmunsky – believed her poetic work in its complexity and depth to be closer to the psychological sensibility of such nineteenth-century writers as Turgenev, Dostoevsky and Leo Tolstoy. In fact, Mandelshtam believed that Akhmatova owed her very creative existence to these writers rather than to any other poetic forerunners: "'The genesis of Akhmatova lies in Russian prose, not poetry.'"[5] One might agree with this evaluation of Akhmatova's poetic sensibility, if it did not exclude the poet Alexander Pushkin.

---

4   The translation is by Judith Hemschemeyer.
5   Quoted in V. M. Zhirmunsky, *Tvorchestvo Anny Akhmatovoy* (Leningrad, 1973), p. 45.

Evening and *Rosary*

Akhmatova's first two books of love lyrics published before the outbreak of World War I – *Vecher* (Evening, 1912) and *Chetki* (Rosary, 1914) – made an impact on Russian society with their haunting images of abandoned love. But they were, in retrospect, too emotionally self-centred to serve the spiritual needs of an impending barbaric age. It was, perhaps, the *personal experience of pain* in these two volumes of poetry which would help her transcend the eroticism of her poetry and move her onto a much more profound level of poetic consciousness:

> Slava tebe, bezyskhodnaya bol'![6]
> (Hail to thee, everlasting pain!)

White Flock

Akhmatova had married the Acmeist poet Nikolay Gumilev in the spring of 1910, but divorced him in 1918. Their only son, Lev, born in 1912, spent most of his time with Gumilev's mother at her estate in Slepnevo.[7] It was there, on a visit in the summer of 1915, that Akhmatova wrote a poem to Gumilev who had volunteered for army service. One of its lines carried the name of her next collection of poems, *Belaya Staya* (White Flock, 1917: I, 460).

This third collection of her poetry gives us occasional glimpses of a more mature poet at work, though an increasingly repetitive and by now monotonous prevalence of love motifs – the emotional vibrancy of her first two collections having been lost – runs interference. Nor do the intermittent religious motifs or the echoes of contemporary war and death undercut the general monotony of the whole.

But there *are* new aspects to her collection. The most central seems to be the romantic conceit that the poet's memory, though a burden, is both witness and prophetic receptacle of impending catastrophe. And it was again in Slepnevo, in the summer of 1916, that she wrote:

> Iz pamyati, kak gruz otnyne lishniy,
> Ischezli teni pesen i strastey.

---

6 I have used *The Complete Poems of Anna Akhmatova,* Translated by Judith Hemschemeyer, Edited and with an Introduction by Roberta Reeder (2 vols.; Somerville, Massachusetts, 1990), I, 258. The translations are Judith Hemschemeyer's unless otherwise indicated. Any further references to quotations from this collection will be given in the text and footnotes.

7 See, for example, Roberta Reeder, "Mirrors and Masks: The Life and Poetic Works of Anna Akhmatova," in *ibid.,*pp. 21- 183, here pp. 51, 52, 73.

Ey – opustevshey – prikazal Vsevyshniy
Stat' strashnoy knigoy grozovykh vestey. (I, 450)
(And the shadows of song and passion/ Have disappeared from memory like an unwanted burden./ And God has ordered this now emptied memory/ To become the frightening book of dreadful events.) *My translation*

Somehow, this now emptied memory – emptied of her first two collections of poems – could finally begin to be charged with a deep sense of guilt. In the autumn of 1916 she wrote:

I tol'ko sovest' s kazhdym dnem strashney
Besnuetsya: velikoy khochet dani. (I, 392)
(And only conscience rages more terribly/ With each new day: it wants huge tribute.) *My translation*

Plantain

Akhmatova's next collection of poems *Podorozhnik* (Plantain) which appeared in 1921, strikes one as if her poetic vision had been arrested in flight. Perhaps the choice of title was fitting for the seeming impasse she had reached: for, one of the other meanings of *podorozhnik* suggests someone who is on the road, but has not yet reached her destination.

And indeed, Akhmatova's attempt to ride out her old erotic imagery – be it in new and even profound love relationships – led nowhere, all the more since the "erotic" images of *Plantain* could hardly have captured the reality of the civil war years.

But there were a few, perhaps unguarded, moments when a much more sombre poetic vision broke through her poetic camouflage. It was again in Slepnevo, in July of 1917, that she wrote the lines

Ne laski zhdu ya, ne lyubovnoy lesti
V predchuvstvii neotvratimoy t'my, (I, 512)
(I do not wait for tenderness, or love's flattery,/ Overcome as I am by a foreboding of inevitable darkness) *My translation*

Once again, in the winter of 1919, she wrote

A zdes' uzh belaya doma krestami metit
I klichet voronov, I vorony letyat. (I, 518)
(White death already marks the houses with her crosses/ And calls her ravens, and the ravens come) *My translation*

These lines are much closer to the mark of a revolutionary time.

Anno Domini MCMXXI

In the year of our Lord 1922, Akhmatova published her *Anno Domini MCMXXI*. This book of poems, following so closely on the heels of *Plantain,* expressed her grief and lament over Gumilev's death, who had been executed by the Soviets in the summer of 1921.

In Gumilev's last book of poems *Ognennyy Stolp* (Pillar of Fire) published shortly after his death – a book that Akhmatova considered his best[8] – there is a poem called "*Dusha i Telo*" (*Soul and Body*) – which captured well Gumilev's conflict between the ideal and the real, or between the romantic exoticism of his poetry and the realism behind the Acmeist aesthetic.[9]

This was a conflict not unfamiliar to Akhmatova herself. In *Anno Domini MCMXXI,* we see movement away from her former romantic self towards a more realistic awareness of life. One can trace this shift in two of her poems. In the one, with its well-known first line "Vse raskhishcheno, predano, prodano," (Everything has been plundered, betrayed, sold out, I, 578), which she wrote in the early summer of 1921, before Gumilev's execution, the conflict seemed resolved in favour of some Symbolist ideal. In the other, at the very end of the cycle, written in September of 1922, Akhmatova seemed to be in the process of transcending her former romantic subjectivism and becoming a kind of collective social conscience in historical time. The poem was duly entitled "Mnogim" (To the Many):

> Ya – golos vash, zhar vashego dykhan'ya,
> Ya – otrazhenie vashego litsa, (I, 618)
> (I am your voice, the fever of your breathing,/ I am the reflection of your face,/)
> *My translation*

She was now on her way to writing her *Requiem* and her *Poem without a Hero.* But, as irony would have it, these most important poems of her life would, in the end effect, continue, in different form, the personal and intimate theme of her life and work – conscience.

The Reed

From 1925 to 1940 Akhmatova's poetry was officially banned as unsuitable to the political dictates of the Soviet totalitarian state. Apart from her longer

---

8   See Lidiya Chukovskaya, *Zapiski ob Anne Akhmatovoy, Volume I, 1938-1941* (Paris, 1976), I, 35.

9   See N. Gumilev, *Sobranie Sochineniy,* edited by G.P. Struve and B.A. Filippov (4 vols.; Washington,1962-68), II, 40.

poem *Requiem,* only some thirty-three poems have come down to us from this period. She called them *Trostnik* (The Reed), which is a suggestive metaphor for survival while being submerged. These poems were only published in the summer of 1940 as part of her *Iz shesti knig* (From Six Books), a collection of poems which, however, was almost immediately withdrawn from circulation. Still, *The Reed* was a milestone in Akhmatova's creative development.

Since Akhmatova is known to have destroyed many of her poems as politically and, therefore, personally dangerous during the time that she was out of favour, her extant poems in this collection do not present a poetic whole and seem disparate. *The Reed* is interspersed, however, with poems on her creative process, which are in turn connected to the theme of conscience and guilt (II, 90, 122), whose burden she must now carry:

> Ya govoryu: "Tvoe nesu ya bremya
> Tyazheloe, ty znaesh', skol'ko let".
> No dlya nee ne sushchestvuet vremya,
> I dlya nee prostranstva v mire net. (II, 82)
> (I say: "I've been carrying your/ Heavy burden, you know, for so many years." / But for it [conscience] time does not exist,/ And for it there is no space [in this world].

The realm of conscience was, in fact, a poetic space: "Chtob ne spugnut' prostranstva chutkiy son." (II, 84) (So as not to disturb the light sleep [or "the sensitive dream"] of space). Akhmatova's poetry now resounded in a *new* space:

> Za to, chto mir napolnil novym zvonom
> V prostranstve novom otrazhennykh strof, – (II,86)
> (Because he [the poet] filled the world with the new sound/ Of his verse reverberating in new space –)

Requiem

This new space of conscience and guilt in the two poems above – written in the mid-thirties – began to be filled in by her longer poem *Requiem* which she wrote between 1935 and 1940. It was first published abroad in 1963 in an unauthorized edition in Munich, Germany. It took another quarter century for it to be published in Russia in 1987.[10]

Akhmatova's *Requiem,* a lament over her son's arrest in 1938, may already have been triggered by his first arrest and release in the spring of 1934.

---

10 *Tsarstvennoe slovo. Akhmatovskie chteniya. Vypusk I* RAN IMLI (Moscow, 1992), p. 175.

There is little doubt that Akhmatova had neglected her son when she left him as a child in the care of her mother-in-law. On a number of occasions in her poetry she saw herself as an unfit mother. Nor was she the marrying kind: her three failed marriages to Gumilev, then to the Assyriologist Vladimir Shileyko, and then her common-law marriage to the art historian and critic, Nikolay Punin, proved that.

We know far too little about her relationship to her son during his child-hood years at his grandmother's estate in Slepnevo from 1911 to 1917. For example, in her autobiographical notes written in 1957, in the section on Slepnevo there is *not one mention* of her son, it is as if he did not exist.[11] Yet when he was arrested for a second time in March of 1938 and released only seventeen months later, it was Akhmatova who kept vigil, day in and day out, in the long lines of women waiting to hear any news of their loved ones imprisoned by the Soviet regime.

His father's execution in 1921 and, one might add, his mother's officially banned poetry, cast a long shadow on the tragic life of their son, Lev Gumilev. After his second release from prison, he lived in exile until 1944. He volunteered for army service at that time, but was rearrested after the war in 1949, and not released until February of 1956 which coincided with Khrushchev's destalinization speech. Notwithstanding all her efforts on his behalf in the 1930s and later on, he seems to have never forgiven her.

In respect to Lev Gumilev, Jelena Kusmina spoke of what psychologists today would call a post-traumatic stress disorder which must have afflicted all those returning from the Stalinist concentration camps. And she quoted Lidiya Chukovskaya to the effect that Lev's feeling of neglect as a child contributed to his own sense of abandonment and lack of self-esteem. His resentment of his mother, in Chukovskaya's eyes, explained why even on his return in 1956 and after, he avoided his mother and continued to believe that she had actually done nothing on his behalf while he was in prison.[12] György Dalos, in his remarkable study of Akhmatova's relationship with Isaiah Berlin, described her son as emotionally crippled as a result of his perception of having been neglected by his mother. And Akhmatova herself, Dalos

---

11   *Anna Akhmatova and her Circle,* Compilation and Notes by Konstantin Polivanov, Trans-lated from the Russian by Patricia Beriozkina (Fayetteville, 1994), pp. 1-50, here pp. 12-14.

12   See Jelena Kusmina, *Anna Achmatova. Ein Leben im Unbehausten,* translated from the Russian by Swetlana Geier (Berlin, 1993), pp. 280-81. See also Solomon Volkov, *Conversations with Joseph Brodsky. A Poet's Journey through the Twentieth Century,* Translated by Marian Schwartz with Photographs by Marianna Volkov (New York, *et al.,* 1998), pp. 228, 236-37.

added, was haunted by guilt.[13] This recalls Akhmatova's words in the poem after her son's arrest:

U menya segodnya mnogo dela :
Nado pamyat' do kontsa ubit',
Nado, chtob dusha okamenela,
Nado snova nauchit'sya zhit', – (II, 104)
(Today I have so much to do:/ I must kill memory once and for all,/ I must turn my soul to stone,/ I must learn to live again –)

Though Akhmatova alluded a couple of times to the fact that *Requiem* was the expression of the collective Russian experience (II, 110, 112), the major thrust in the poem was a lament over her son's fate and the state of her spiritual being.

From this vantage point, *Requiem* has always been overestimated especially in the West – perhaps for political reasons – as the collective outcry of an oppressed Russia. Indeed, it was Akhmatova herself who contributed to this interpretation of the poem – she was, in any case, forever filing away at and rearranging her poems – by writing two prefaces to *Requiem* years later, in 1957 and 1961 (See II,94).

Poem without a Hero

During the Second World War Akhmatova was evacuated from Leningrad in 1941, ending up in Tashkent, where she remained until her return to her beloved city in the summer of 1944. But in 1946 she again fell into official disfavour, and it was only in 1958 that she was able to publish a heavily censored collection of poems. It was her *Poema bez geroya* (Poem without a Hero, 1940-62) however, – first published in the Soviet Union in 1976 – which would become her greatest poetic legacy to Russian culture.

David Wells quite rightly saw the *Poem without a Hero* as autobiographical from beginning to end and the theme of guilt as central to the poem.[14] And speaking of the years 1941-56, Amanda Haight also singled out guilt as an endemic part of Akhmatova's personality:

---

13 György Dalos, *Der Gast aus der Zukunft. Anna Achmatova und Sir Isaiah Berlin. Eine Liebesgeschichte,* in collaboration with Andrea Dunai, German revision by Elsbeth Zylla (Hamburg, 1996), pp. 126-29.

14 David N. Wells, *Anna Akhmatova. Her Poetry* (Oxford-Washington D.C., 1996), p. 115.

Akhmatova again experienced that feeling of guilt that she always seemed to carry with her: guilt at being the person she was, from whom however there was no escape.[15]

The autobiographical sweep of the poem is perhaps even contained in the title: for it *was* a poem without a hero, since at the centre of it stood the poet, Akhmatova, the "heroine". Akhmatova herself pointed to this autobiographical sweep when she said of the poem's gestation period:

It is impossible to determine when I began to hear the poem within me. It may have been when I was standing with my companion on Nevsky Prospekt (after a dress rehearsal of the *Masquerade,* February 25, 1917) …[16]

Akhmatova and Pushkin

Although there are many inter-textual allusions to other writers and poets in Akhmatova's later works – particularly to Dostoevsky, Blok, Mayakovsky, Dante and Shakespeare, among others[17] – it was Pushkin in particular who captured her poetic imagination.

The crucial importance of the theme of conscience and guilt in Pushkin's work bears a direct relation to Akhmatova's *Poem without a Hero.* Inna Chechelnitsky wrote a pivotal paper on Akhmatova and Pushkin:

In Akhmatova, the Silver Age found its final truth, the truth of conscience. And it is not by accident, of course, that conscience is the sole hero of her poetry and of the wonderful *Poem without a Hero.* In 1966, A. Pavlovsky wrote in his book on Akhmatova that "unbridled conscience … in *Poem without a Hero* organized the entire action, theme, and all the inner turns of the work."[18]

Chechelnitsky went on to suggest that it was especially in Pushkin's *Little Tragedies* that Akhmatova found the "inner hidden theme" of conscience:[19]

---

15 Amanda Haight, *Anna Akhmatova. A Poetic Pilgrimage* (Oxford-New York, 1990), p. 133.

16 Anna Akhmatova, *My Half Century. Selected Prose,* Edited by Ronald Meyer (Ann Arbor, 1992), p. 127.

17 See Susan Amert, *In a Shattered Mirror. The Later Poetry of Anna Akhmatova* (Stanford, CA, 1992).

18 Inna Chechelnitsky, "Akhmatova and Pushkin: *Apologia Pro Vita Sua,*" in *Anna Akhmatova 1889-1989. Papers from the Akhmatova Centennial Conference, Bellagio Study and Conference Center, June 1989,* Edited by Sonia I. Ketchian in *Modern Russian Literature and Culture Studies and Texts,* Vol. 28 (Berkeley, 1993), pp. 29-42, here p. 29.

19 *Ibid.,* p. 30.

> In Akhmatova's formulation the *Little Tragedies* are a "dramatic embodiment of Pushkin's inner personality." ... Akhmatova writes that the *Little Tragedies* not only pose "immense moral problems," but most of all reveal the secret confession of the poet to himself.[20]

One might say that Pushkin was, in a sense, to Akhmatova, what Alexander Radishchev had been once to Pushkin.[21] Indeed, Akhmatova's work on Pushkin[22] served her well, providing her with psychological insight into herself as the author of *Poem without a Hero.* The vital point of attraction for Akhmatova was Pushkin's troubled conscience which found obsessive and profound reflection in his *Little Tragedies.* Not too surprisingly, it was Pushkin's *Kamennyy gost'* (The Stone Guest) with its themes of love and retribution, guilt and atonement, which fascinated her most of all.

Isaiah Berlin

Isaiah Berlin in his memoir of Anna Akhmatova, said of her *Poem without a Hero* that it was "a mysterious and deeply evocative work," but that "A tumulous of learned commentary is inexorably rising over it. Soon it may be buried under its weight." (II, 30)

He suggested, furthermore, that the poem could only be understood in the context of both Akhmatova's life (II, 33) and her literary biography (II, 35). Akhmatova herself emphasized the personal and autobiographical aspects of her poem:

> I asked her if she would ever annotate the *Poem Without a Hero:* the allusions might be unintelligible to those who did not know the life it was connected with; did she wish them to remain in darkness? She answered that when those who knew the world about which she spoke were overtaken by senility or death, the poem would die too; it would be buried with her and her century; it was not written for eternity, nor even for posterity: the past alone had significance for poets – childhood most of all – those were the emotions that they wished to re-create and relive. (II, 41)

Akhmatova said this to Berlin in the spring of 1965 during her visit to Oxford to receive an honorary degree.

And so, as surely as Pushkin used his poetry to express his personal moral dilemmas – and Akhmatova read him "constantly" (II, 41) – her *Poem without a Hero* had a similar function for her. Her continuous allusions in the poem to Pushkin's work and, in particular, to his *Little Tragedies,* created a

---

20 *Ibid.,* p.36.

21 See P. N. Sakulin, *Pushkin I Radishchev. Novoe reshenie starogo voprosa* (Moscow, 1920).

22 See Akhmatova, *My Half Century, op. cit.,* pp. 145-214.; see also Anna Akhmatova, *Sochineniya,* vol. 3, edited by G. P. Struve, N. A. Struve, B. A. Filippov, (Paris, 1983),pp. 169-318.

reciprocal context in which she, by alluding to Pushkin's poetry, could at the same time express metaphorically and indirectly her own moral concerns. As Akhmatova herself pointed out, the real meaning of the poem lay not *in,* but beyond its complexity. Thus, in her "In Place of a Foreword" to the poem, she wrote: "Nikakikh tret'ikh, sed'mykh i dvadtsat' devyatykh smyslov poema ne soderzhit" (II, 400), (The poem does not have any third, seventh, or twenty-ninth meanings).

Leitmotifs, Dedications, Introductions, Subtitles

The leitmotif of the *Poem without a Hero* evoked Pushkin's little tragedy *The Stone Guest*: "Di rider finirai/ Pria dell' aurora" (You will stop laughing before dawn, II, 396). This reference to Mozart's *Don Giovanni* even suggested furthermore, in an indirect way, Pushkin's other little tragedy *Mozart and Salieri.*

The poem's "Third and Last" dedication written on the sixth of January, 1956, the Day of the Three Kings, was essentially dedicated to Akhmatova's relationship with Isaiah Berlin. But its references to the Russian tradition of fortune-telling on New Year's Eve (II, 406) set the theme of guilt and conscience in motion, a theme that was to be sustained throughout the poem.

S. P. Il'ev, speaking of New Year's Eve divinations, while looking into a mirror flanked by two burning candles, quoted the ancient Russian saying that "' ... kto zrit' v zertsalo, toy vidit' svoya grekhi ...'"[23] (Whoever looks into the mirror, sees his or her sins; my translation). Akhmatova herself reminded the reader of her poem that "The feeling of New Year's Eve and Christmas Eve is the *axis* on which the whole thing revolves ..."[24] (Akhmatova's italics).

Thus, the setting of the poem suggested that the whole festive occasion had to do with guilt and conscience. Even the poem's subtitle "A Petersburg Tale" alluded to Pushkin's poem *The Bronze Horseman* (II, 410), thus reemphasizing the theme of conscience. The brief Introduction to the poem, written out of a besieged Leningrad in the summer of 1941 – shades of Pushkin's *Pir vo vremya chumy* (The Feast during the Plague) – also brought to mind Pushkin's little tragedy *Skupoy rytsar'* (The Covetous Knight),

---

23 S. P. Il'ev, "'Peterburgskie povesti' Andreya Belogo i Anny Akhmatovoy (*Peterburg – Poema bez geroya)*" in *Tsarstvennoe slovo, op. cit.,* p. 154.
24 In *My Half Century, op. cit.,* p. 137.

especially the knight's memorable soliloquy on conscience, as he surveyed his ill-begotten riches in his vaulted cellar:[25]

> IZ GODA SOROKOVOGO
> KAK S BASHNI, NA VSE GLYAZHU.
> …
> KAK BUDTO PEREKRESTILAS'
> I POD TEMNYE SVODY SKHOZHU. (II, 408; Akhmatova's capitalization)
> (FROM THE YEAR NINETEEN FORTY/ AS IF FROM A TOWER, I SURVEY EVERYTHING./ … AS IF CROSSING MYSELF/ AND THEN DESCENDING TO DARK VAULTS.)

In a poem of 1940 "Podval pamyati" (The Cellar of Memory), she had been even more direct about this connection to Pushkin:

> No sushchiy vzdor, chto ya zhivu grustya
> I chto menya vospominan'e tochit.
> Ne chasto ya u pamyati v gostyakh,
> Da i ona menya vsegda morochit.
> Kogda spuskayus' s fonarem v podval,
> Mne kazhetsya – opyat' glukhoy obval
> Uzhe po uzkoy lestnitse grokhochet.
> Chadit fonar', vernut'sya ne mogu, (II, 124)
> (But it is pure nonsense, that I live grieving/ And that reminiscence gnaws at me./ I don't often visit memory/ And it always surprises me./ When I descend with a lamp to the cellar,/ It seems to me – a landslide/ Rumbles again on the narrow stairs./ The lamp smokes, I can't turn back,)

Part One, Chapter One

The second epigraph to chapter one also recalled the New Year's Eve divinations of Tatyana in Pushkin's *Evgeny Onegin,* and the third epigraph, taken from Byron's *Don Juan,* once again harked back to the theme of guilt and conscience in *The Stone Guest* II, 410).

Akhmatova, too, like Pushkin's Don Juan pulled down to hell by the statue of Doña Anna's husband, felt herself turning to stone, freezing and burning as her doorbell rang announcing the arrival of her New Year's Eve guests, who all were shades:

> I ya slyshu zvonok protyazhnyy,
> I ya chuvstvuyu kholod vlazhnyy,

---

25 See Eugene M. Kayden's marvellous translation of scene II of *The Covetous Knight* in Alexander Pushkin, *Little Tragedies* (Yellow Springs, Ohio, 1965), pp. 13-17.

Kameneyu, stynu, goryu … (II, 412)
(And I hear the insistent bell,/ And I break into a cold sweat,/ I turn to stone, I freeze, I burn …)

Her ghostly guests all turned out to be either associated with New Year's Eve, like doctor Dapertutto, or they carried a heavy burden of guilt, like Faust, Don Juan, Hamlet and Dorian Gray, among others (II, 412). But it was especially she herself who needed to "ask forgiveness for an old sin" (Zamalivat' davniy grekh, II, 414); and, it was probably herself as that "goat-legged nymph" (Kozlonoguyu, II, 412), who was associated with the "Prince of Darkness" who, like Mephisto in Goethe's *Faust,* also limped (II, 414). Small wonder, if she did not want to meet her former self until the Last Judgement, which was close at hand:

S toy kakoyu byla kogda-to,
 V ozherel'i chernykh agatov,
  Do doliny Iosafata
   Snova vstretit'sya ne khochu … (II, 414)
(I don't want to meet again/ The woman I was then,/ Wearing a necklace of black agate/ Until the Valley of Jehosephat …)

Akhmatova opened the festivities (II, 416), very much like like Pushkin's Chairman in *The Feast during the Plague* must have done, who also was a poet and whose conscience was also burdened by guilt[26] As if in a dream, she heard a biblical cock crow (II, 418) and faced her as yet "still unlamented hour" (I eshche ne oplakannyy chas, II, 420). Tongue-in-cheek she maintained that

Poetam
Voobshche ne pristali grekhi. (II, 418)
(Poets/ And sinning just don't go together.)

At the end of chapter one, in her "Interlude," Akhmatova again appeared as the "goat-legged nymph" (II, 422), as "the time of madness nears" (I bezum'ya blizitsya srok, II, 422). After this echo of Pushkin and his last little tragedy *A Feast during the Plague,* we are confronted with the tell-tale line

"Que veut mon Prince Carnaval?" (II, 424)
("What does my Prince Carnival want of me?")

This reference to carnivals, a week before Lent, suggested that the time was fast approaching when she, the poet, would have to fast and repent. And, of

---

26 See A. S. Pushkin, *Sobranie sochineniy,* edited by D. D. Blagoy, S. M. Bondi, V. V. Vinogradov andYu. G. Oksman (10 vols.; Moscow, 1959-62), IV,380.

course, it was she who appeared in the last lines of chapter one among the New Year's satanic celebrants: "And simultaneously in the depths of the hall, on stage, in hell or on the peak of Goethe's Brocken, She appears (or perhaps – her shade)," (II, 424), – appears, like some fallen Beautiful Lady straight out of Alexander Blok's poetry.

Chapter Two

At the opening of chapter two, conscience still haunted the poem. Of the three portraits of the "mistress of the house" that hung in the "Heroine's bedroom," one was of the goat-legged nymph, the other of "Confusion-Psyche," both of whom Akhmatova's close friend, Olga Glebova-Sudeykina, – who had left Russia after the Revolution – used to portray on stage, and who, in this poem, was also "one of Akhmatova's doubles" (II, 771). The third portrait, in shadow, resembled Doña Anna – or Columbine – (II, 426). Doña Anna, whose name was also Akhmatova's, once again recalled Pushkin's *The Stone Guest.*

This Doña Anna, however, as Akhmatova tells us (II, 426), came from one of Blok's poems, "Shagi Komandora," (The Steps of the Commendatore), that statue-ghost who took revenge on Don Juan for Doña Anna's death.[27] As the New Year's Eve festivities continued, one wonders whether the "blackamoors … throwing snowballs" (II, 426) were not in effect emanations of Pushkin also. Indeed, in Akhmatova's world of shadows, identities were forever shifting, and people's likenesses could change from one moment to the next.

The heroine, almost immediately, connected this second chapter to the first:

> Ne tebya, a sebya kaznyu.
> Vse ravno podkhodit rasplata – (II, 426)
> (I blame [punish] myself, not you./ In any case, the day of reckoning is at hand –)

She appeared no longer certain whether it was Gabriel or Mephisto who was her knight errant (II, 428). Good and evil were no longer distinct, and beauty and purity had become tainted, like Lermontov's Tamara or Blok's Beautiful Lady (II, 428, 430). Then, just as suddenly, Akhmatova, the heroine, was ready to suffer the consequences:

---

27 See Alexander Blok, *Sobranie sochineniy* (8 vols.; Moscow/Leningrad, 1960-63), III, 80-81.

Ya zhe rol' rokovogo khora
  Na sebya soglasna prinyat'. (II, 430)
(And the role of the fateful chorus/ I agree to take on.)

But it was not easy at all to take on the function of a Greek-like chorus in order to elucidate the tragic incompatibility of the poet with her social and political environment: for Akhmatova's revolutionary time was deaf to conscience; and she, like Pushkin's negative heroes in the *Little Tragedies,* had a crime on her conscience and retribution was at hand:

Ved' segodnya takaya noch'
Kogda nuzhno platit' po shchetu ...(II, 430; her italics)
(For this is the kind of night/ When one must pay one's debts ...)

Just for a fleeting moment, quite ironically, she saw herself as an innocent bride but knew, as she looked at the phantom-like festivities at her residence on New Year's Eve, that her heart would remain burdened with a curse:

  Vizhu tanets pridvornykh kostey ...
Oplyvayut venchal'nye svechi,
  Pod fatoy potseluynye plechi,
    Khram gremit: "Golubitsa, gryadi!"
Gory parmskikh fialok v aprele –
  I svidanie v Maltiyskoy kapelle,
    Kak proklyat'e v tvoey grudi.
Zolotogo li veka viden'e
  Ili chernoe prestuplenie
    V groznom khaose davnikh dney? (II, 432)
(I see the dance of court skeletons .../ The wedding candles gutter,/ Veiled are the kissable shoulders,/ The temple thunders: "Come, oh Innocent One!"/ Mountains of Parma violets in April – / And that meeting in the Maltese Chapel/ Like perdition in your breast./ Is it a vision of the golden age/ Or a black crime/ From the terrible chaos of long-gone days?)

Chapter Three

The next chapter echoed Akhmatova's by now familiar theme of approaching retribution for sins committed. But she still had difficulty looking squarely at herself. An ominous time came with New Year's Eve of 1913: "A shadow was drawing near" (Priblizhalas' medlenno ten' –, II, 436); and "As before an execution, the drum rolled ..." (Kak pered kazn'yu bil baraban ..., II, 436). But how almost impossible it was to look at her own guilt:

Slovno v zerkale strashnoy nochi
  I besnuetsya i ne khochet

Uznavat' sebya chelovek, –
A po naberezhnoy legendarnyy
 Priblizhalsya ne kalendarnyy –
Nastoyashchiy Dvadtsatyy Vek. (II, 436)
(It was just as if a human being in a rage/ Refused to recognize himself/ In the mirror of this
terrifying night, –/ While along that legendary embankment/ It was the real Twentieth
Century approaching/ Not its calendar year.) *My translation*

Chapter Four

The last chapter of part one recapitulated the theme of guilt. It did so, for one,
by its reference again to Vsevolod Knyazev's suicide in 1913 (II, 438, 440)
over his rejection by Akhmatova's friend Sudeykina: but Akhmatova used
this story for her own purposes. For another, Akhmatova heard, in the midst
of the palace ball, "And invisible hooves ring out …" (I nevidimykh zvon
kopyt, II,438) – a reference to the guilt motif in Pushkin's *The Bronze Horseman*. And Akhmatova exclaimed:

"'Pomogite, eshche ne pozdno!'" (II, 438)
("'Help [me], it's not too late!'")

And so, as part one came to a close, we hear the line: "'It is I – your old
conscience'" (Eto ya – tvoya staraya sovest' –, II, 440) – a voice which, this
time, directly addressed the poet herself.

Part Two

The second part of the poem – (and the epilogue that makes up part three) –
both read like epilogues to the spiritual and psychological work that
Akhmatova undertook in part one. She was now in a position to ask the crucial question whether or not she had overcome and survived the moral ordeal:

Kto pogib, I kto zhiv ostalsya,
 I kto avtor, i kto geroy, – (II, 446)
(Who perished and who survived,/ And who is the author, and who is the hero –)

leaving only Satan knowing nothing about conscience –

Kto ne znaet, chto sovest' znachit
 I zachem sushchestvuet ona. (II, 448)
([Satan] who doesn't know what conscience means,/ And why conscience exists.)

This, in turn, was followed by non-existent stanzas, where dots were sub-stituted for lines to indicate, in the best Pushkin tradition, that for personal reasons or for reasons of state censorship she could no longer express herself. In any case, the dotted lines were an eloquent metaphor to suggest that she, the poet, could no longer speak:

> I prokhodyat desyatiletiya :
>   Pytki, ssylki i kazni – pet' ya
>   Vy zhe vidite, ne mogu. (II, 450)
> (And the decades pass by me:/ Tortures, exiles and executions – don't you see/ That I can no longer sing.) *My translation*

She divulged that her poem had "a triple bottom" (U shkatulki zh troynoe dno, II, 452) and that she had no other way open to her but to write "in invisible ink" and "in mirror writing". Though she had earlier in the poem denied any complexity, it was clear that such writing in invisible ink had its own difficulties for the reader. In any event, her reference to mirror writing seemed especially suited for a poem expressing her personal difficulty in giving voice to her conscience. So, in the end, she again tried to get off the hook by playing the innocent, as if she were at a loss to know how her life could have taken such a turn:

> Nu, a kak zhe mozhet sluchit'sya,
>   Chto vo vsem vinovata ya?
> Ya – tishayshaya, ya – prostaya,
>   *Podorozhnik, Belaya staya ...*
>   Opravdat'sya ... no kak, druz'ya? (II, 452)
> (But how does it come to pass/ That I am totally guilty of everything?/ I – the quietest of women, I – the simplest one, –/ *White Flock, Plantain* .../ To vindicate myself ... but how, my friends?)

Part Three (Epilogue)

There were only faint echoes in the Epilogue of the theme of conscience in the *Poem without a Hero* (II, 458-64). It is curious that Akhmatova should have used an "epilogue" dated in Tashkent, in August of 1942, for a poem that she was to finish only in 1962. But perhaps the following lines on ever wakeful poetry liberating the burdened conscience and healing the self, give us a clue as to why she might have decided to use that early material as an epilogue:

> Vse, chto skazano v Pervoy chasti
>   O lyubvi, izmene i strasti,

Sbrosil s kryl'ev svobodnyy stikh,
I stoit moy gorod zashityy ...
 Tyazhely nadgrobnye plity
 Na bessonnykh ochakh tvoikh. (II, 462)
(Everything recounted in Part One/ About love, betrayal and passion,/ Free verse [poetry] flung from its wings,/ And my city stands, mended .../ Heavy are the gravestones/ On your sleepless eyes.)[28]

Seventh Book

In Akhmatova's *Sed'maya kniga* (Seventh Book, 1936-64), it was perhaps the poems in memory of her meeting and "non-meeting" with Isaiah Berlin[29] – in *Cinque* (1945-46) and *Shipovnik tsvetet* (Sweetbriar in Blossom, 1946-62) – which seemed most inspired. Of course, other poems too echoed some of the main themes of her *Poem without a Hero* on which she worked during the same period of time (e.g., II, 168,174, 178, 202, 204, 216, 224), but it was in *Cinque* and in *Sweetbriar in Blossom* that the motif of conscience was most strongly expressed. Take for example the lines:

Ili vyshedshiy vdrug iz ramy
Novogodniy strashnyy portret ? (II, 236)
(Or the terrible New Year's portrait/
Suddenly hurled from its frame?)

It was in one of the *Sweetbriar* poems that Akhmatova, harking back to the motif of conscience in Pushkin's little tragedy *Mozart and Salieri,* went beyond her meeting with Isaiah Berlin, to express the tragic theme of her life:

Ni vrach ne istselit, ni utolit poet, –
Ten' prizraka tebya I den' I noch' trevozhit. (II, 248)
(A doctor cannot cure, a poet cannot comfort –/ A shadowy apparition haunts you night and day.)

---

28 As for Akhmatova's other longer poems, such as her *Severnye Elegii* (Northern Elegies, 1921-55), and *U samogo morya* (At the Edge of the Sea, 1914), they lack the more direct poetic impact of her shorter lyrical poems, with the exception, perhaps, of *Putem vseya zemli* (The Way of all the Earth, 1940). The few verse fragments (Prologue) that remain of her play *Enuma elish* (There Above, 1942-44; Akhmatova's translation of the Babylonian title), which she destroyed, make it impossible to see the intended whole.

29 Akhmatova met Isaiah Berlin in Moscow in the autumn of 1945 and on January 5, 1946. On his next visit to Moscow in the summer of 1956, Akhmatova talked with him on the telephone, but decided against a meeting, for fear of jeopardizing her son's recent release from the camps.

Her *Polnochnye stikhi* (Midnight Verses, 1963) for one last time recaptured her meeting with Isaiah Berlin. The epigraph to the poems was a direct quote from the second part of her *Poem without a Hero* (II, 266). If Isaiah Berlin had stirred up past memories, two haunting lines about the passage of time remind us of what was still morally at stake in her life:

Nad skol'kimi bezdnami pela
I v skol'kikh zhila zerkalakh. (II, 268)
(I have sung over so many abysses,/ And lived in so many mirrors.)

In the last part of her *Seventh Book – Nechet* (Odd Number) – there was a 1960 poem called "Echo" which once again gave voice to Akhmatova's uneasy conscience:

Ili ekho, chto eshche ne mozhet
Zamolchat', khotya ya tak proshu ...
S etim ekhom priklyuchilos' to zhe,
Chto i s tem, chto v serdtse ya noshu. (II, 298)
(Or an echo that still can't be / Still, no matter how I plead .../ It's the same story with the [this] echo/ And the echo that I carry in my heart.)

Finally – she was in poor health – we see Akhmatova losing her will to live: in a poem she wrote during the summer of 1962 in her small rural cabin at Komarovo, which the Soviet state had given her in the spring of 1955, she confessed –

Gospodi! Ty vidish', ya ustala
Voskresat',i umirat' i zhit'. (II, 316)
(My God! You see that I am tired/ Of being resurrected, and of dying, and of living.)
My translation

Small wonder if she gave her last collection of poems published in 1965 – made up of *The Reed* and *Seventh Book* – the name *Beg vremeni* (The Flight of Time), a name she took out of a 1962 poem where the passage of time was described as sheer horror:

No kto nas zashchitit ot uzhasa, kotoryy
Byl begom vremeni kogda-to narechen? (II, 216)
(But who will defend us from the horror/ That once was named the flight of time?)

Literary Critics on Akhmatova

Without a doubt, it will be Akhmatova's later poetry for which she will be remembered. And chief among her work will be the *Poem without a Hero* on which she worked during the last twenty-five years of her life.

The literary critical tendency has been to set her poetic work into a historical and cultural context. But we may remind ourselves of her comment to Isaiah Berlin (see p. 28 above). With this admission, Akhmatova pointed to the personal and subjective context of her *Poem,* and of her poetry in general. But the majority of literary critics have not been dissuaded from reading her work, and particularly her *Poem,* from a much larger historical and cultural vantage point than she intended,[30] *even when* they too have been struck by the pervasiveness of the theme of conscience, especially in her *Poem without a Hero*.

Thus, Johannes Holthusen, for example, pointed out how conscience played the main role in her *Poem without a Hero* ("in ihr spielt das Gewissen die Hauptrolle") which, however, did not prevent him from objectifying conscience as a function of historical process, in his words, seeing the poem "overrun by visions of an epochal analysis of Russia's future destiny." (überwuchert von den Visionen einer epochalen Auseinandersetzung um das weitere Schicksal Russlands).[31] Similarly, though A. I. Pavlovsky wrote that

> "indomitable conscience" which made up the central psychological content of many and many of Akhmatova's poems, in the *Poem without a Hero* conscience organized all the action, all the meaning and all the inner turns of the poem.[32]

he still finished off his study by focusing on the historical and social implications of her poem.[33]

Jeanne Van der Eng-Liedmeier is another case in point in her study of *Poem without a Hero*. Having suggested that Akhmatova was at the "mercy

---

30 See, for instance, Renato Poggioli, *The Poets of Russia 1890-1930* (Cambridge, Mass., 1960), p. 233; Viktor Frank, "Anna Akhmatova," (1968) in his *Po Suti Dela* (London, 1977), p. 114; Kees Verheul, "Some Marginal Observations on the First Version of *Poema bez Geroja*," in *Tale Without a Hero and Twenty-Two Poems by Anna Akhmatova* (The Hague-Paris, 1973), pp. 135-41; Deming Brown, *Soviet Russian Literature since Stalin* (Cambridge, 1978), pp. 26-27; A. I. Pavlovsky, *Anna Akhmatova. Ocherk tvorchestva* (Leningrad, 1982), pp. 150-61; David Wells, *Akhmatova and Pushkin: The Pushkin Contexts of Akhmatova's Poetry, Birmingham Slavonic Monographs No, 25* (Birmingham, 1994), pp. 86-92, see also pp. 13, 14, 33, 75, 81, 109, 110.

31 Johannes Holthusen, *Russische Gegenwartsliteratur* (2 vols.; Berlin-Munich, 1963, 1968), II, 54. My tr.

32 A. I. Pavlovsky, *Anna Akhmatova, op. cit.,* p. 145. My tr.

33 *Ibid.,* pp. 150-61.

of her conscience," that in the poem her "feeling of guilt predominates,"[34] she too, ultimately, saw the root of this guilt in a historical context:

> We are faced here again with the poet's obsessive sense of guilt to which we referred in our discussion of the first part. She cannot resist her passionate longing to look back at the lost paradise of her youth, "the vision of a golden age" as she calls it, but by giving in to this temptation she is confronted with the horrifying reproaches of her conscience. The conflict between a more romantic view of the past based on aesthetic delight in its art, and a profoundly tragic interpretation which implies a moral judgement of her former life, seems to lie at the root of her ambivalent attitude. This contradiction is indicated by the symbolic figures of demon, muse and conscience who, in a sense, appear as her doubles and play a part in the genesis of the *poèma*.[35]

Consequently, the reader is led to believe that Akhmatova's agonized conscience had in effect to do with her romanticization of a socially and historically unacceptable pre-revolutionary reality. David Wells came to a similar conclusion as regards Soviet, post-revolutionary reality:

> As has already been noted, Akhmatova's poetry from the late 1920s onwards and particularly *Poem Without a Hero* shows a strong theme of guilt about the past and the responsibility of Akhmatova's generation for the excesses of revolutionary terror and Stalinism.[36]

Kees Verheul's historical slant on Akhmatova's *Poem without a Hero* tended in the same direction:

> In her picture of the year 1913 her remorseful preoccupations with personal memories are enlarged and generalized into a vision of the sinfulness of an entire historical milieu and an age which did not recognize its guilt, but which already lived under the spell of an impending retribution.[37]

She might as well have been writing about the year 1931!

To Verheul's credit, he did enter a proviso in connection with the *Poem without a Hero* which, in referring to the poem's "literary process, a development in the form of a continuous expansion of a certain poetical impulse,"[38] suggested that the poem did not allow for any straightforward interpretation:

---

34 See *Tale Without a Hero, op. cit.,* pp. 93, 95 respectively.

35 *Ibid.,* p. 99.

36 Wells, *Anna Akhmatova. Her Poetry, op. cit.,* p. 134.

37 Kees Verheul, *The Theme of Time in the Poetry of Anna Akhmatova* (The Hague-Paris, 1971), pp. 191-92.

38 Verheul, "Some Marginal Observations on the First Version of *Poèma bez Geroja*," *op. cit.,* p. 137.

In many ways [he wrote] *Poèma bez Geroja* is a strangely unique and peculiar work. One of the most striking peculiarities is formed by the fact that it is almost impossible to tie its composition to any definite date or even period, and, stranger still, that the reader remains at a loss to decide what actually is to be considered as its "real" text.[39]

Other Longer Poems

Even Akhmatova's other longer poems – though they lacked the personal impact of her shorter lyrics – reflected the subjective momentum of her lyrical poetic output. For example, in "U samogo morya" (At the Edge of the Sea, II, 356-72) which she wrote in 1914, there was already the tragic experience of Pushkin's sense (in *Evgeny Onegin)* of failed happiness: "A schast'e bylo tak vozmozhno" (Yet happiness was so close)[40] in her lines:

Bukhty izrezali nizkiy bereg,
Vse parusa ubezhali v more,
A ya sushila solenuyu kosu
Za verstu ot zemli na ploskom kamne.
Ko mne priplyvala zelenaya ryba
Ko mne priletala belaya chayka,
A ya byla derzkoy, zloy i veseloy
I vovse ne znala, chto eto – schast'e. (II, 356)
(Bays cut into the low-lying shore,/ All the sails were fleeing [had fled] out to sea,/ And I was drying my salty braid/ On a flat rock a mile from land./ A green fish swam up to me,/ A white gull flew up to me,/ And I was daring, vexed and merry,/ And completely unaware that this – was happiness)

In "Putem vseya zemli" (The Way of all the Earth, II, 374-82) which she finished in 1940, her existential tragic awareness had deepened so that she could now see how life could suddenly turn nightmarish and become filled to the brim with choked up screams, broken mirrors and pain (II, 378, 380, 382).

Nadezhda Mandelshtam, whose objectivity as regards Akhmatova has been – rightly – questioned,[41] was, however, at times, quite perceptive as to Akhmatova's poetic vision. Thus she was not far off the mark when she saw Akhmatova as a poet of "oblivion" and "renunciation" but "not love".[42] In this she reemphasized her friend's tragic subjectivity.

---

39 *Ibid.,* p. 135.
40 Pushkin, *Sobranie sochineniy, op. cit.,* IV, 176. My tr.
41 See Dalos, *op. cit.,* pp. 213-14; Anatoly Nayman, *Remembering Anna Akhmatova,* Introduction by Joseph Brodsky. Translated by Wendy Rosslyn (London, 1991), pp. 76-77; and Nadezhda Mandelshtam, *Vospominaniya* (New York, 1970), pp. 480-81, 490, 491, 497, 608.
42 See Nadezhda Mandelshtam, *Vtoraya Kniga* (Paris, 1978), pp. 174-75, 256 respectively.

Akhmatova herself pointed to her personal culpability when she wrote in one of her uncollected poems of the mid-fifties that

Neuzhto ya vsekh vinovatey
Na etoy planete byla? (II, 640)
(Am I really more guilty than anyone/ Who ever lived on this planet?) (See also II, 580, 600, 654, 722)

As if in answer to her question, there was an even more tell-tale line in her cycle of poems *Cherepki* (Potsherds, 1946):

Ya vsekh na zemle vinovatey.[43]
(On this earth I am more guilty than any one else)

a line which was set in the context of her relationship to her son –

The short and apparently unfinished cycle "*Cherepki*" (Potsherds, III, 73-74) repeats in miniature the central theme of *Requiem:* the grief of a mother for her son separated from her by political imprisonment.[44]

It comes as no surprise to hear that Akhmatova was attracted to Shakespeare whom she read "to the end of her days" and especially *Macbeth.*[45]

Potsherds

Potsherds which Akhmatova wrote between the end of the forties and early fifties was both a poignant reflection of the perennial guilt that was always with her over abandoning her child as well as – in this particular poem – the expression of the love she felt for him (II, 632-34). As she put it in this unfinished endeavour of hers:

Ne uslyshish' kak mat' zovet
V groznom voe polyarnogo vetra,
V tesnote obstupivshikh nevzgod, (II, 632)
(And you won't hear your mother's calls/ In the threatening wailing of the polar wind,/ In the crush of misfortunes) *My translation*

Though during the years of post-revolutionary Russia her son lived with her, beginning in 1927 as a student of Leningrad University until the late 1930s (I,

---

43 Quoted in Wells, *Anna Akhmatova. Her Poetry, op. cit.,* p. 132. My tr.
44 *Ibid.,* p. 131.
45 Naiman, *Remembering Anna Akhmatova, op. cit.,* p. 95.

98); and then again after his return in 1945 (I, 121); finally, again, after his return from prison in 1956, mother and son could never quite find to each other:

> They tried to live together [after 1956], but had trouble getting along. After many quarrels, Lev moved out, and they rarely saw each other. (I, 125)

In the end her mother's intuition was right: he did not hear and, perhaps, for all we know, after a tragic life that was equal to millions of others, he did not want to, or could not, hear Akhmatova's lone voice.

Conclusion

Roberta Reeder, paraphrasing Jeanne Van der Eng-Liedmeier, reminded us that

> salvation is possible only through one's conscience, by returning in memory to the time of one's guilt to expiate and atone for one's actions. (I, 136)[46]

It was Pushkin, above all, who prodded her conscience. And for over fifty years it was the memory of having failed her child that pursued her relentlessly.

Perhaps, too, she found some solace in transmuting her profound personal grief into more manageable historical, social and political contexts, but there was no escape from the awareness of her own moral responsibility.

Akhmatova was able to transmute her sense of grief and of guilt into her poetry because, as Efim Etkind has put it so aptly, her poems were deeply existential rather than literary or, for that matter, historical. Writing of Akhmatova's poem in memory of her life-long friend V. S. Sreznevskaya, Etkind used it as a touchstone for all her poetic work:

> we have here in front of us poems which do not wish to become a fact of literature that is turned towards the eye and ear of outsiders: all this – like all of Akhmatova's poems – is a link in her poetic diary, which resembles more a piece of life than a manifestation of literature. In her contempt for the literariness of a work of art lies the particular power of Akhmatova's lyrical poetry which, let us say it immediately, is typical for the poetry of the twentieth century.[47]

---

46 See Roberta Reeder, "Mirrors and Masks: The Life and Poetic Works of Anna Akhmatova," in *The Complete Poems of Anna Akhmatova, op. cit.,* pp. 21-183.

47 E. Etkind, *Materiya Stikha* (Paris, 1978), p. 124. My tr.

In the final analysis, however, we can also appreciate Akhmatova's poetic work with its spiritual concentration on the power of conscience and of pain in human life for its organic link to the best of nineteenth-century Russian literature.

Marina Tsvetaeva's Mystic Path

Und wenn dich das Irdische vergass,
zu der stillen Erde sag: Ich rinne.
Zu dem raschen Wasser sprich: Ich bin.
[And if earthly life has passed you by,
to the tranquil earth declare: I'm flowing.
To the rushing water say: I am.]
(Muzot, February19/23, 1922)
Rainer Maria Rilke: *The Sonnets to Orpheus*[48]

For a year I have been trying on death. ... I don't
want *to die,* I want *not to be.*
Marina Tsvetaeva: An Entry of 1940 (her italics)

Essays, Translations and Reminiscences

Although Russia has historically possessed a religious culture, she has produced few, if any, mystic poets.[49] Marina Tsvetaeva is the exception.

For Tsvetaeva the poetic process was always primarily a special kind of intuitive love reaching out for nature and the eternal. This is why the poets she felt closest to were Konstantin Balmont and Maksimilian Voloshin, Boris Pasternak and Alexander Blok, Goethe and Pushkin, and especially Rainer Maria Rilke.[50] That is also why the symbolist poet Valery Briusov was alien to her for, in her eyes, his poetic work was labour without love, work without inspiration.[51] As she put it even more pointedly: "Balmont and Briusov. One

---

48 My translation. See "The Mystic Way in Blok and Rilke," in my *The Spiritual Geography of Modern Writing. Essays on Dehumanization, Human Isolation, and Transcendence* (Amsterdam-Atlanta, GA,1997), pp. 77-80, here p. 79. The translations of Tsvetaeva's prose and poetry are mine, unless otherwise indicated.

49 See "The Mystic Dimension in Russian Poetry," in my *In the Shadow of the Holocaust & Other Essays* (Amsterdam-Atlanta, GA, 1998), pp. 75-97.

50 See her essays written between 1922 and 1933 in Marina Tsvetaeva, *Izbrannaya proza v dvukh tomakh. 1917-1937,* Compiled and Edited by Alexander Sumerkin, Preface by Joseph Brodsky (2 vols; NewYork, 1979), I, 135-48, 171-75, 221-41, 251-73, 367-406; II, 7-79, 247-79. Further references to this edition will be given as *Izbrannaya Proza.*

51 See "Geroy truda (zapisi o Valerii Bryusove), (1925), in *Izbrannaya proza,* I,176-220.

could write a whole book about it, – the poem has already been written: Mozart, Salieri."[52]

In this context it is not too surprising if Tsvetaeva had very little tolerance for prosodic and formalist analyses of poetry.[53] What was of far greater creative significance for her was the profound spiritual connection she felt to German culture, a feeling she shared with Voloshin.[54] This common ground between them enabled her to see in him a "concealed mystic" (skrytyy mistik),[55] while she herself espoused art as an eternal manifestation of the sacred (svyatost' iskusstva) and therefore "truly contemporary".[56] For her as a poet all these aspects of the creative process defined the true life and, in this sense, she could claim that her specialty was Life.[57]

In line with her view of the transcendental nature of art were her aesthetics with the stress on the moral and therapeutic function of art, which came to her from German romanticism.[58] And so, in the end, though she began to correspond with Rilke only in the last half year of his life when he was already very ill,[59] it was the romantic and mystic Rilke whose poetic sensibility came closest to hers.

In fact, the few letters she chose to translate into Russian in 1929 from Rilke's *Briefe an einen jungen Dichter* (Letters to a Young Poet, 1903-08) strongly suggests the spiritual and creative affinity they both shared. Thus, Rilke's emphasis on creative existence as the only real life, his view that love and joy were an integral part of the creative process, and that the poetry coming out of the lonely depths of the individual was in effect a way of creating God,[60] must have found a profound resonance in her own poetic being. Small wonder, if she saw him as a poet-priest with a sacred mission, a spirit who was the guiding will and conscience of his time.[61] Tsvetaeva's yearning for the sacred was well expressed when she wrote in 1932: "No

---

52   *Ibid.,* I, 210.
53   *Ibid.,* I, 136, 240.
54   *Ibid.,* II, 72, 73.
55   *Ibid.,* II, 74.
56   *Ibid.,* I, 381, 377 respectively.
57   *Ibid.,* I, 136.
58   *Ibid.,* I, 382-86, 388-90, 394-99.
59   See Patricia Pollock Brodsky, *Rainer Maria Rilke* (Boston, 1988), p. 27; and "Neskol'ko pisem RaineraMaria Rilke," in *Izbrannaya proza,,*I,272.
60   "Iz pisem Rainera Maria Rilke," in *Izbrannaya proza,,* I, 276-78.
61   "Poet i vremya," in *ibid.,* I, 378, and "Tvoya smert'," I, 266. See also her longer poem "Novogodnee" (New Year's, February 1927) on Rilke's death, in Marina Tsvetaeva, *Stikhotvoreniya i poemy v pyati tomakh,* Compiled and edited by Alexander Sumerkin (with Victoria Schweitzer in vol. 2), with an Introductory essay by V. Schweitzer and a Preface by I. Brodsky (4 vols.; New York 1980-84), I, 263-67, IV, 273-77, 379-82. Further references to this edition will be given in the text and footnotes as I. The translations are mine.

matter how much you feed the wolf, he will always look to the forest. We are all wolves of the deep forest of Eternity."[62]

Evening Album, Magic Lantern and Adolescent Poems

Tsvetaeva published her first book of poetry *Evening Album* (Vecherniy Al'bom) at the age of eighteen – or sixteen[63] – in 1910. In it there were only fleeting glimpses of the transcendental motif, be it in the mention of paradise or paradise lost; in the haunting evocation of death, especially in the moving poem in memory of her mother; in the remembrance of dreams that brought with them signs from another realm; and in the poem "One More Prayer" (Eshche Molitva) which spoke of Christ in His starry kingdom (I, 3, 37; I, 21; I,40; and I, 71-72, respectively).

Voloshin was the first to notice the transcendental focus of Tsvetaeva's early poetry. In a poem of December 1910, in response to her first book of poetry, he wrote:

Vasha kniga – eto vest' *ottuda*, (I, 278)
(Your book brings tidings *from that other world,/*). His italics.

Her second book of poems, *Magic Lantern* (Volshebnyy Fonar') was published in 1912. In this collection of poems the death motif had become more pervasive while, here and there, a certain weariness of humanity crept into the text, and her spirit seemed to be yearning for a miracle (toska po chudu; I, 81, 134, respectively).

The spiritual and creative significance to Tsvetaeva of these two early books of poetry was made evident by her decision to republish a selection from both books in 1913 in a publishing house that she and her husband, Sergey Efron, had founded. Her preface to this publication allowed her to articulate the chemistry behind her poetic vision.

Poetry would outlast mortality, she wrote. But the function of poetry should be to record all the minutiae of animate and inanimate nature, all the possible details of human life in its daily routines. Poetry should catch all those evanescent and seemingly unimportant moments in human speech and in human relationships, be they a sigh or a smile, or the lips that uttered a word. Nor should poetry forget the upholstery of a sofa or the curtains, the carpets and flowers, perhaps a precious stone on a ring. For, these were the

---

62 "Poet i vremya," in *Izbrannaya proza*, I, 379.
63 See Marina Tsvetaeva, *Lebedinyy stan. Stikhi 1917-1921 gg.*, edited by G. P. Struve with an introduction by Yu. P. Ivask (Munich, 1957), p. 3.

details of human existence that helped to mark the spiritual location of the soul in this world. "– all this," she wrote, "will be the body of your poor, poor soul abandoned in this huge universe." (I, 289.)

Tsvetaeva's *Adolescent Poems* (Yunosheskie Stikhi, 1913-15), intended by her as a third book of poems were never published during her lifetime (see I, 291-92). In retrospect, it is perhaps just as well, since most of these poems were exactly what she called them, adolescent.

Mile after Mile I

Mile after Mile I (Versty I), completed in 1916, was finally published in 1922. It represents, as Victoria Schweitzer has suggested, Tsvetaeva's first mature work and reveals a shift in her poetic vision (I, 299).This may perhaps explain the new-found confidence in Tsvetaeva that allowed her to devote the greater part of this collection of poems to three of her great contemporaries: Osip Mandelshtam, Alexander Blok and Anna Akhmatova.

Poems to Akhmatova

Even though Tsvetaeva felt emotionally close to Mandelshtam (I, 216) and idolized Blok as a poet (I, 305, 229), she found a certain poetic distance between her work and theirs (I, 202, 230). This was not the case with Akhmatova.

As early as February of 1915 Tsvetaeva had expressed her love for Akhmatova and her work (I, 191). In the eleven poems she wrote to Akhmatova between June 19 and July 2, 1916, it was ultimately the transcendental and religious focus of Akhmatova's poetry which made the most spiritual impact on Tsvetaeva. In this beautiful Muse of tragedy (I, 232) what attracted Tsvetaeva most was Akhmatova's poetic power to imbue her readers with a deep sense of the immortal and eternal. From her Moscow Tsvetaeva responded in kind to the poet of St. Petersburg:

> I tot kto ranen smertel'noy tvoey sud'boy,
> Uzhe bessmertnym na smertnoe skhodit lozhe.
> V pevuchem grade moem kupola goryat,
> I Spasa svetlogo slavit slepets brodyachiy ...
> I ya daryu tebe svoy kolokol'nyy grad,
> Akhmatova! – i serdtse svoe v pridachu. (I, 232)
> (And whoever is wounded by your fatal fate,/ Lies down on his mortal bed an immortal.// In my melodious city the cupolas burn,/ And the blind wandering beggar gives praise to the

radiant Saviour .../ And I make you a present, Akhmatova, of my city filled with the chiming of bells,/ And give you my heart in addition.).

Tsvetaeva saw Akhmatova as unique, a cross between an eagle and an angel drawn to the Garden of Eden (I, 233), a sorceress who could bring down natural disasters and fevers and wars upon humanity (I, 235). Half demon, half angel, she still possessed the sectarian Virgin's power to heal:

> Pomolis' za menya, krasa
> Grustnaya i besovskaya,
> Kak postavyat tebya lesa
> Bogoroditsey khlystovskoyu. (I, 236)
> (Pray for me, beautiful woman/ Sad and demonic,/ As soon as the forests/ Make you a Khlyst Virgin.)

In the end, Akhmatova personified a "heavenly cross" (nebesnyy krest) and became synonymous and interchangeable with the Sacred itself:

> Tebe odnoy nochami kladu poklony, –
> I vse *tvoimi* ochami glyadyat ikony! (I,237, her italics)
> (To you alone I bow in prayer at night,/ And all the icons look at me *with your* eyes!)

We are reminded of an earlier poem Tsvetaeva had written in March of 1916, – "Still more and more songs" (Eshche i eshche pesni) – in which she had reenacted Christ's Golgotha in her own person as the sanctified poet and healer being led to the cross by archangels (I, 206).

Love Poems

The rest of the poems in the book after the Akhmatova cycle were, according to Schweitzer, love poems (I, 301-02). The third-last poem of the book, written on November 15, 1916, was yet another sacred reenactment in her own person – but this time – as the Virgin Mary and Child:

> Po dorogam, ot moroza zvonkim,
> S tsarstvennym serebryanym rebenkom
> Prokhozhu. Vse – sneg, vse – smert', vse – son.
>
> Na kustakh serebryanye strely.
> Bylo u menya kogda-to telo,
> Bylo imya, – no ne vse li – dym?
>
> Golos byl, goryachiy i glubokiy ...
> Govoryat, chto tot golubookiy,
> Gornostaevyy rebenok – moy.

I nikto ne vidit po doroge,
Chto davnym-davno uzh ya vo grobe
Dosmotrela svoy ogromnyy son. (I, 247)

(On the country roads ringing in the frost,/ With my regal silver child/ I pass. All is snow, and death, and sleep.// Silver arrows on the bushes./ Once upon a time I had a body,/ Had a name, – but is it not all smoke?// Had a voice, passionate and deep .../ And they tell me that that ermine child,/ With the pale-blue eyes is mine.// No one realizes on the road,/ That I've long ago already in my grave/ Finished watching my enormous dream.)

With this poem in mind, we are not surprised to hear Tsvetaeva say that her favorite day of the year was the church festival of the Annunciation, a day she considered her own (I, 209). But in this somewhat nightmarish poem, her metaphorization of the poet as the embodiment of the divine also stood for her poetic journey through life viewed from a transcendental or supernatural vantage point (e. g., lines 2, 8, 9, 12). Consequently, she wanted her readers to see her poetic life in a transcendental, religious context, where a higher spiritual reality was set off against the insubstantiality of human existence.

Mile after Mile II

The second volume of *Mile after Mile* (Versty II) was dedicated to Akhmatova and contained poems written between 1917 and 1920. It was, however, only in the second part of this book of poems that Tsvetaeva continued the spiritual quest of the preceding volume.

These poems recorded her encounter with God: how she appeared before Him weighed down by millstones, how she handed over the ragged remains of her mortal body of which only two wings had remained whole, and how she asked Him to save and forgive her and place her mortal remains in the sacristy (II, 20-21). Her only justification for salvation, she said, was that she was a poet who had always sought the otherworldly reaches lying beyond human existence:

Stan razgibaya nad strokoy upornoy,
Iskala ya nad lbom svoim prostornym
Zvezd tol'ko, a ne glaz. (II, 25)
(Bent over a stubborn line,/ I sought only the stars above my spacious brow, not the eyes.)

Transcendental Intermission

It is interesting to note that in Tsvetaeva's poetry leading up to her collection of poems *After Russia*, the transcendental theme sounded only intermittently and was much diminished in resonance. There was very little indeed of that otherworldly focus either in her *Poems to Blok* (Stikhi k Bloku, 1922), in *Psyche* (Psikheya, 1923), in *The White Swan's Camp* (Libedinyy stan, first published abroad in 1957) or in her *A Poet's Craft* (Remeslo, 1923).

Perhaps it was Tsvetaeva herself who best explained this sudden muting of a theme when she said of herself that "Generally speaking, you could single out at least *seven* poets in me" (II, 335; her italics).

After Russia

Tsvetaeva left Russia in May of 1922, and the poems she wrote between 1922 and 1925 made up her next book of poetry *After Russia* (Posle Rossii, 1928). It is this collection of poems that Alexander Sumerkin has described as "the apex of Tsvetaeva's lyrical output" (III, 433). It was also in this volume of poetry that Tsvetaeva found back to her transcendental theme (e. g., III, 38, 39, 47, 56, 72, 92, 104).

What is especially striking here is that for the first time in her work her sense of a transcendental reality was deepened to a more cosmic and mystic sensibility:

> – ibo put' komet
> Poetov put'...
> (April 1923, III, 67)
> (– for, the path of comets/ Is the path of poets ...)

she wrote. And in May of the same year there was the line

> Vremya! Ya tebya minuyu (III, 75)
> (Time! I pass you by)

There were a number of poems in particular that brought out this deeper layer of Tsvetaeva's poetic vision. One of these was "The Sibyl" (Sivilla) written in Prague between May and August of 1922, a poem which celebrated the Assumption (III, 24-26). Another poem, even more mystic in sensibility, was "Trees" (Derev'ya, September 1922 to May 1923, III, 29-35), which Janet

King described as expressing a "pantheistic exaltation".[64] Here the forest was her Elysium, a refuge from everyday reality, the "great peace" (velikiy pokoy) where one might see God. This forest was a

Vvys' sorvavshiysya les! (III, 32)
(A forest breaking loose from earth and falling upward into the depths!).

It was a "light lit by a luminescence" (Kakim-to svechen'em svetyas'), a place more blissful than death, beyond all causal connections, the beginning of mysteries, sacraments and truths. Indeed, the windy breath of the forest trees brought healing:

Chto v vashem veyan'i?
No znayu – lechite
Obidu Vremeni –
Prokhladoy Vechnosti (III, 35)
(What is there in your soughing?/ Yet I know that you heal/ The wounds of Time / With the cool of Eternity).

Tsvetaeva gave full vent to her mystic sensibility in her poem "To Steal By ..." (Prokrast'sya, May 1923). I give the poem in full:

A mozhet, luchshaya pobeda
Nad vremenem i tyagoten'em –
Proyti, chtob ne ostavit' sleda,
Proyti, chtob ne ostavit' teni

Na stenakh...
    Mozhet byt' – otkazom
Vzyat'? Vycherknut'sya iz zerkal?
Tak: Lermontovym po Kavkazu
Prokrast'sya, ne vstrevozhiv skal.

A mozhet – luchshaya potekha
Perstom Sevastiana Bakha
Organnogo ne tronut' ekha?
Raspast'sya, ne ostaviv prakha

Na urnu...
    Mozhet byt' – obmanom
Vzyat'? Vypisat'sya iz shirot?
Tak: Vremenem kak okeanom
Prokrast'sya, ne vstrevozhiv vod... (III, 76)

---

64 See *Handbook of Russian Literature*, Edited by Victor Terras (New Haven and London, 1985), p. 486.

(Perhaps, the best victory/ Over time and gravity/ Is to pass by without leaving a trace,/ Pass by, without leaving a shadow// On the walls.../ Perhaps, the best way to do it is to refuse?/ To cross oneself out from the mirrors?/ Like Lermontov, steal by through the Caucasus/ Without disturbing the cliffs.// Or, perhaps, the best way to amuse oneself/ Is to avoid touching the organ's echo/ With Sebastian Bach's fingers?/ To fall apart , without leaving any bodily remains// For the urn.../ Perhaps, the best way to do it is through deception? To sign and write oneself out of the latitudes?/ To steal by in the form of Time, like an ocean, without disturbing the waves...).

Poem of the Mountain

In her longer *Poem of the Mountain* (Poema Gory, 1926; revised 1938-40, IV, 161-67), Tsvetaeva went on to develop and articulate her mystic sensibility.

The motif of the Mountain had sounded elsewhere too in her poetry of the 1920s. Thus, for example in her poem on Rilke's death (1927), she referred to him as a "mountainous paradise" (Rainer – ray goristyy, I, 266, my tr.). And even earlier, in connection with her poem "The Pupil" (Uchenik, 1922, II, 95-99) dedicated to her friend Prince Sergey Volkonsky, she remarked that the pupil (herself) was "not on earth, but on the mountain. And the mountain was not on earth, but in heaven" (II, 366). In "The Sibyl" (1922), the motif of "Gore goré" (Woe to the mountain or, perhaps more accurately, Leave suffering to the mountain, III, 25), had already anticipated the main theme of her *Poem of the Mountain:*

Gore goré! Pod tolshchey
Vek, v prozorlivykh t'makh –
Glinyanye oskolki
Tsarstv i dorozhnyy prakh

Bitv ... (III, 25)

(Leave suffering to the mountain!/ In the intuitive dark below the eyelids,/ There are clay splinters of kingdoms/ And the bodily remains of battles// On the way ...).

From the outset the Mountain – in the *Poem of the Mountain* – was connected to human suffering and possessed the spiritual power to lighten the poet's burden of earthly pain:

Vzdrognesh' – i gory s plech,
I dusha – goré.
Day mne o góre spet':
O moey gore!
...

Day mne o góre spet'
Na verkhu gory. (IV,161)

(I need only to feel a shiver – and the weight of mountains falls off my shoulders,/ And my soul is the mountain's./ Let me sing of the sorrow:/ Let me sing of my mountain!// ... Let me sing of my sorrow/ On the top of the mountain).

Tsvetaeva's use of the mountain metaphor served her mystic journey well, for it became a vantage point from which to approach the Sacred. Speaking of the hill in Prague – she had rented an apartment on top of that hill – which she metaphorized into her Mountain, she wrote:

Otchego zhe glazam moim
...

Ta gora byla ray? (IV, 162)
(What made that hill/ In my eyes into paradise?).

And added

Gora kak svodnya – svyatosti,
Ukazyvala: zdes'... (IV, 162)

(The hill was like a procuress of the sacred,/ Marking the place of the sacred ...).

Related to the Sacred, men and women had come into this world as heavenly beings of love (IV, 163), leaving the Mountain to grieve for them:

Gora gorevala o nashey druzhbe: (IV, 163)
(The mountain grieved for our friendship:).

The Mountain was not only open to our sorrow but also stood for mystic fulfillment in the future to come:

Gora gorevala o nashem gore:
Zavtra! Ne srazu! Kogda nad lbom –
Uzh ne memento, – a prosto – *more*!
Zavtra, kogda poymem. (IV, 164, her italics)
(The mountain grieved for our sorrow:/ The time will come – tomorrow! Not right away!/ When above your brow will only be *sea*, no memento mori!/ The time will come tomorrow, when we'll finally understand).

In this stanza with its play on memento mori (remember that you must die), Tsvetaeva echoed two lines of a poem in *Mile after Mile II* where she had sought the stars above her spacious brow (II, 25). And now she sought non-being:

> Zhizn' svoyu – kak kartu b'em!
> Strastnye – *ne byt'* uporstvuem. (IV, 164, her italics)
> (We play our life, the way we play at cards!/ Full of passion and intent on *not being).*

Her yearning for non-being summed up the otherworldly current of the poem. And she knew that the Mountain would take our lives into account and not forget:

> Ne zabudet gora – igry. (IV, 166)
> (The mountain won't forget our play).

Epilogue

Tsvetaeva's epilogue to her *Poem of the Mountain* was like a biblical *Song of Songs*, a love poem to the Deity beyond the mountains and seas of human existence:

> Est' probely v pamyati – bel'ma
> Na glazakh: sem' pokryval.
> Ya ne pomnyu tebya otdel'no.
> Vmesto chert – belyy proval.
> ...
>
> Nebosvod – tsel'nym osnovan.
> Okean – skopishche bryzg?!
> Bez primet. Verno – osobyy –
> Ves'. Lyubov' – svyaz', a ne sysk.
> ...
>
> Ty kak krug, polnyy i tsel'nyy:
> *Tsel'nyy* vikhr, *polnyy* stolbnyak.
> Ya ne pomnyu tebya otdel'no
> Ot lyubvi. Ravenstva znak. (IV, 166-67, her italics)

(There are gaps in my memory – cataracts/ On the eyes: seven veils deep./ I don't remember you distinctly./ Only a white yawning abyss in place of your features.// ... The vault of heaven is all one./ The ocean a collection of spray?!/ You are featureless. Truly, you're special –/ All of you. Love is a bond, not a criminal investigation.// ... You are like a circle, complete and of one piece:/ An *integral* vortex, stunning in your *totality./* I don't remember you distinctly/ Apart from love. For you are balance and equality.)

Although, according to Marc Slonim, the *Poem of the Mountain* was based simply on a love affair,[65] the mystic imagery of the poem suggests otherwise.[66]

Lyrical Poems after 1926

Tsvetaeva would never again reach the spiritual intensity of *After Russia* or of her *Poem of the Mountain*,[67] but the mystic theme continued to haunt her poetry especially in the years between 1932 and her suicide in 1941.

---

65 I am aware that Marc Slonim, in his insightful essay on Tsvetaeva "O Marine Tsvetaevoy," (III, 341-85), saw her *Poem of the Mountain* only in the context of her love affair with Konstantin Rodzevich and of her failure to raise this amorous experience to ideal heights. At the same time, he himself admits that Tsvetaeva's romantic nature was prone to use such passionate material and transmute it into "images and feelings of unreal proportions and tremendous power" (III, 351). One might also add here that she was not the first poet ever to utilize the material of everyday life for her own poetic, idealistic or, for that matter, mystic ends. As G. Gorchakov has said of Tsvetaeva: "As usual, she utilizes anymaterial in order to express what is of innermost value to her." See his "K istochnikam tragicheskogo u Mariny Tsvetaevoy," (1989) in Marina Tsvetaeva, *Stat'i i Teksty*, edited by Lev Mnukhin, *Wiener Slawistischer Almanach*, special issue vol. 32, Series editor Aage A. Hansen-Löve (Vienna, 1992), pp. 147-59, here p. 151. See also G. S. Smith, "Marina Cvetaeva's *Poema gory: An Analysis*," *Russian Literature* 6, no. 4 (October, 1978), pp.365-88, here p. 365; but see also p. 383. See also Lily Feiler, *Marina Tsvetaeva. The Double Beat of Heaven and Hell* (Durham and London, 1994), pp. 144-51.

66 Tsvetaeva's mystic poetry, with its sense of eternity, its ultimate disregard of the everyday world, its by-passing of Time, its orientation towards nature as a conduit to the Sacred, its deep yearning for the "great peace" with its powers of healing, reminds us of what William James said of the mystical experience and of his belief that we belonged to the mystical world "in a more intimate sense than that in which we belong to the visible world," and that the mystical dimension could actually shape and improve our human self. See William James, *The Varieties of Religious Experience. A study in Human Nature*, Foreword by Jacques Barzun (New York, 1958), pp. 388-89. Walter Stace, in his *The Teachings of the Mystics*, wrote that the mystical experience brought one to a world of "ineffable peace", allowed one to identify oneself with the divine and pass "beyond all sorrow"; see pp. 20, 31,respectively. As to Tsvetaeva's Mountain metaphor, ancient wisdom had it that the mountain symbolized the "ascent to the realm of the spirit"; that there was always a sacred aspect to the mountain,for it represented the "point of contact between heaven and earth"; it was, furthermore, a point "through which all things temporal and spatial must pass in order to divest themselves of their worldly characteristics"; it was also the point where life and death, mortality and immortality crossed, where good and evil, love and hate, affirmation and negation coexisted and, ultimately, it stood for salvation and health. See J. E. Cirlot, *A Dictionary of Symbols*, Translated from the Spanish by Jack Sage, Foreword by Herbert Read (London, 1962), pp. 208-11.

67 Her long poem *The Poem of the End* (Poema Kontsa, IV, 168-87, 1924) can be seen as a companion piece to her *Poem of the Mountain*, but its mystic strain is much weaker (e. g.,

Not surprisingly, it was in a poem of October, 1932 – "Ici-Haut" (Here, High Above) – written just after Voloshin's death, that she could, once again, give expression to the mystic motif of her earlier poetry. Voloshin's grave, on a hill high above Koktebel in the Crimea, became a metaphor for her spiritual quest:

Pokhoronili poeta *na*
Samom vysokom meste.
...

Vyshe kotorogo – tol'ko Bog!
Bog – i ni veshchi bole. (III, 165, her italics)

(They buried the poet/ *In the highest place./* ... Only God is higher!/ Nothing but God.)

It was a place paid up to the end of time (III, 166) and had become a mountain that had "turned into the soul's throne" (III, 166). In fact, Voloshin's place of rest became a mystical point of transformation and transfiguration:

Preobrazhenie na gore?
Gory – preobrazhenie.
...
Dnes' Vechnoy Pamyati Gora,
Dokole solntse svetit – (III, 167)

(Is this a Transfiguration on the mountain?/ It is the mountain's transfiguration.// ... Now the Mountain is the keeper of his Eternal Memory,/ For as long as the sun will shine –).

Four other poems kept the mystic theme alive during Tsvetaeva's last, lonely years. In "Rodina" (Homeland, May 1932. III, 164), she was thinking not so much of Russia as of the cosmic distance that separated her from her *real* spiritual home:

Dal', govoryashchaya "Vernis'
Domoy!"
  So vsekh – do gornykh zvezd –
Menya snimayushchaya mest!

Nedarom, golubey vody,
Ya dal'yu obdavala lby. (her italics)

IV, 169, 170, 172, 184), much like the fading of a musical theme in a symphony. Tsvetaeva's other longer poems – perhaps with the exception of her *Poem of the Air* (Poema Vozdukha, 1930) – written mainly between 1925 and 1936, some of which were revised as late as 1938 and 1939, concentrated on more worldly themes (see IV, 188-338).

(The distance tells me "Come back / *Home*!/ Removing me from all the places on and between earth and the mountain stars!// No wonder, I splashed people's brows/ With this distance whose colour was a paler blue than water).

Her poem "The Bush" (Kust) of August 1934 tried to capture the stillness in nature that lay somewhere between silence and speech (III, 176), and in October of that year she wrote her poem "The Garden" (Sad) which she metaphorized into a garden of Eden that would absolve her soul in recompense for all her suffering (III, 178).

It was in January of 1940 that she wrote one of her most beautiful poems which summed up a lifetime of seeking that mystic love on top of the mountain:

– Pora! dlya *etogo* ognya –
Stara!
  – Lyubov' – starey menya!
– Pyatidesyati yanvarey
Gora!
  – Lyubov' – eshche starey:
Stara, kak khvoshch, stara kak zmey,
Starey livonskikh yantarey,
Vsekh prividenskikh korabley
Starey! – kamney, starey – morey...
No bol', kotoraya v grudi, –
Starey lyubvi, starey lyubvi. (III, 212, her italics)

(It's time to realize! for *this* fire -/ I am too old!/ Much older is this love than I!/ Than my Mountain of fifty Januaries!/ Much older is this love than I/ Who look as old as a mare's tail, as old as a serpent,/ This love is older than Livonian ambers,/ Or all the ghostly ships that ever sailed the seas/ Much older than the stones and older than the oceans .../ But in my breast, the pain/ Is older still, is older still).

Only the pain of her mystic longing felt more ancient than this love.

Critics on Tsvetaeva

On the whole, critics have not dealt specifically with the mystic perspective in Tsvetaeva's poetry. For some, in fact, as for example Marc Slonim, there is absolutely no religious or mystic tendency in Tsvetaeva's work at all, not even in the context of her Romanticism (III, 355). But for our purposes it is useful to look at critics whose observations about her poetry were, in varying degrees, relevant to her mystic orientation, yet who stopped short of following up the spiritual implications of their findings because their critical concerns took them elsewhere.

Thus Simon Karlinsky, though he commented on Tsvetaeva's "continuous driving urge to escape from bounds of time and of human condition" and spoke of her "lasting affinity with the Russian Symbolist poets," saw her ultimately as longing "for a dimly perceived Romantic past of the eighteenth century and the Napoleonic age."[68]

A very interesting critic of Tsvetaeva's poetic work was Joseph Brodsky. In his perceptive essay on Tsvetaeva's "New Year's" dirge to Rilke,[69] he too made comments that were relevant to her mystic perception, but was sidetracked by his profound appreciation of her poetics. Looking at her poetic texture, he drew attention to her tonality which he saw as the "purely spiritual aspect of [her] creativity," or as "a pure voice soaring upward".[70] Then he pointed to her sense of space which allowed her – in his words – to undertake a "spiritual flight precipitated not so much by the presupposed location of the 'next world' as *by the overall poetic orientation of the author*" (my italics).[71] Nonetheless, in his ultimate analysis, he interpreted Tsvetaeva's poetry as a whole in terms of *time*, and with this he pulled her right back into the orbit of the known rather than the unknown:

> And the whole poem (as, essentially, her oeuvre in general) is a development, an elaboration of this theme [time] – better still, of this state, i. e., of drawing nearer to time – expressed in the only palpable spatial categories: height, the next world, paradise.[72]

D. S. Mirsky also stopped short of the mystic connection, though he recognized the ontological roots of Tsvetaeva's art and herself as an "idealist" for whom the "material world is ... only an emanation of essence."[73] He wrote in 1926:

> For Tsvetaeva the word cannot be a sign of a thing, for the thing itself is only a sign. Words for her are more ontological than things; they bypass things and are directly connected with essences: absolute, self-contained, irreplaceable, untranslatable.[74]

---

68 Simon Karlinsky, *Marina Cvetaeva. Her Life and Art* (Berkeley and Los Angeles, 1966), pp. 221, 288, 287, respectively.

69 See Joseph Brodsky, "Footnote to a Poem," Translated by Barry Rubin in 1981, in his *Less Than One.Selected Essays* (New York, 1986), pp. 195-267.

70 *Ibid.*, pp. 208, 207 respectively.

71 *Ibid.*, p. 235.

72 *Ibid.*, p. 248.

73 D. S. Mirsky, "Marina Tsvetaeva," in Simon Karlinsky and Alfred Appel, Jr., eds., in *The Bitter Air of Exile: Russian Writers in the West 1922-1972* (Berkeley *et al.*, 1977), pp. 88-93, here p. 89.

74 *Ibid.*, p. 90.

A number of other critics have likewise touched on Tsvetaeva's transcendental perspective without developing it as a theme in its own right. For example, though Alyssa Dinega was not unaware of Tsvetaeva's otherworldly focus, her book as a whole was much more earth-bound and inspired by a feminist perspective that explored Tsvetaeva's attempt through her art to restructure a male-oriented poetic tradition.[75] Svetlana Elnitsky found an inner conflict in Tsvetaeva's poetry between a higher, authentic reality and an earthly reality that fell far short of it[76] and two years later, in her paper on *mifotvorchestvo*, came fairly close to pinpointing the spiritual space of Tsvetaeva's creative focus, but did not refer to her poetic perception as mystic:

> The creation of a new world in Tsvetaeva's work is realized in an ideal space of the soul and spirit, and the transformation takes the form of a transfiguration of the earthly into another, higher reality.[77]

In Irma Kudrova's eyes, Tsvetaeva's spiritual link to the "world of the Absolute" was essential for her writing,[78] but her greatest poetic imperative was to root this transcendental feeling not beyond but within the limits of this world which conditioned her poetic experience: "All of Tsvetaeva's creative work, if one is to see it without prejudice, is precisely a witness to a most profound attachment of the poet to earthly love and earthly nature, to people and books, to mountains and valleys.[79] Lily Feiler, too, bypassed the mystic aspect of Tsvetaeva's poetry even when she commented on her responsiveness to Rilke's "nonreligious mysticism," spoke of her poems "From the Sea" and "Attempt at a Room" as "evidence of a move toward mysticism," yet at the same time saw her as living in a world of "fantasy" and interpreted her poetic process not in spiritual but poetic terms, as a striving for "the freedom of new creative forms."[80]

---

75 See Alyssa W. Dinega, *A Russian Psyche. The Poetic Mind of Marina Tsvetaeva* (Madison, Wisconsin, 2001).

76 Svetlana Elnitskaya, *Poeticheskiy mir Tsvetaevoy: Konflikt liricheskogo geroya i deystvitel'nosti,* in*Wiener Slawistischer Almanach*, Special issue vol. 30, Literary Series, edited by Aage A. Hansen-Löve (Vienna, 1990), pp. 304-05.

77 Svetlana Elnitskaya, "'Vozvyshayushchiy obman'. Mirotvorchestvo i mifotvorchestvo Tsvetaevoy," in *Marina Tsvetaeva 1892-1992*, Edited by Svetlana Elnitsky and Efim Etkind, Norwich Symposia on Russian Literature and Culture, Vol. II (Vermont, 1992), pp. 45-62, here p. 47, my tr.

78 Irma Kudrova, "Formula Tsvetaevoy: 'Luchshe byt', chem imet''," in *ibid.*, pp. 74-86, here pp. 79, 80,82.

79 *Ibid.*, p. 83, my tr.

80 Lily Feiler, *Marina Tsvetaeva. The Double Beat of Heaven and Hell, op. cit.*, pp. 169, 176, 266, 176.

One final example. Olga Peters Hasty, in her penetrating chapters focussing on the poetic connection between Tsvetaeva and Rilke, had this to say:

> Tsvetaeva demands of the poet not that he transfigure the world, but that he enlarge on the perceptual possibilities it affords. In providing a bridge to the other world, the poet encourages not escapism, but the admission of new frames of reference. Travel to the other world that poetry makes possible enhances the returning wayfarer's capacity to recognize in the earthly signs surrounding him indicators of that other world. The ability to derive transcendent meaning from the signs of this world is one that – as Tsvetaeva was at pains to underscore in her letters [to Rilke] – she shared with Rilke.[81]

Nevertheless, Peters Hasty found nothing mystical in Tsvetaeva's otherworldly focus and regarded this "new frame of reference" not as a spiritual journey but as a creative adventure in the ongoing process of the poetic word.[82]

The foregoing shows how unintentionally close critics came to Tsvetaeva's mystic poetic perception. It also brings out the variety of literary criticism on her work and proves her right in thinking that there were at least seven poets in her (II,335).[83]

---

81 Olga Peters Hasty, *Tsvetaeva's Orphic Journeys in the Worlds of the Word* (Evanston, Illinois, 1996), pp. 134-222, here p. 158.

82 *Ibid.*, pp. 170-71, 212, 224. See also Bettina Eberspächer, *Realität und Transzendenz – Marina Cvetaevas Poetische Synthese* (Munich, 1987).

83 There have of course been other noteworthy critics of Tsvetaeva's work who have, however, not dealt with her transcendental side at all. Thus Gleb Struve found it difficult to pigeonhole her art, but saw her as a great and original poet with a strange mix of romantic excessiveness and a sense for classical form.See Gleb Struve, *Russkaya literatura v izgnanii. Opyt istoricheskogo obzora zarubezhnoy literatury* (New York, 1956), pp. 149-54. Michael Makin was primarily interested in the function of an inherited literary tradition in Tsvetaeva's poetry and the creative use he made of it. See Michael Makin, *Marina Tsvetaeva: Poetics of Appropriation* (Oxford, 1993). V. Admoni looked at the parallels between Tsvetaeva's poetry and twentieth-century poetry as a whole, not least of which was the dissonant poetic structure of her work which reflected the catastrophic events of the century. See V.Adoni, "Marina Tsvetaeva i poeziya XX veka," (1982) in *Marina Tsvetaeva. Stat'i i teksty, op. cit.*, pp. 17-28. There is also G. Gorchakov's intriguing paper on Tsvetaeva's infant and childhood years before the age of seven, which suggest a psychological trauma to do with her feeling of not being loved by her mother which, in turn, in Gorchakov's view, left profound traces in some of her work and shaped her personality. See G. Gorchakov, in *Marina Tsvetaeva. Stat'i i teksty, op. cit.* See also Makin, *op. cit.,*who gives an extensive bibliography of literary criticism on Tsvetaeva in his Introduction, pp. 1-15; and Anya Motalygo-Krot, "Marina Tsvetaeva i o ney: bibliograficheskiy ukazatel' sovetskikh publikatsyy (1985-1990)," in *Marina Tsvetaeva 1892-1992, op. cit.,* pp. 267-78.

Rilke's Elegy to Tsvetaeva

In the end it was Rilke more than anyone else who, as one kindred spirit to another, – in his elegy to Tsvetaeva "Elegie an Marina Zwetajewa-Efron" written on June 8, 1926[84] – bore witness to his own and to Tsvetaeva's mystic journey.

The very first line of the elegy suggested the mystic enterprise between them:

> O die Verluste ins All, Marina, die stürzenden Sterne!
> (Oh, our losses into the universe, Marina, the falling stars!)

Yet, even failed attempts to connect with the sacred centre of the universe did not diminish the holy source and brought healing in its wake:

> So auch, wer fällt, vermindert die heilige Zahl nicht.
> Jeder verzichtende Sturz stürzt in den Ursprung und heilt.
> (Yet even those who fall, do not diminish the sacred number./ With each sacrificial fall we plunge into the source and are healed.)

That Rilke included Tsvetaeva in his mystic pilgrimage is clear from the following:

> Wellen, Marina, wir Meer! Tiefen, Marina, wir Himmel.
> Erde, Marina, wir Erde, wir tausendmal Frühling, wie Lerchen,
> die ein ausbrechendes Lied in die Unsichtbarkeit wirft.
> (Waves, Marina, and we the sea! Depths, Marina, and we the sky./ Earth, Marina, and we the earth, we the thousandfold celebration of spring, like larks,/ that are thrown into the invisible by their rising song.)

Their only possession was this joyous and gentle link to nature:

> Nichts gehört uns. Wir legen ein wenig die Hand um die Hälse
> ungebrochener Blumen. ...
> (Nothing belongs to us. Gently we put our hand around the necks/ of unplucked flowers. ...)

And they themselves were but

> ... Zeichengeber, sonst nichts.
> (We only give signs, nothing more.)

---

84 See Rilke's letter and elegy in *Rainer Maria Rilke und Marina Zwetajewa. Ein Gespräch in Briefen*, Edited by Konstantin M. Asadowski (2nd ed.; Frankfurt am Main and Leipzig, 1993), pp. 70-72. My tr.

Their poetic and mystic longing for non-being, however, had its dangers:

> Dieses leise Geschäft, wo es der unsrigen einer
> nicht mehr erträgt und sich zum Zugriff entschliesst,
> rächt sich und tötet. Denn dass es tödliche Macht hat,
> merken wir alle an seiner Verhaltung und Zartheit
> und an der seltsamen Kraft, die uns aus Lebenden zu
> Überlebenden macht. Nicht-Sein. ...
> (This quiet business, when one of us/ can no longer endure it and decides to make his move,/ revenges itself and kills. That our business has deadly power,/ we have all noticed by the poet's behaviour and gentleness/ and by that strange power which makes us the living/ into survivors. Non-Being.)

Once more he saw Tsvetaeva as taking part in the same mystic journey:

> O wie begreif ich dich, weibliche Blüte am gleichen
> unvergänglichen Strauch. ...
> (Oh, how I understand you, womanly blossom/ part of the same immortal bush.)

The elegy finished with the knowledge that, ultimately, the key to their successful spiritual journey lay in themselves, in their inner creative self:

> ... Wir in das Kreisen bezogen
> füllten zum Ganzen uns an wie die Scheibe des Monds.
> Auch in abnehmender Frist, auch in den Wochen der Wendung
> niemand verhülfe uns je wieder zum Vollsein, als der
> einsame eigene Gang über der schlaflosen Landschaft.
> (... We who are drawn into this orbit/ filled out and became whole like the moon's disc./ And even in waning, or in the weeks of our transformation/ no one could ever help us again to become whole/ except our own lonely passage over the sleepless landscape.)

Rilke's elegy to Tsvetaeva, as we can appreciate from the above, shows us that he must have recognized his own mystic longing in her letters to him and in her poetry.[85] His poetic witness gives additional credibility to Tsvetaeva's mystic spirituality. That Rilke was a mystic poet in his own right is evident from his major poetic work, his *Duino Elegies* (Duineser Elegien, 1912-22) and *The Sonnets to Orpheus* (Die Sonette an Orpheus, 1922-23). But critics drew attention to his mystical orientation even in his earliest book of poetry, *The Book of Hours* (Das Stunden-Buch, 1899-1905), which summed up his

---

85 Rilke had sent her his *Duino Elegies* and *The Sonnets to Orpheus* and she responded by sending him her *Poems to Blok* and *Psyche*. See Maria Razumovsky, *Marina Zwetajewa. Eine Biographie* (Frankfurt amMain, 1989), pp. 209-19. See also *Nebesnaya Arka. Marina Tsvetaeva i Rainer Maria Rilke*, edited by Konstantin Azadovsky (St. Petersburg, 1992), photocopies between pp. 64-65.

spiritual experience of Russian religious life. Jacob Steiner had this to say about Rilke's *The Book of Hours*:

> [Rilke's] main conception is however one of God in the process of becoming (des werden-den Gottes), and it is artists above all who work on the completion of this God ... One could say that such relativity expresses precisely the attitude of the *mystic* who is not so much interested in a clearly delineated image of God as he is in an immediate union with what God is at any one moment.[86] (My italics)

Konstantin Azadovsky has also drawn attention to the spiritual affinity between Rilke and Tsvetaeva as it is expressed in his elegy to her: "The *Elegy* presents us with 'ciphered writing,' as it were, which can be fully understood only by the two participants of the correspondence".[87] Maria Razumovsky, also referring to the elegy, made a similar observation: "We have here a meeting between two people who understand each other and who speak the same language ..."[88]

Conclusion

In retrospect, it is noteworthy that just as Tsvetaeva's life journey was about to come to an abrupt end, she was meditating on mystic transformation which she described using the exact words – in Russian "ne byt'" – that Rilke had used in his elegy to her: "Nicht-Sein":

> For a year I have been trying on death. ... I don't want *to die,*
> I want *not to be.* (III, 391, her italics).

Anna Saakyants, who quoted the same remark, added: "How are we to ex-plain this comment? But it is precisely about this that Tsvetaeva wrote all her life."[89]

The critics who have not shied away from applying the word "mystic" to Tsvetaeva are few and far between. One was Kristina Orlova. Speaking of the poet's love of mountains, she said that Tsvetaeva was in effect "hinting at their sublime nature, precisely in the mystic sense of the word."[90] And she

---

86 Jacob Steiner, "Rainer Maria Rilke," in *Deutsche Dichter der Moderne. Ihr Leben und Werk,* edited by Benno von Wiese (3rd expanded edition.; Berlin, 1975), pp. 161-85, here p. 171; my tr.

87 See *Nebesnaya Arka, op. cit.,* p. 32, my tr.

88 Razumovsky, *op. cit.,* p. 214, my tr.

89 Anna Saakyants, *Marina Tsvetaeva. Zhizn' i tvorchestvo* (Moscow, 1997), p. 756, my tr.

90 Kristina Orlova, "Poeticheskoe prostranstvo poezii Mariny Tsvetaevoy," in Marina Tsvetaeva, *Trudy Igo mezhdunarodnogo simpoziuma (Lozanna, 30. VI.–3. VII.,1982),* edited

concluded her paper –given at the international colloquium in Lausanne in 1982 – with these words:

> The poetic space of Tsvetaeva's poetry is cosmic space perceived through the poet's prism (I and the universe); the external in Tsvetaeva's poetic work becomes inward in focus. In the measureless and immense space, the human being becomes a part of the cosmos, he is united with the elements that make up earth, water, fire and air. Rilke expressed this thought in his *Elegy for Marina*:
> Wellen, Marina, wir Meer! Tiefen, Marina, wir Himmel! Erde, Marina, wir Erde, wir tausendmal Frühling ...[91]

Tatyana Kuznetsova, writing on Rudolf Steiner's influence on Tsvetaeva's poetry – especially after Tsvetaeva heard his lecture in Prague in April of 1923 on "The Eternity of the Soul in the Light of Anthroposophy,"[92] – made the following observation:

> Tsvetaeva's poetry of the Prague period [1922-25] as a whole startles one especially by its tendency towards higher worlds, and it is here that one can even call her a "mystic" who receives her revelations directly from the spiritual reaches of the universe.[93]

This has all the earmarks of Romanticism. Indeed, Tsvetaeva's working out of a German romantic tradition may have been but a stepping stone to the discovery through her poetry of a mystic sensibility within her which empowered her over time to articulate a profound sense of the Sacred through an equally profound feeling of love. This mystic strain in her poetic work brings to mind the medieval Sufi woman saint, mystic and poet Rābi'a al-Adawiya whose "mainspring of mysticism [was] love" and who expressed her mystic love also through poetry:

> But that purest love, which is Thy due,
> Is that the veils which hide Thee fall, and I gaze on Thee,[94]

---

by Robin Kemball in collaboration with E. G. Etkind and Leonid Heller (Bern, *et al.,*1991), pp. 337-44, here p. 341, my tr.

91 *Ibid.,* p. 343, my tr.

92 See Tatyana Kuznetsova, *Tsvetaeva i Shteyner* (Moscow, 1996), pp. 36-41, 28-29, 32 respectively. She singles out Tsvetaeva's poems "The Trees," "The Sibyl" and "The Poem of the Air."

93 *Ibid.,* pp. 35-36, my tr.; see also p. 52. But see also Ieva Vitins, "Escape from Earth: A Study of Tsvetaeva's Elsewheres," *Slavic Review* (December 1977), pp. 644-57, who interprets Tsvetaeva's emotionally compensative flights into transcendence as *mental* journeys into realms of "abstractthought," "nothingness" and "death"; see pp. 647-48, 654, 652, 657 respectively.

94 See Sir Hamilton A. R. Gibb, *Mohammedanism. An Historical Survey* (New York, 1953), pp. 99-113, here p. 103.

Though to date critics have paid little attention to it, the mystical aspect of Tsvetaeva's poetic vision certainly enriches her poetic legacy. It makes this great and original poet, sui generis, with a cultural and thematic richness all her own, even more complex and adds another poetic dimension to her work.

Tsvetaeva's complexity will continue to haunt the critical imagination. Gleb Struve's difficulty to pigeon-hole her art is a good example of this. In his words: "Essentially Tsvetaeva is her own poet (sama po sebe), without contemporaries, without ancestors."[95]

Tsvetaeva did not live to see the international critical acclaim of her work, but her place in twentieth-century Russian poetry is secure. In fact, Joseph Brodsky, who was once Akhmatova's protégé, considered her the foremost Russian poet of the last century: "I consider Tsvetaeva to be the first poet of the twentieth century. Of course. Tsvetaeva."[96]

95 Struve, *Russkaya literatura v izgnanii, op. cit.,* p. 152, my tr; see also pp. 149-51.
96 See Solomon Volkov, "O Tsvetaevoy: dialog s Iosifom Brodskim," in *Brodsky o Tsvetaevoy*, Literary Criticism Series (Moscow, 1997), pp.23-55, here p. 55, my tr.

Vladislav Khodasevich's Nightmare World

> ... bol'no
> Zhit' v etom mire! Zachem ty menya rodila?
> (It is painful/ To live in this world! Why did you
> give birth to me?).
>
> "To My Mother" (Autumn of 1910)

> Etot mir lyubit' ne perestanu.
> Khorosho mne v sumrake zemnom!
> (I'll never stop loving this world./ I feel good
> in the terrestrial dusk!).
>
> "Paradise" (December 1913)

Early Poems, 1907-13

Vladislav Khodasevich was born in Moscow in 1886 into a Catholic family of Polish-Jewish descent. Born with a weak and ailing constitution that was to mark him for life, no one thought he would survive his infancy. He owed his life to a Russian peasant wet nurse, who sacrificed her own child in order to save him. She became his nanny and was very close to him. Though he remained a Catholic all his life, his intense identification with Russia was no doubt in part due to her influence.

Though Khodasevich's first two collections of poetry – *Youth* (Molodost', 1908) and *A Happy Little House* (Schastlivyy domik, 1914) – were, for the most part, poems about his love affairs, the overall tone of this early poetry – give or take a few poems in the second book – was one of depression, not joy: a depression riddled by feelings of sorrow and anger, pain and existential despair. A poem of June 1907, expressed his state of mind well:

V moey strane, ni zim, ni let, ni vesen,
Ni dney, ni zor', ni golubykh nochey.
Tam kruglyy god vladychestvuet osen',
Tam – seryy svet bessolnechnykh luchey.[97]

---

97 Vladislav Khodasevich, *Sobranie sochineniy v chetyrekh tomakh,* edited by V. P. Kochetov in collaboration with others (4 vols.; Moscow, 1996-97), I, 61. Further references to this

(In my land there are no winters and no summers and no springs,/ Nor days, nor dawns or sunsets, and no pale blue nights./ There only autumn all year round holds sway,/ And the grey light of sunless rays.)

It is curious that when Khodasevich published his *Collected Poems* in 1927, he did not include his first two books of poetry.[98] David Bethea has suggested that this was an aesthetic act of "disowning" the Symbolist influence on his work.[99] But the reasons may lie far deeper, in the psychological reaches of Khodasevich's personality.

The Grain's Way

Khodasevich published his *The Grain's Way* (Putem zerna) in 1920. Though, on the surface, *The Grain's Way* seems to be intent on developing the idea that the grain's "death" brings life in its wake – and a number of lines, especially in the title poem, do foster this line of thinking – at a deeper, psychic level, the metaphorical process of the whole seems to go in an opposite, life-negating direction. This inner dichotomy of *The Grain's Way* does much to cast the poems into an ironic mould.

We can see this process at work in his poem "The Acrobat" (Akrobat, 1913, 1921, I, 143). The acrobat, who is likened to the poet, walks "lightly and calmly" (legko i spokoyno) across a tightrope that is firmly and securely attached to two rooftops. The sky above is clear and transparent. The cane in his hands is his only means of keeping balance. Below him an impatient crowd of onlookers are all but waiting for him to fall. And should this acrobat or clown (figlyar) fall, the deceitful people below will just go through the motions of crossing themselves. This ironic turn in the poem only deepens the sense of a world whose reality is not always what it appears to be.

In this poem, though the poet was still full of confidence, the imagery suggested his precarious balance between life and death as he walked that fine line dividing the two realities of human existence. But the stage was also set for his possible fall into the abyss. The image of hurtling to one's death, potentially or in fact, was repeated in two other poems – "To the Aviator" (Aviatoru, 1914, I, 183) and "Solitude" (Uedinenie, 1915, I, 185), the last of which spoke of a sailor fallen to the bottom of the sea.[100]

---

edition will be given in the text and footnotes as I. Translations from Khodasevich's poetry and prose are my own unless otherwise indicated.

98 See Tomas Venclova's contribution in *Handbook of Russian Literature, op. cit.,* p. 223.

99 David M. Bethea, *Khodasevich. His Life and Art* (Princeton, New Jersey, 1983), p. 49.

100 These two poems with a few others, excluded from the 1927 edition of his collected poems, were still part of the 1920 edition. See Bethea, p. 138, fn. 66.

"The Acrobat" would prove indicative of the disturbing nature of Khodasevich's poetic vision. Indeed, it can be said that the whole of *The Grain's Way* did in effect express and develop this imagery of the poet caught between being and non-being, between a daily existential reality and one that could turn phantasmagoric and nightmarish.

Life could thus be like a scarf that was being knitted one minute, only to be undone in the next moment by death, that "guest" who might without warning come silently out of the dark and, "with a slightly terrifying smile" (s ulybkoy strashnoyu nemnozhko), undo all the knitting (I, 144). Or the poet might live amidst the everyday cares of life while his soul, hidden under a bushel (pod spudom), as if by some miracle, lived a life apart from him (I, 146). This sense of dissociation and otherness was expressed in his poem "Dreams" (Sny, 1917, I,149):

Eshche tomyas' v moem bessil'nom tele,
Skvoz' grubyy sloy zemnogo bytiya
Uchis' dyshat' i zhit' v inom predele,
Gde ty – ne ya;
(Still languishing in my powerless body,/ Learn how to breathe through the coarse layer of earthly existence/ And how to live in another dimension/ Where you are not I;).

This sense of duality was expressed in other poems as well. In one he was torn between life and the pull of some debilitating force, between the familiar pulse of life and something inside of him that overpowered him with a feeling of weakness and fading (I, 152). Death could take on a hallucinatory form as in his poem "At the Sea" (U morya, 1917, I, 158):

Von – belaya vskrutilas' pyl'
I proletela.
(There, look – a cloud of white dust has whirled up/ And passed.)

Sometimes the earthly sounds of his environment came to him as if through a sleep or a dream, as if he were in another circle of existence in another world (1919, I, 162).

The sense of self as other was hauntingly revealed in Khodasevich's beautiful poem "Look for Me" (Ishchi menya, I, 164) which he wrote between December 20, 1917 and January 3, 1918:

Ishchi menya v skvoznom vesennem svete.
Ya ves' – kak vzmakh neoshchutimykh kryl,
Ya zvuk, ya vzdokh, ya zaychik na parkete,
Ya legche zaychika: on – vot, on est', ya byl.

(Look for me in the transparent light of spring./ I'm all like flapping of invisible wings,/ I am a sound, a sigh, the play of sunlight on the parquet floor,/ I'm lighter than this play: for, it is here, it is, I was.).[101]

Increasingly, Khodasevich was moving away from adult humankind and closer to children, to flowers and wild animals. In "Stanzas" (Stansy, 1918, I, 177) he confessed:

Zato slova: tsvetok, rebenok, zver' –
Prikhodyat na usta vse chashche.
(But then words like flower, child, wild animal/ Come to
my lips more and more often.)

And again, in a poem of March 1921, we read:

Yazyk moy stal zverinym ili ptich'im,
Usta molchat. (I, 186)
(My language has become a wild animal's or a bird's,/ My lips are silent.)

There were six striking longer poems in this collection written between 1918 and 1920. One of these, the deservedly famous "The Monkey" (Obez'yana, June 7, 1918-February 20, 1919, I, 172-73), also recorded this shift in Khodasevich's poetic vision from the human to the non-human.

As the Serb busker's monkey thanked the poet for bringing it water by shaking his hand, the poet remembered shaking hands with beautiful women, poets, leaders of nations, but none of those hands had had such nobleness of outline and

... Ni odna ruka
Moey ruki tak bratsky ne kosnulas'!
I, vidit Bog, nikto v moi glaza
Ne zaglyanul tak mudro i gluboko,
Voistinu – do dna dushi moey.
(... No hand had ever/ Touched my own with such fraternal feeling!/ As God is my witness, no one had ever looked into my eyes/ so wisely and so deeply,/ In truth – to the very bottom of my soul.)

---

101 This poem, whose first stanza was excluded by Khodasevich (I, 508), was written in the wake of the suicide of one of his closest friends, Muni, in March of 1916 (see IV, 68-79). With Muni's death in mind, – viewed logically – without the first stanza, the voice of the poem would be Muni's. But if the excluded stanza is added to the poem, the voice would clearly be Khodasevich's: for, the first stanza depicts Khodasevich in *his* room discovering that he has himself – like Muni – become invisible: "Here's the mirror, but I'm not reflected in it." (Vot zerkalo, no v nem ne otrazhayus' ya, I, 508). Consequently, the following three stanzas would then clearly refer to Khodasevich , not to Muni.

As if to distance himself even more from humanity, the last line of the poem, standing alone and apart from the rest of the poem, read:

V tot den' byla ob''yavlena voyna.
(On that day war was declared.) [July 19, 1914]

Along with Khodasevich's shift towards the non-human came a parallel shift to a world of estrangement, to what Wolfgang Kayser defined as the *grotesque*: a world suddenly become strange and alien, distorting the familiar and destroying the human order of things, "so that the categories which apply to our world view become inapplicable."[102]

Khodasevich's poem "The Second of November" (2-go Noyabrya, June 1, 1918, I, 165-67), written in the aftermath of the Revolution, was a good example of a world in the process of turning strange. Thus, the image of the coffin being painted red by a joiner, a friend of the poet's, had the quality of the grotesque about it, and all the more so after the poet bowed to him through the cellar window:

... ya poklonilsya nizko
Petru Ivanovichu, ego rabote, grobu,
I vsey zemle, i nebu, chto v stekle
Lazur'yu otrazhalos'. ... (I, 166)
(... I bowed deep/ To Petr Ivanovich, to his work, to the coffin,/ And to all the earth, and to the sky, which was reflected/ Azure in the glass. ...).

Just as grotesque was the description of a boy of four sitting on a stone amidst a Moscow torn to pieces, fallen and suffering. A couple of pigeons had just been released from their basket and children were whistling and clapping, watching the pair disappear. Only this one little boy seemed oblivious to it all and, having spread wide his hands, was looking up into the sky and smiling:

Kak idol malen'kiy, sidel on, ravnodushnyy,
S bessmyslennoy, svyashchennoyu ulybkoy.
I mal'chiku ya poklonilsya tozhe. (I, 167)
(Like a small idol, he sat, indifferent,/ With a senseless, sacred smile on his face./ And to him I also bowed.)

Khodasevich's poem "An Episode" (Epizod, January 1918, I, 159-61), reminiscent of his "Look for Me", recorded what must have been an out-of-body experience lasting less than a second. Outside he could hear children

---

102 Wolfgang Kayser, *The Grotesque in Art and Literature*, Translated from the German by Ulrich Weisstein (New York-Toronto, 1966), pp. 184-85.

shouting, while at the same time a streaming and flowing (struenie) went through him from head to foot and out of his body. Whereupon he saw himself sitting alone in his room. When this experience was about to end, he remembered that he had not wanted to return to his body:

Mne bylo trudno, tesno, kak zmee,
Kotoruyu zastavili by snova
Vmestit'sya v sbroshennuyu kozhu ... (I, 160)
(I found it difficult, I felt as cramped as a snake,/ That would have been forced once again/ To fit into its shed skin.)

If this poem of self-estrangement brought out Khodasevich's yen to transcend and to escape from his earthly form, his poem "The House" (Dom, July 1919, 1920, I, 174-76), using realistic detail, suggested metaphorically a similar process of the dissolution of life as we know it. The house, once a place of human habitation, was now a ruin of its former self, one emptiness leading into another, marked by war, plague, revolt and time. Man in time was like a half-wild nomad. And Khodasevich, the poet, welcomed this disintegration of society. Addressing time, he burst out:

... Khorosho
Vdokhnut' ot tvoego uzhasnogo prostora. (I, 175)
(How good it feels/ To get a whiff of your terrifying wide open spaces.)

His yen for leaving human existence behind was well expressed in the following lines:

I chelovek dushoy neutolimoy
Brosaetsya v zhelannuyu puchinu. (I, 175)
(And man, with his insatiable soul/ Throws himself into the longed for deep.)

Not surprisingly, the poet lent a hand in this process of dissolution: at the end of the poem, as it began to grow dark and a green crescent appeared in the sky, he helped an old woman come to tear hemp fibres and shingles off the walls of the house.

The Heavy Lyre

Khodasevich left Russia in June of 1922 and *The Heavy Lyre* (Tyazhelaya lira), in its definitive version, came out in Berlin, in 1923. It is considered by some his best book of poetry.

This collection of poems could be called Dostoevskian, in that the central concern of the whole seems to revolve around spiritual salvation from an earth contaminated by Adam (I, 221-22), a world both loved by the poet for its demonic beauty and rejected for its banality, vulgarity and triviality of human existence. The spiritual and poetic conflict with an unacceptable earth made for a sometimes ambivalent and ironic undercurrent, but this did not undercut the book's primary objective of reestablishing through poetry man's lost links with his sacred beginnings in Paradise. *The Heavy Lyre,* with its Gogolian and Sologubian undertones, reads like an exorcism, as if Khodasevich had wanted to counteract the tendency to nightmare of *The Grain's Way.*

Hence, almost every poem in *The Heavy Lyre* referred to the soul (dusha) and its more earthly emanations, psyche and spirit (psikheya, dukh). The idea of the soul shedding its earthly shell to commence its spiritual journey into the reaches of cosmic night was clearly expressed in the poem "From My Diary" (Iz dnevnika, 1921, I, 214; 515). It was far better to sleep, he wrote, than to listen to the "malicious speeches of human life", for sleep might bring one closer to that other, purer, world (1921, I, 210,). But it was not easy for the human psyche to bear the inspired and prophetic words of poetry:

Prostoy dushe nevynosim
Dar taynoslyshan'ya tyazhelyy. (1921, I, 200)
(The simple soul cannot endure/ The heavy gift of secret hearing).

Yet only poetry had the power to free one from mortality, from the plague-ridden sting of vice, sickness and death:

I tol'ko tot ikh yazvy ubezhit,
Kto taynoe khranit na serdtse slovo –
Uteshnyy klyuch ot bytiya inogo. (1921, I,229)
(And only he can escape their contagion,/ Who keeps the secret word safe in his heart – /
The word that is the consoling key to an other reality.)

Come what may, the soul was fearless and would reach that other world of being, be it a heaven or a hell (!) (1921, I, 230).

The spiritual struggle to free oneself from earthly existence, however, was not an easy one because, on occasion, this earth – that in moments of delirium he hated so tenderly and mocked so lovingly (1922, I, 212), that he felt was God's incredible gift to him, a world that he recreated in his poetry only to destroy it the very next minute as if in jest, the way a small child will destroy a fortress built of cards (1921, I, 223) – this earth could at times seem like a paradise: as in the poem where the triangular sails of fishing boats going out to sea looked like winged angels walking on the water (1922, I, 239).

But ultimately – as he put it so starkly and graphically in his apocalyptic and nightmarish poem "Looking Out the Window" (Iz okna, 2: August 1921, I, 209) – the soul would have its way, even if the angels themselves would have to step in and put an end to human existence:

> Prervutsya sny, chto dushu dushat,
> Nachnetsya vse, chego khochu,
> I solntse angely potushat,
> Kak utrom – lishnyuyu svechu.
> (The dreams that choke the soul will stop,/ Everything I wish for will begin,/ And the angels will extinguish the sun,/ The way one snuffs out a superfluous candle in the morning.)

European Night

In *European Night* (Evropeyskaya noch') published in 1927 as part of his *Collected Works,* Khodasevich returned to the depressive atmosphere of his first two books of poetry and, in the process, intensified the grotesque vision of *The Grain's Way.* In fact, his *European Night* reminds one very strongly of Alexander Blok's cycle of poems *The City* (Gorod, 1904-08) which expressed such profound poetic disillusionment through the deformation of Blok's ideal, the Beautiful Lady.

The world of *European Night* was one of ugliness and terror, a world where human life was reduced to a kind of freakish and obscene purposelessness and where images of suicide, masturbation, rape and murder seemed to make up the high points of a monotonous round of human existence. The Blokian resentment and destruction of the poetic ideal found its own angry expression in the nightmarish lines of a poem of 1923:

> I v etoy zhizni mne dorozhe
> Vsekh garmonicheskikh krasot –
> Drozh', pobezhavshaya po kozhe,
> Il' uzhasa kholodnyy pot,
> Il' son, gde, nekogda edinyy, –
> Vzryvayas', razletayus' ya,
> Kak gryaz', razbryzgannaya shinoy
> Po chuzhdym sferam bytiya. (I, 250)
> (And in this life what I value/ More than all the harmonious beauties of life,/ Are the shivers running across my skin,/ Or the cold sweat of terror,// Or the dream where I – once upon a time a whole being – / Explode and am scattered all over/ Like some mud splashed by a tire/ Over alien spheres of being.)

Increasingly, the poems of this collection recorded a mounting despair over the tedium and futility of the poet's life (e. g., I, 254,256). Life had become so unendurable, in fact, that Khodasevich *wanted* to go mad (I, 282), all the more so since it was now so difficult and painful to live the life of the soul:

> I kak-to tyazhko, bol'no dazhe
> Dushoyu zhit' – (1924, I, 268).
> (And it has somehow become hard, even painful/ To live the life of one's soul –).

He had lost his way in the metropolitan desert of Paris, Khodasevich wrote in the summer of 1924, and could not find back to his tracks (I, 277), he had become deaf to the sounds of poetry and was spell-bound by his silence (I, 278). In a rage he even beat the angels:

> I angelov naotmash' b'yu, (1925, I,282).
> (And I strike the angels with swinging blows,).

His poem "Berlinian" (Berlinskoe, I, 258) written in Berlin in the autumn of 1922, had already given notice of his nightmarish and bankrupt poetic imagination. Bringing to mind both Blok's poem "The Stranger" (Neznakomka, 1906) and Nikolay Gumilev's "The Streetcar that Lost its Way" (Zabludivshiysya tramvay, 1921), "Berlinian" described how Khodasevich, one evening, sitting in the Prager Diele café over a cognac and looking out through a huge polished window, saw himself reflected in a passing streetcar window:

> I tam, skol'zya v nochnuyu gnilost',
> Na tolshche chuzhdogo stekla
> V vagonnykh oknakh otrazilas'
> Poverkhnost' moego stola, –
>
> I, pronikaya v zhizn' chuzhuyu,
> Vdrug s otvrashcheniem uznayu
> Otrublennuyu, nezhivuyu,
> Nochnuyu golovu moyu.
>
> (And there, sliding into the rottenness of night,/ The surface of my table was reflected/ In the thick and alien glass of the streetcar windows, – // And looking into someone else's life,/ I suddenly recognize with disgust/ My own chopped off and lifeless head in the night.)

Khodasevich's Berlin poem signalled the death of poetic vision. Perhaps it is not too surprising to find out that his favorite poem in the whole collection – phonically speaking (I, 522) – was "Sorrento Photographs" (Sorrentinskie fotografii, March 5, 1925 to February 26, 1926, I, 270-75), the only poem that cast a ray of sunshine over his gloomy and decaying poetic landscape.[103]

Necropolis

Though Khodasevich did write reviews of contemporary living writers, his penchant seems to have been for obituaries in essay form either of writers and poets who had been his contemporaries, as in his *Necropolis* (Nekropol', 1939), or of the more ancient dead such as the countess Evdokiya Rostopchina (the forgotten poet), Gavrila Derzhavin and Alexander Pushkin in his *On Russian Poetry* (Stat'i o russkoy poezii, 1922). Given Khodasevich's dark poetic vision, his interest in the dead rather than the living was certainly in character.

In *On Russian Poetry* he was drawn particularly to poetic themes that were relevant to his own work. Hence, in "Derzhavin" (1916, II, 39-47), his eye was caught by the inner conflict – evident in Khodasevich's poetry as well – between Derzhavin's fear "of the eternal cold and emptiness of interstellar spaces" (II, 47) and the quiet, rural existence on an earth that he loved so deeply (II, 43), between that "genuine terror, that genuine and terrifying sense of death spread throughout nature" (II, 41) and a world of plenty that he lived so sensuously (II, 45, 46).[104]

Khodasevich – though he could on occasion also be more lighthearted – turned his attention to similar themes in the works of Pushkin. This was especially true of those works in which terrestrial happiness was threatened by the dark, demonic and destructive forces lying in wait for us, ready to push us into insanity and/or death: such were Pushkin's "The Stone Guest (1830), "The Bronze Horseman" (1833) and "The Queen of Spades" (1833). (See II, 48-70).

Khodasevich's memorable collection of essays in *Necropolis* was published in Brussels just before his death. Apart from two essays on his close friends Muni (Samuil Kissin) and Mikhail Gershenzon, and two on Sergey Esenin and Maxim Gorky, his main focus fell on Russian Symbolism and its major practitioners Valery Briusov, Andrey Bely, Alexander Blok and Fedor Sologub. Leaving Sologub aside for the moment, Khodasevich's recurring

---

103 See also Vladimir Weidlé's fine essay on Khodasevich's poetry where he found two instances in his "Sorrento Photographs" where he felt that Khodasevich had reached the "peak of [his] poetry" as a whole. See V. Veydle, "Poeziya Khodasevicha," in *Sovremennye Zapiski*, Vol. 34, N.D.V., 1928, pp. 452-69, here pp. 467-68.

104 See also Khodasevich's biography *Derzhavin* (1931, III, 119-394, here p. 214).

concern was with the other Symbolists and how their art, in his estimation, *had lost all contact with life.*

Thus, in his "Briusov" (1924, IV, 19-41), he focussed on how the idolization of art could lead to the destruction of human lives, including Briusov's own (see IV, 27). In "Andrey Bely" (1934-38, IV, 42-67), he explored how the demonization of reality through a deranged psyche, transcribed into artistic form, could in the end only undermine the will to live life as it was in actuality (IV, 55, 60, 66, 67). In "Gumilev and Blok" (1931, IV, 80-94), he was especially shaken by Blok's death, the tragedy of a great poet who could no longer keep step with a revolutionary Russia that had taken away his creative freedom (IV, 91, 93).

In "Esenin" (1926, IV,120-50), – a romantic, neo-Symbolist poet – Khodasevich saw Esenin's refusal to recognize "the disparity between dream and reality" (IV, 146) and his involvement with a variety of agrarian ideologies, as the root cause that took him away from his one, real love, that was Russia and, in the end, destroyed him as a poet (IV, 150). In this context, the inclusion of Gorky was not surprising. Not only had they been close at one time, but Gorky, the official socialist realist figurehead of the new, revolutionary Russia was, essentially, like Esenin or the Acmeist Gumilev, a romantic whose support of the Bolshevik cause in Russia made him ultimately also lose contact with the social and humane needs of the poor and disadvantaged Russian people to whom he had been profoundly committed. In "Gorky" (1936, IV, 151-82), Khodasevich explained this tragic process in Gorky in the light of the latter's fateful predisposition for the lie rather than the truth, and for illusion rather than reality (IV, 166-67, 178).

Khodasevich's profound concern with writers and poets whose art had lost touch with life – a problem that, as we shall see, concerned him as well – was well expressed in his critique of Russian Symbolism as a whole in "The End of Renata" (Konets Renaty, 1928, IV, 7-18):

> The miserly knights of Symbolism were dying of
> spiritual hunger on their sacks of saved up "experiences". (IV, 10)

The Solitary Poet

In his unfinished autobiographical fragments *Infancy* (Mladenchestvo, 1933, IV, 190-209), Khodasevich wrote of his and Tsvetaeva's isolation as poets:

> But I and Tsvetaeva – who is, by the way, younger than I – having come out of Symbolism, have not attached ourselves to anything or anybody, have remained forever solitary, "wild" (IV, 190)

Khodasevich's sense of isolation among the Russian émigrés in France[105] was probably one reason for his decision to stop writing after 1927. Bethea, speaking of Khodasevich's biography of Derzhavin, came to a similar conclusion:

> But, as the biographer knew, there was bound to be a waning of Derzhavin's creative and civic energies. Thus, as Khodasevich came to describe the last years of Derzhavin and the inevitable decline that set in, his thoughts must have turned to himself. These final pages, I believe, are as close as the reader comes to an "explanation" of Khodasevich's silence as a poet. Like Derzhavin, Khodasevich had fallen out of touch with the epoch to which he had given his life.[106]

But Derzhavin was not only a mirror for Khodasevich's loss of confidence in himself as a poet. He was also a prime example of a writer whose poetry had always been rooted in existential reality (see, e. g., III, 351-52, 541). And it was the same aspect that drew him to Pushkin's work in his highly interesting exploration of Pushkin's poetic mind in *On Pushkin* (O Pushkine, 1937, III, 395-511):

> [Pushkin] loved this connection between life and creative work and loved, just for himself, to firm up this connection by way of sly hints which were scattered all across his writings (III, 493).

Finally, in "Sologub" (1928, IV, 106-19), Khodasevich found a *modern* poet whose original poetic genius, philosophic reach and creative solitude had allowed him to remain *relevant* beyond the political and artistic confines of a hostile revolutionary society.

But the exemplary lives and works of three poets dear to Khodasevich's heart – Derzhavin, Pushkin, Sologub – were not able to vanquish his own sense of being a superfluous man and poet no longer connected to his time. This would also explain the intensity of his critique of the Russian Symbolist poets even though he never quite lost the sense of still being a part of the Russian Symbolist movement.[107]

---

105 See Khodasevich's rather pessimistic view in 1933 of the present and future of Russian émigré literature in his "Literature in Exile" (Literatura v izgnanii, II, 256-67); see also his obituary of the poet Boris Poplavsky in 1935, where he drew attention to the "general despair"among the younger generation of Russian émigré writers (II, 362-67); and his forebodings in 1938 about both Russian émigré and European literatures in "The Dying of Art" (Umiranie iskusstva, II, 444- 48).

106 See Bethea, *op. cit.,* p. 336; and also pp. 15, 18, 255, 324-41.

107 *Ibid.,* pp. 189, 248, 315, 348, 349, 350. See also the Introduction to volume I by S. Bocharov, "'The Monument' of Khodasevich" ('Pamyatnik' Khodasevicha, I, 5-56), here pp. 27-28, 32, 40, 53. See also Khodasevich's "On Symbolism" (O simvolizme, 1928, II, 173-76), esp. pp. 175-76.

There may, however, be another reason for Khodasevich's poetic silence. It lay in the very nature and process of his poetic vision. We have seen, for example, how his depressive beginnings in *Youth* and *A Happy Little House* opened up to a life-negating poetic imagination in *The Grain's Way* whose disturbing, ironic and nightmarish perspective began to shift towards a world of estrangement and of the non-human. The presence of a few, more life-affirming, poems, such as the title poem itself (1917, I, 137), or the poems "Noon" (Polden', 1918, I, 168-69) and "The Encounter" (Vstrecha, 1918, I, 170-71), could not stem the metaphorical process towards dissolution.

Nor was this process stopped by Khodasevich's *The Heavy Lyre*. For, though it reads like an exorcism of the evils of earthly existence and recorded Khodasevich's spiritual attempt to free himself of his negative poetic vision, in the end he failed, as we could see from his poem "Looking Out the Window" (1921, 2: I, 209).

His last book of poetry *European Night* – after which he essentially fell silent as a poet – only intensified his dark poetic perspective which ultimately led to the death of his poetic vision altogether, as can be gathered from his poem "Berlinian" (1922, I, 258).

Conclusion

Hence, a number of factors may have contributed to Khodasevich's decision to stop writing poetry: his sense of isolation as a poet, his feeling that his art was out of touch with contemporary life, that contemporary literature, both Russian émigré and European was, in any case, in decline and, finally, his own dark, life-negating poetic vision. Gleb Struve has put the case well. Of Khodasevich's stopping to write poetry he said:

> Was it a drying out of the creative source or the conscious dooming of oneself to silence? I think it was both. Khodasevich's path from *The Grain's Way* to *The Heavy Lyre* and *European Night* foreshadowed this end, this irreparable poetic impasse. Even if we see this path ... as one of maturing and perfecting his art. But this maturing was connected with a continuously growing realization of a tragic split and as tragic a discord with the world – and an equally sharp realization of the impotence of poetry. Khodasevich's feel for human existence (mirooshchushchenie) was tragic through and through. In his poetry, with all its remarkable concreteness, its corporeal spirituality, Khodasevich did not respond spontaneously and directly to events, but our epoch weighed heavily on his poetry with some kind of oppressive nightmare.[108]

---

108 Struve, *Russkaya literatura v izgnanii, op. cit.,* p. 144. My tr.

We can be fairly certain that the metaphorical language of Khodasevich's poetry in particular, was an accurate reflection of his state of mind. David Bethea has observed quite correctly that "Khodasevich's poems nearly always tell the story of 'where he was' psychologically at the moment of writing."[109] Even his essays in *Necropolis*, for example, with their critique of Russian Symbolism as an art out of touch with real life, may have in effect reflected his own creative impasse.

Before he left Russia, Khodasevich gave a speech on Pushkin – "The Shaken Tripod" (Koleblemyy trenozhnik, II, 77-85) – in the Writer's House in Petersburg on February 14, 1921 – Blok had just given his Pushkin speech the day before in the same venue – in which he saw Russian culture being engulfed by a darkness that was fast approaching. His life in exile did not brighten this vision and the nightmare world of his poetry only intensified his sense of gloom. In June of 1939, a few days before his death from cancer in a Paris hospital, and on the eve of a World War that even he could not have quite imagined, his fear of being alone, cut off from everybody, overpowered him with a vengeance. To his former wife Nina Berberova who had remained a close friend, he said:

> "To be somewhere," he said, tears pouring, "and to know nothing of you!"
> I wanted to say something to him, to comfort him, but he continued:
> "I know I am only an obstacle in your life ... But to be somewhere, in a spot where I would never again know anything about you! ... Only about you ... Only about you ... I love only you ... All the time about you,day and night about you alone ... You know ... How will I be without you?
> ... Where will I be? ... It doesn't make any difference. Only you be happy and well, drive slowly. Now farewell."[110]

In an unfinished poem he called "Monument" (Pamyatnik, I 362), written in Paris in 1928 and published there in 1939, he had written:

> Vo mne konets, vo mne nachalo.
> Mnoy sovershennoe tak malo!
> No vse zh ya prochnoe zveno:
> Mne eto schastie dano.
>
> V Rossii novoy, no velikoy,
> Postavyat idol moy dvulikiy
> Na perekrestke dvukh dorog,
> Gde vremya, veter i pesok ...

---

109 Bethea, *op. cit.,* p. 92.
110 Nina Berberova, *The Italics Are Mine,* Translated from the Russian by Philippe Radley (London, 1991), p. 363.

(I am the end and the beginning./ I've done so little!/ But still I am a solid link:/ This happiness is given me.// In a new but great Russia,/ They'll put my Janus-faced idol/ At the crossing of two roads,/ A place of time and wind and sand ...).

His poetic legacy was small but was assured a place in Russian letters, this much knowledge and happiness was his. He would not be forgotten.But at the same time there was something alien and heathen in the two-faced and deceptive idol tha a *new* Russia would erect in his memory, and something precarious about the place where he would stand at the crossroads, like some homeless wanderer not knowing which way to turn and at the mercy of time, wind and sand. As we can see, Khodasevich's humble estimate of and belief in his poetic achievement was almost immediately torn apart by self-doubt and an ironic sense of human immortality. If only he had had a stronger sense of being a "solid link", of *belonging* and not being alone, a greater sureness of the durability of his poetic work and that his poetic day would yet come. No one less than Vladimir Nabokov, in a Foreword to his novel *The Gift*, would write in 1962: "Gone is Vladislav Khodasevich, the greatest Russian poet that the twentieth century has yet produced."[111] Today, Khodasevich is no longer alone.

---

111 Vladimir Nabokov, *The Gift*, Translated from the Russian by Michael Scammel with the collaboration of the author (New York, 1963), n. p. See also Vladimir Nabokov, "On Khodasevich," (1939) where he called him "the greatest Russian poet of our time", in *The Bitter Air of Exile: Russian Writers in the West 1922-1972, op. cit.,* pp. 83-87, here p. 83.

Boris Poplavsky: Poet of Unknown Destination

> The entire horizon is blindingly occupied by God; in every sweaty creature He is right there again. Eyesight grows dim and there is no shade anywhere, for there is no home of my own, but only history, eternity, apocalypse. There is no soul, no personality, no I, nothing is mine; from heaven to earth there is only the fiery waterfall of universal existence, inception, disappearance.
>
> Boris Poplavsky: *Homeward from Heaven*[112]

The Life of a Poet

In her excellent essay on Poplavsky's life[113] Elena Menegaldo gives us meaningful insights into Poplavsky's childhood years:

> ... but it is noteworthy, nonetheless, [she wrote] that Boris always felt himself to be a child who had no mother, – this is confirmed by key images in his poems and in his search for the ideal woman who would be both mother and wife to him. There is no doubt that what contributed to his feeling of bitter loneliness was, in no small way, his mother's imperious character, and her demands could not but conflict with the embittered opposition of the child who was defending his inner self. It was an irreconcilable conflict that in the end led to open warfare. (*N.*, 27)

Menegaldo continued:

> Without any doubt Boris's mother never thought about her responsibility in the shaping of her son's character, did not give any thought to how her innumerable moralizing forays, her reproaches and demands and, what is most important, her lack of affection made her sensitive child suffer and triggered an inferiority complex in him which in turn had a decisive influence in developing a sense of social inadequacy which caused Sofia Valentinovna so much grief. (*N.*, 27)

---

112 Translated from Poplavsky's novel by Simon Karlinsky in his "In search of Poplavsky: a collage," in *The Bitter Air of Exile, op. cit.*, pp. 311-33, here p. 323.

113 See Elena Menegal'do, "Liniya zhizni," in Boris Poplavsky, *Neizdannoe. Dnevniki. Stat'i. Stikhi. Pis'ma,* edited by A. Bogoslovsky and E. Menegal'do (Moscow, 1996), pp. 26-52. Page references to this edition in the text or footnotes will be given as *N.* All translations are mine.

Though his mother was herself interested in theosophy, – she was a distant relative of Madame Blavatsky – she could not make peace with the fact that her child's spiritual tendencies were incompatible with a life bent on material gain and status, insisting that both could coexist, side by side (*N.,* 28). "She neither understood her son, nor his poetry, and after Boris's death was the only close family member who did not participate in the publication of his book of poetry *The Snowy Hour.*" (*N.,* 27; see also *N.,* 241)

Fortunately, he had a loving and tolerant father. But he too did not fully understand his son. He never read even one of his poems, though he respected his artistic work:

> Throughout Boris's lifetime he would give him ten francs a day and did everything possible to insure his son's well-being and freedom. His son, in return, adored his father and, when they lived apart, would write to him daily, whereas over his lifetime he did not even send one letter to his mother. (*N.,* 28)

His father came from Polish peasant stock and Boris inherited his athletic build, his physical strength and his love of boxing but not, it seems, his father's ability to fully take in the joys and the down-to-earth pleasures of life. In contrast, his mother came from the gentry in the Baltic States, suffered from psychological ills (chelovek s bol'noy dushoy) and was haunted by all kinds of terrors which pushed her into spiritualistic pursuits. (*N.,* 26-29)

Boris inherited his mother's neurotic disposition, for he was prone to outbursts of praying and crying which often lasted for hours (*N.,* 9, 36, 37, 234, 437-38 and *passim*) and would as often spend long hours sleeping during the daytime (*N.,* 37, 42 and *passim*). His state of mind probably explained his seeking comfort in God and in Russian Orthodoxy, though ultimately, he rejected both the Russian Church and esoteric pursuits – which he felt lacked genuine religiousness – in favour of a more personal, spontaneous, mystic experience of God (*N.,* 46). His addiction to drugs to which his sister Natasha presumably introduced him by the time he was twelve, – probably opium, followed by cocaine in Constantinople and later by heroin in France – could not but have aggravated his state of health.[114]

In 1918, when he was fifteen, he and his father escaped the violence of the Revolution of 1917 by going to the south of Russia which they left in November of 1920, crossing the Black Sea to Constantinople. There they stayed till May of 1921 at which time they went on to Paris.

---

114 See Karlinsky, "In Search of Poplavsky ....," who wrote that Natasha "introduced Boris to drugs by the time he was twelve" and that she died from a "hopeless opium addiction," *op. cit.,* p329. See also *N.,* 29, 35, 40, 41.

In his father's October 1935 reminiscence of him (*N., 423-25*) – not always accurate – Boris became profoundly religious and mystical in Constantinople. The money his father gave him, and often Boris's own food and belongings, were given away to the less fortunate – Russian students, officers, monks, sailors and other refugees – whom he would often put up for the night at their place. He sketched and read a great deal. In 1921 they both left for Paris where, with the exception of a few months in Berlin in 1922 (!), Boris lived out the days that were left to him ... Boris actually lived in Berlin from 1922 to 1924 studying painting (*N., 25, 38, 462*). One of the reasons why he left Paris was probably also his wish to avoid his mother who arrived with his brother in Paris in 1922.

His father finished his recollections saying that Boris's close friends thought of him as a "religious mystic, a seeker after God, and a lucid and profound philosopher." (*N., 425*)

The details about Poplavsky's life in Paris are much better known. He visited museums, was active in sports, had an omnivorous yearning for knowledge and wrote. He would occasionally drop into the Academy of Art at La Grande Chaumière on Montparnasse and sit in unofficially on life drawing classes (*N., 441*), enrolled at the Sorbonne in history and philology, studied philosophy and theology, and would spend many hours in the rare manuscript room of the Library of Sainte Geneviève. He was deeply involved in the Russian cultural life of Paris, took part in literary debates and conferences, read papers and was very well known. But he was probably happiest in the cafés of Montparnasse where he would spend his nights discussing and arguing about literature and metaphysical subjects. He was a very articulate and impressive speaker, always wearing his sunglasses, and in the view of many, "one of the most educated writers of his generation" (*N., 43*).

But the family lived in dire poverty. Boris's brother Vsevolod, his mother's favorite, was forced to quit his courses at the Sorbonne and become a taxi driver. His sister Natasha left the family in the late 20s, going off to the island of Madagascar, then to Africa and India, and ending up in China where she died from an overdose of opium (*N., 29*). Boris himself, would now and again, look for a job, but his inability to hang on to it would be followed by bouts of severe depression (*N., 40, 42*).[115] Day after day, he lived like a beggar in the streets of Paris doing his best not to let on publically how dire his straits were.

---

115 Gleb Struve has suggested that Poplavsky, though he was in good health, "did not know how and did not want to work"; see Struve, *Russkaya literatura v izgnanii, op. cit.,* pp. 310-14, here p. 314. It is ironic that Struve should, among other things, have ignored the amount of work that Poplavsky put into his studying and writing, work that was both academic and creative.

There was one bit of sunshine in his life, and that was the love of his life, Natalia Stolyarova, who became his fiancée. He had met her in 1931 and dedicated a cycle of poems to her in his *The Snowy Hour* collection of poems. But her departure to the Soviet Union in December of 1934 left him totally bereft (*N.,* 10, 17, 49-50, 69-78) and his depressions returned with a vengeance. It is not clear, why she decided to accompany her father back to the Soviet Union. She and Poplavsky had plans to reunite in a year's time. But things turned out differently. Poplavsky died, her father was executed and she herself was arrested in 1937. Released in the spring of 1945, she was rehabilitated only after 1956. She was able to visit her sister and friends in France in the 1960s, and spent her last years in the Soviet Union translating French writers into Russian. She died in August of 1984.

There seems to be no doubt that Poplavsky suffered from mental illness of which his recurring depressions were symptomatic (*N.,* 40, 42, 113, 117). His early death in Paris, in October of 1935 at the age of thirty-two, either from an overdose of heroin, or it may have been a suicide or murder (*N.,* 51-52, 404-18, 425), finally put an end to his suffering.

Poplavsky's Views on Contemporary Life and Literature

Between 1929 and 1934 Poplavsky wrote a number of articles on religious, philosophical and literary matters, book reviews and responses to question-naires (see *N.,* 249-306).

Reading this material, it becomes clear that Poplavsky was indeed a child of two cultures. He was not only involved in Russian cultural life but was equally attracted to French and European cultures. But he was quick to add that his French perspective was based on his Parisian experience.

He was particularly impressed by the "French respect" for individual rights of expression which he contrasted with the oppression of the individual in the Soviet Union (*N.,* 304). On the other hand, he was also perturbed by a European world which he believed was on the verge of destruction. Already in 1932 he was uneasy about the relationship between capitalism and fascism, especially as it pertained to the armament manufacturer Krupp in Hitler's Germany (*N.,* 289, 245). "Already now we are living not in historical but in eschatological times ...," he wrote (*N.,* 289). It was almost as if he sensed the coming of the Holocaust. His vision was just as grim a year earlier:

An abstract inhuman epoch is on the rise, a new Assyria, a kingdom of huge masses and of flatness merciless to individuality. It is not for nothing that the newest architecture is carried away by purely Assyrian schematic and monumental proportions. From this abstract point of view the human being is but an ephemeral unit, easily moulded or liquidated one way or another. (*N.*, 264)

Poplavsky's main concern was therefore how to protect the individual's spiritual life from this coming devastation, and this is where the poet and writer came in.

Dynamic, mystic energy was at the centre of Poplavsky's world view (*N.*, 277), and of poetry in particular: "The theme of a poem," he wrote, "its mystic centre, lies beyond initial comprehension ...", which made a poem into a revelation that surpassed the poet (*N.*, 251, 252). Russian literature as a whole was "deeply mystical", he believed, and Blok, for example, who "listened to time", was in a sense the personification of this mystic energy (*N.*, 255).

The cornerstone of Poplavsky's philosophy of being seems to have been a "mystical compassion for human beings" (*N.*, 263). Though traditionally associated with Dostoevsky and Chekhov, and the Russian Orthodox Christ, this mystical compassion was a "new note" that countered Bolshevik cruelty and could, for example, be found in Nabokov's Luzhin [*Luzhin's Defence*, Russian ed., 1930] (*N.*, 263). Compassion, Poplavsky maintained, was synonymous with Russian humanism. (*N.*, 282). In this context, Lermontov was "the first Russian Christian writer" (*N.*, 273). James Joyce's *Ulysses* was also an expression of "immense compassion", as was the poetry of Arthur Rimbaud and Blok (*N.*, 276, 253, 259).

Poplavsky saw himself – and those who, like him, were associated with the journal *Numbers* (Chisla)[116] – as the "avant-garde of Russian Westernism" based on a "literature of truth about our day and age, a literature that like some eternal music of hunger and happiness sounds to us on the boulevard Montparnasse" (*N.*, 300).

But this eternal music came out of a creative process that was at bottom acutely painful, because the artist could describe the world's deteriorating human fabric only in terms of his own experience (*N.*, 277, 283). Poplavsky's focus on the artist's self and the creative process explains his interest in dreams, Freudian psychoanalysis and French surrealism (*N.*, 264, 274, 459). As he put it in an essay of 1930 entitled "On the Mystical Atmosphere of the Young Literature in Emigration": "There exists only the document, only the

---

116 This apolitical journal, edited by Nikolay Otsup, came out in ten issues between 1930 and 1934. It was comparative in the sense that it focussed not only on poetry and literature, but also on painting and sculpture, music and dance, and on past and contemporary literatures, on Virgil and Goethe, and Proust and Joyce. The literary section of the journal was mostly made up of young writers and poets who advocated simplicity and humanity and who shared a sense of impending catastrophe. See Struve, *Russkaya literatura v izgnanii*, pp. 213-18. See also *N.*, 47-48.

fact of spiritual life. The private letter, the diary and the psychoanalytical shorthand report are the best means to express this." (*N.,* 257)

Perhaps the most alarming point in Poplavsky's vision of European society and its art was the idea that a return to "Christian Orthodox" spirituality was to be achieved even at the price of great social suffering and pain. Compassion for humankind demanded that, if necessary, even unimagineable pain should be inflicted by the writer and poet on the present social order as a way of shocking it into humane awareness. Almost paradoxically and enigmatically he wrote:

> Does man help anyone through sorrow? Yes, probably. It is necessary to increase the world's pain in order to make that pain more tolerable. The world's pain must become unendurable before one can come to love that pain. (*N.,* 268)

Writings on Painting

Between 1929 and 1932 Poplavsky also wrote articles on contemporary painters and reviewed art exhibits in Paris (*N.,* 307-45).

In the history of European art he was particularly drawn to painters who were original, unconventional and avant-garde. His favorites were Leonardo da Vinci, Rembrandt, Claude Lorrain and Gustave Moreau (*N.,* 464), the latter of which is considered to have been a forerunner of surrealism. Poplavsky was attracted to the French impressionists Claude Monet, Auguste Renoir and especially Paul Cézanne and Camille Pissaro (*N.,* 333, 340-42, 464).

Among contemporary European painters he had high praise for French painting, for example the work of André Derain, Maurice Utrillo and Raoul Dufy (*N.,* 310, 315, 327, 335, 344). But he also admired the works of Amedeo Modigliani, Pablo Picasso and Giorgio de Chirico (*N.,* 464). As for the Russian émigré painters he was especially fond of Marc Chagall, a forerunner of surrealism, of the rayonists Mikhail Larionov (his best friend among the painters, *N.,* 37) and his wife Natalia Goncharova, of Ivan Puni (Jean Pougny) and of the expressionist Chaim Soutine.

In Poplavsky's view of painting, art did not only have to depict the world as it was, but as it should be – by which he meant that a painting should express the artist's "live entelechy", that is, it should be bent on the actualization of creative potentiality. Hence in *deforming* the world, the artist was actually transforming it in the light of some inner ideal (*N.,* 328, 329). In trying to describe this process visually, Poplavsky used words that bring to mind Larionov's *Blue Rayonism* and Goncharova's *Green-Yellow Forest*, both painted in 1912[117]:

> Doesn't every mortal feel ... that everything is half-bound to stagnation and yearning for form? And once again the artist helps out, helps the tree to melt in the air, the noonday garden to bloom and be radiant, the reflections of rivers to turn green, he continues creation, he helps God. (*N.*, 328-29)

Poplavsky went on to define what the French called "esprit", the spirit of painting, in the following words:

> The spirit of a painter is the plastic expression of all his ideas, all his reveries and beliefs and, to a very large extent, even the expression of his life and, what is the main thing, of a greater or lesser attitude to art as something sacred and prayerfully important (molitvenno vazhnomu, *N.*, 332).

Art as such was a seeking out of the "'form' of God" (*N.*, 333), and Rembrandt was exemplary here:

> All one's struggles, all despair, all seeking after the most important, as well as all well-being and amusements find their reflection on canvas. And ... it is not charm or fascination only that we see through the eyes of Rembrandt but the tragic nature of the world, its tendency towards ruin, its illusoriness, and death and compassion. (*N.*, 333)

In this sense, Cézanne with his "superior soul" and "immense pain," was a "titan and genius, Renoir merely a beautiful painter ..." (*N.*, 333).

It is interesting to note that Poplavsky devoted a whole article on the Russian émigré painter Abram Minchin, in the wake of his sudden death in 1931 when he was only thirty-three (*N.*, 325-26). Minchin collaborated with the journal *Numbers* and was considered even a "genius" by some (*N.*, 336, 463, 496). Alexander Bogoslavsky in his enlightening commentary on Poplavsky's articles on painting (*N.*, 461-65), made a very interesting analogy between Minchin's paintings and Poplavsky's poetry:

> And so, one of [Poplavsky's] articles is dedicated to the work of Abram Minchin whom B. Sosinsky [writer, literary critic, close friend of Poplavsky] described as a "genius who died prematurely," and who was spiritually and artistically close to Poplavsky. In essence, Poplavsky himself strove for the same kind of "rare combination of realism and the fantastic" that we find in Minchin. Sometimes one even has the feeling that in describing the magical world of Minchin's paintings, Poplavsky is really speaking about the magical atmosphere (stikhiya) of his book of poetry *Flags*. (*N.*, 464)

---

117 See Camilla Gray, *Die russische Avantgarde der modernen Kunst 1863-1922,* Translated from the English by Dr. Eva Rapsilber (Cologne, 1963), pp. 119, 121.

Modernism

Reading Poplavsky's poetry, one is particularly reminded of Rimbaud and of the French surrealists. Rimbaud's famous "Le Bateau ivre" (The Drunken Boat, 1871) with its metaphorical critique of European civilization, its poetic exaltation and ultimate disillusionment captures much of Poplavsky's tragic poetic spirit.[118] And Rimbaud's thoughts on his creative process had much in common with Poplavsky's own. At the age of sixteen, in a letter to his teacher George Izambard, Rimbaud wrote in May of 1871:

> Je veux être poète, et je travaille à me rendre *voyant.* ... Il s'agit d'arriver à l'inconnu par le dérèglement de *tous les sens.* Les souffrances sont énormes, mais il faut être fort, être né poète, et je me suis reconnu poète.[119] (His italics)
> (I want to be a poet and I am working to make myself a *seer.* ... It is a question of reaching the unknown by the derangement of *all the senses.* The sufferings are enormous, but one has to be strong, one has to be born a poet, and I know I am a poet.)

Poplavsky's contemporary Yury Terapiano, writer, poet and critic, observed in 1953 that Poplavsky "was the first and the last Russian surrealist."[120] Indeed, there is much in the subatomic world of Poplavsky's poetry that reminds one of André Breton's thoughts on surrealism which hit out against our world of cause and effect, negating predictability, logic and consciousness, in favour of the spontaneous flow of the imagination, the fluidity of the dream and the creative potential of our subconscious.[121] Apart from Poplavsky's Russian romantic and modernist poetic inheritance (Lermontov, Fedor Tyutchev, Blok, Bely, Tsvetaeva), and the influence of German romanticism on his work (Friedrich Hölderlin and Heine among others), Menegaldo singled out his poetic debt to the French modernists (Baudelaire, Lautréamont, Rimbaud, Verlaine, Guillaume Appolinaire and Jules Laforgue) and the French surrealists (Louis Aragon, André Breton, Paul Eluard, Philippe Soupault and Tristan Tzara), the last three of whom Poplavsky knew personally (*N.,* 21).[122]

---

118 See *Rimbaud. Complete Works, Selected Letters,* Translation, Introduction and Notes by Wallace Fowlie (Chicago and London, 1966), pp. 114-20.

119 "Lettres du voyant", *ibid.,* p. 302. The translation is on p. 303.

120 Yury Terapiano, "Boris Poplavsky," in *Boris Poplavsky v otsenkakh i vospominaniyakh sovremennikov,* edited by Louis Allain and Olga Grise (St. Petersburg-Düsseldorf, 1993), pp. 134-38, here p. 136. All translations from this volume are mine.

121 See André Breton, "Manifesto of Surrealim," (1924) in *Manifestoes of Surrealism* (Ann Arbor, 1969), pp. 3-29. See also Boris Poplavsky, *Avtomaticheskie stikhi,* edited by Vladimir Kochetov, introduction by Elena Menegal'do (Moscow, 1999), pp. 5-30.

122 For modernism see *Modernism 1890-1930,* edited by Malcolm Bradbury and James McFarlane (Harmondsworth, 1983); see also Arthur Symons, *The Symbolist Movement in Literature,* with

A Difficult Poet

I have looked at Poplavsky's social and aesthetic ideas in order to create a possible context of reference for his poetry which is a difficult poetry to read and understand. His Russian émigré contemporaries thought so too. The poet, critic and friend Georgy Adamovich, for example, observed in 1955 that even admirers of Poplavsky's poetry did not always understand him. Perhaps it was the intentional haziness and obscurity of his poetry, or the "obsessive, drugging melodiousness" of his poems which contributed to the difficulty of interpretation.[123] In his obituary of Poplavsky in October of 1935, Adamovich had also drawn attention to the "incredible muddle" in Poplavsky's head due "in part to his insatiable thirst for knowledge" which he never had the time to digest properly. Caught between two cultures, without any "inner structure," "unbalanced by nature [he] rushed about without ever quite knowing what cause to espouse." The "musical basis" of his poetry also ran interference with making sense of it.[124]

Nikolay Tatishchev, writer, critic, a longtime friend of Poplavsky's who looked after the latter's archive and helped bring out Poplavsky's works, said essentially the same thing in 1938. It may also have been his "mysticism" which aggravated the situation for, as Tatishchev put it a decade later, Poplavsky's mystic reaching out for God imbued his poetry with a kind of "dulled, muddied music and unintelligible chaos." Still his poetry made an unforgettable impact on the reader and

> ... gradually the chaos would begin to lift and, out of a seeming piling up of images and dreams, a landscape would arise, mysterious but distinct, like Claude Lorrain's evening harbours with ships.[125]

The literary critic and future scholar Marc Slonim wrote an illuminating review of Poplavsky's first book of poetry *Flags* in 1931 which he also described as "unclear and at times incomprehensible" but went on to say that

> It is full of fantastic visions of monsters, moonlit dirigibles, deranged young women, dwellers of heaven and demons ... The connection between ideas and words is very often lost in Poplavsky's poems – in any case, ideas are not important for his poetic connections, and one should not look for logical meaning in this motley world populated with

---

an Introduction by Richard Ellman (New York, 1958); and Jean Pierrot, *The Decadent Imagination 1880-1900*, Translated by Derek Coltman (Chicago and London, 1981).

123 G. Adamovich, "Poplavsky," in *Boris Poplavsky ..., op. cit.*, pp. 13-18, here pp. 13, 14-15 respectively.

124 G. Adamovich, "Pamyati Poplavskogo," *ibid.,* pp. 18-22, here pp. 19, 20, 21.

125 See N. Tatishchev's "O Poplavskom," (1938) and "Poet v izgnanii," (1947), *ibid.,* pp. 92-108, here pp. 98, 100, 101 respectively.

conventional images. All this play of the imagination, all these sometimes vague and sometimes unexpectedly vivid dreams live and are moved by the power of music, and flow at the bidding of those rhythmic combinations that Poplavsky commands. Music, i. e., that element of poetry which makes up its primary nature, everything that it is impossible to express in words, that lies ... *outside* rational understanding and the five senses, this is what makes Poplavsky's poems most remarkable.[126] (His italics)

Flags

Poplavsky's *Flags* (Flagi) was published in Paris in 1931 and was the only book of poetry to come out during his lifetime. It included poems written between 1923 and 1930.

Menegaldo has pointed out that for Poplavsky life experience cut across all fictional and non-fictional lines (*N.,* 7, 10). We should therefore expect to find his experiences and concerns reflected, to some degree at least, in his poetry which became central to his life.

And indeed, what seemed to be the cornerstone of his humanism, i. e., pity and compassion (zhalost'), was contained in the very title poem of the collection:

Vsekh nas flagov osenyala zhalost'.[127]
(We were all protected by the flags' compassion.)

One suspects that references to compassion (which is a feminine in Russian) occur in several guises throughout this collection of poems: sometimes as a direct reference by using the word "compassion" itself (*S.,* 71, 72, 78, 83, 86); sometimes by a capitalized "You" in its pronominal and possessive forms (*S.,* 57, 60, 63, 89, 93); at other times by way of personification where, for example, his Morella (*S.,* 92-94) and Seraphita (*S.,* 94-96), might very well have been feminine reincarnations of the spirit of compassion. Thus, Seraphita, in Poplavsky a *female* three-winged seraph who has traditionally surrounded God's throne, was weeping out of compassion for man's poor and miserable lot:

I byla Ty tikha, kak rassvet nad fabrichnym kvartalom,
Khorosha tochno pyl'naya vetka v pustykh gorodakh.
Ty u gryaznoy steny prislonivshis' kak p'yanyy stoyala,
I v glazakh Tvoikh slezy siyali kak ptitsy v lesakh. (*S.,* 96)

---

126 M. Slonim, "Kniga stikhov B. Poplavskogo (B. Poplavsky. *Flagi),*" *ibid.,* pp. 169-71, here p. 169.

127 Boris Poplavsky, *Sochineniya,* edited by S. A. Ivanova (St. Petersburg, 1999), p. 62. Further page references to this edition will be given in the text or footnotes as *S.* All translations are mine.

(And You were as quiet as dawn breaking over a workingman's quarter,/ As beautiful as a dusty branch in an empty city./ Like a drunkard You stood leaning against a dirty wall,/ And in Your eyes tears shone like birds in the forest.)

But Poplavsky's *Flags* was not motivated by the feeling of compassion alone, it was also energized by the *conflict* between compassion and music, two seemingly irreconcilable impulses, two incompatible worlds: the ugly world of human misery which brought compassion into being in the first place, and the beautiful world of poetry whose music, after all, might actually make one blind and insensitive to human suffering. This underlying conflict in Poplavsky's poetry may perhaps explain the following two lines in his poem "The Spirit of Music" (Dukh muzyki) written in 1930:

Lomala ruki v pereulki zhalost'
I muzyku ubit' zvala narod. (*S.*, 84)
(Compassion wrung her hands in the alley/ And called on the people to kill music.)

This may also elucidate the rather enigmatic line in his poem "Paysage d' Enfer" (Landscape of Hell) written in 1926:

Dusha molchala na granitse zvuka. (*S.*, 45)
(The soul [a feminine in Russian] was silent at the edge of sound.)

Poplavsky's *deformation* of his imagery was probably an attempt to undercut the power of music in his lines, even though the imagery, to be effective, depended on the music of his poetry. There are a great many instances of this intentional deformation in his work. We have one such instance in his "Starry Hell" (Zvezdnyy ad, 1926), where a deranged star, possibly another meta-morphosis of compassion, erred amid a world of sounds:

Chu! podrazhaya solov'yu poet
Bezumnaya zvezda nad sadom sonnym.
...
Bluzhdaya v zvukakh nad goroy zazhglas',
Gde spal steklyannyy mal'chik v plat'e snezhnom,
Zaplakal on ne raskryvaya glaz,
I na zare rastayal dymom nezhnym. (*S.*, 46)
(Hark! imitating a nightingale/ An insane star sings over a sleepy garden.// ... Erring among the sounds the star caught fire above the hill,/ Where a little boy out of glass was sleeping in his snowy clothes,/ He burst out crying without opening his eyes,/ And then at dawn melted away in delicate smoke.)

Music was dangerous to the poet, for when he was captivated by it, his life resembled a convict's and made him deaf to God's call (*S.*, 37, 35).

In his remarkable poem "The Black Madonna" (Chernaya Madonna) written in 1927, – a close cousin to the insane star – he continued the theme of conflict between music and compassion, this time expressed in terms of transient and eternal categories of being: the loud and hectic sounds of a jazz band – but a brief and flickering moment of earthly time dreamt by the Black Madonna in her restless sleep – and the quiet and eternal passage of cosmic Time. It was the arrogant and dandyish youth, the poet, who suddenly heard

...
Schast'ya kratkiy vystrel, let mgnovennyy,
Leta krasnyy mesyats na volnakh.

Vdrug vozniknet na ustakh trombona
Vizg sharov, krutyashchikhsya vo mgle.
Diko vskriknet chernaya Madonna
Ruki razmetav v smertel'nom sne.

I skvoz' zhar, nochnoy, svyashchennyy, adnyy,
Skvoz' lilovyy dym, gde pel klarnet,
Zaporkhaet belyy, besposhchadnyy
Sneg idushchiy milliony let. (*S.,* 49-50)

(The brief shot of happiness, sudden flying,/ The red moon of summer on the waves.// suddenly on the trombone's lips/ Rise the squeals of balloons spinning in the darkness./ And the frightened outcry of the black Madonna/ Tossing wildly in her mortal sleep.// Through the heat of night, sacred, hellish heat,/ Through the violet smoke where the clarinet was singing,/ The white and merciless snow will suddenly start flurrying/ As it has done for millions of years.)

Poplavsky may have conceived his two Morella poems as a way of countering the fateful pull of poetry. Thus we find Morella standing at the very spot where once "the soul was silent at the edge of sound":

...
Ty, kak chernyy shtandard, razvevalas' *na samom krayu.*

Ty, kak *zhizn' vozvrashchalas',* kak svet uletayushchiy v
    bezdnu
Ty vstupila na vozdukh i tikho skvoz' vozdukh ushla,
A navstrechu sletali ogromnye *snezhnye zvezdy,*
Okruzhali *Tebya,* tselovali *Tebya* bez chisla.
(*S.,* 94, my italics)

(You were like a black banner flying *at the very edge.*// You were like *life returning,* like light flying into the deep/ You stepped out into the air and left through it quietly,/ And enormous *snowy stars* were flying down to meet *You,*/ Surrounded *You* in great numbers and kissed *You.)*

The Snowy Hour

The Snowy Hour (Snezhnyy chas) collection of poems written between 1931 and 1935, appeared in 1936 after Poplavsky's death, though he had already prepared it for publication in the summer of 1935.

In *The Snowy Hour* – with the exception of the poems dedicated to Natalia Stolyarova, which made up the last twenty pages of the collection, – the creative dynamism of Poplavsky's *Flags,* expressed in the clash between music and compassion, was gone. Instead, the poems were written in a plaintive minor key, and there seemed to be a basic giving up on all the things held dear before – life, poetry and spirituality. These poems read as if they had been conceived while the poet was in deep depression.

Poplavsky's poetic world became cold and naked, defenceless before the frigid blasts of winter. The poet's heart was now icy and empty and the blue sky above was ill (*S.,* 107, 108). The poet was exhausted, his soul was dead and silent and he himself was morally ill:

> Bolezneyu, kotoroyu ya bolen,
> Byl bolen mir, ot pervykh dney grekha. (*S.,* 108)
> (I suffer from the same illness/That has plagued the world since sin began.)

It was a time to sleep, to suffer and to die. Poetic inspiration was gone, for the birds had all left (*S.,* 112). The world was as empty as a desert (*S.,* 115) and the poet had no more strength left to live (*S.,* 118). Even his faith was shaken (*S.,* 130), and suicide a distinct possibility (*S.,* 137).

> Pevets Morelly! boysya vody,
> Skol'zit v ney belyy venets luny. (*S.,* 143)
> (Morella's bard! beware of the water,/ The moon's white wreath glides over it.)

The mention of Morella recalled the theme of compassion in *Flags.* But the theme had by now lost much of its power. In fact, compassion could no longer help him now (*S.,* 115). His poem "The Flags are Lowered" (Flagi spuskayutsya, *S.,* 145-46), written perhaps on the 15th of July (*S.,* 384) of 1931, was already a dirge to compassion:

> Ty siyal, teper' soydi s flagshtoka,
> Vozvratis' k obyknovennoy zhizni. (*S.,* 145)
> (You used to be a radiant poet, now come down from the flagstaff,/ And return to ordinary life.)

Poplavsky's judgement of himself and his poetry was equally disillusioned:

> Chto zh padi. Ty ozaryal temnitsu,

Ty siyal, prinyav lazurnyy uzhas.
Spi. Usni. Lyubov' nam tol'ko snitsya,
Ty, kak schast'e, nikomu ne nuzhen. (*S.,* 146)
(Well, fall then. You used to illumine this dark dungeon,/ You were radiant, even when
taking on the azure horror./ Sleep and pass away. We only dream of love,/Like happiness,
you are a poet whom nobody needs.)

But love had been waiting in the wings.

Above the Sunny Music of the Water

It was in the autumn of 1931 (*N.,* 74) that Poplavsky met Natalia Stolyarova
who, for some three years, brought sunshine back into his life. They were
deeply in love and were going to get married. The cycle of poems "Above the
Sunny Music of the Water" (Nad solnechnoyu muzykoy vody) was dedicated
to her and was written during their three years together, from 1931 to 1934.
In these poems Poplavsky celebrated the return of music in his poetry.

The cycle resembled a bright sunny day at the seashore following a dark,
stormy night. The poems expressed a spiritual and emotional, a sensual and
visual awakening. Colour, warmth and feelings streamed back into his
poetry, it was springtime and nature was radiant. The poet's heart was full of
love and joy, and his eyes were open to all things, be they sailboats out at sea,
the leaves in the forest or the flowers and fields of the countryside.

It felt like a resurrection, the world was wonderful, a new happiness had
come his way making him forget the tortures of winter (*S.,* 151). His soul had
come to life again and the birds were back (*S.,* 155, 157, 167). In the title
poem of the cycle, written in 1934, he announced that his soul had once again
risen out of winter's dark (*S.,* 158):[128]

Lozhus' na teplyy veresk, zabyvaya
O tom, kak dolgo muchilsya, lyubya.
Glaza, na solntse greyas', zakryvayu
I snova navsegda lyublyu Tebya.
(I lie down on the warm heather/ And loving You, forget how long I suffered./ Warming
myself in the sun, I close my eyes/ And love You once again forever.)

Love, he wrote, was a universal force, forever accompanied by sacred joy,
and he was now able again to believe and to listen to the waves (*S.,* 161,
162). He now understood that the earth and joy were deeper and more
profound than pain (*S.,* 163), and he realized

---

128 The fact that these poems were written in the same time period as his other depressed winter
poems in *The Snowy Hour* suggests that Poplavsky may have suffered from mood swings.

Chto temnee lzhi pechal' bez very,
A bol'naya zhalost' gorshe zla. (*S.,* 163)
(That sorrow without faith is darker than the lie,/ And that a sick compassion is more bitter than evil.)

In a Wreath of Wax

In a Wreath of Wax (V venke iz voska) is a very short collection of poems, just over twenty pages long. It was also put together by Poplavsky in the summer of 1935. But only the last fifteen pages or so seem to be attuned to the poetic tone and logic of *The Snowy Hour.* Since only two poems of the early 20s were dated, the desperate feeling of these last fifteen pages suggests that they were most likely written in 1935 after Natalia Stolyarova's departure to the Soviet Union.

There is no doubt that Poplavsky had once again sunk back into depression. Spring was gone and he was totally destroyed (*S.,* 181). Snow was again beginning to fall over his poetic landscape through which reverberated the screaching of a bird that had alighted on a bronze statue darkened by time (*S.,* 182).

His poetry became peopled with skeletons (*S.,* 186, 187, 189 and *passim*) and there was no cure for his illness (*S.,* 186). His life was like a boat filling with water and going to the bottom (*S.,* 187). A severe cold spell was on the way and the snowy landscape was turning mute and empty (*S.,* 189, 191). His soul lay ill and delirious in sickbed, laughing wildly and straining to get away to the land of the stars (*S.,* 195-96).

A number of nightmarish poems were a foreboding of the end, as for example the poem dedicated to Georgy Adamovich (*S.,* 188-89), where skeletons at the bottom of a river still had the human faces of guests and were hanging from the ceiling. In another poem (*S.,* 192-93), dedicated to Minchin, you could hear the horrifying screams of violets as the sunset blazed scarlet over an insane asylum and a leaf on a tree screamed its imminent demise in a shrill and terrifying voice. An imagery of death and departure was in the air:

Byla zima vo mne i ya v zime.
Kto mozhet sporit' s etim morem alym,
Kogda dusha povesilas' v tyur'me
I chernyy mir rodilsya nad vokzalom. (*S.,* 192)
(I was in winter and winter was in me./ Who can argue with this scarlet sea,/ When the soul has hanged itself in prison/ And a dark world is born over the railway station.)

Poplavsky's poem "Green Horror" (Zelenyy uzhas, *S.,* 193-94) was a final leave-taking, the poet a sick corpse, the world in a delirium, and all the clocks in an unhealthy hurry. He had just taken his seat in a streetcar of unknown destination, and even his music, filthy at its source, had succumbed to illness and absinthe:

Temneet den', vesna kipit v zakate,
I muzykoy bol'noy zevaet sad.
Tam zhenshchina na rozovom plakate,
Smeyas', rukoy ukazyvaet ad.

Voskhodit noch', zelenyy uzhas schast'ya
Razlit vo vsem, i lunnyy yad kipit.
I my uzhe, u muzyki vo vlasti
U gryaznogo fontana prosim pit'. (*S.*, 194)

(The day grows darker, spring is seething in the sunset,/ And the garden yawns its sick music./ There a woman on a rose-coloured placard/ Is laughing and pointing to hell.// Night comes, the green horror of happiness/ Fills up everything and the moon poison seethes./ We are already in the music's power/ And beg to drink from the filthy fountain.)

Farewell to life, he wrote –

Proshchay, epicheskaya zhizn',
Noch' salyutuet neizvestnym flagom. (*S.*, 190)
(Farewell to epic life,/ The night salutes with an unknown flag.)[129]

Conclusion

In 1939, in Paris, Nikolay Berdiaev reviewed a book of selections from Poplavsky's diaries that had just appeared. He thought it "a sad and tortured book" and a "document of a contemporary soul, a young Russian soul in emigration."[130] Berdiaev went on to suggest that Poplavsky was a man of *ressentiment,* deeply resentful of his failure in life, a man who felt himself to be marginalized, immured, having neither spiritual nor social anchorage. He saw him as "a victim of his striving for holiness," and a tragic example of the "disintegration of personality."[131] I think, Berdiaev saw clearly. Poplavsky's

---

129 Though Poplavsky had planned to bring out *A Dirigible of Unknown Destination* (Dirizhabl' neizvestnogo napravleniya) in the mid-twenties, the collection as brought out by Tatishchev in 1965 (*S.*, 207-46) contained poems already previously published. Moreover, we cannot be sure that the other poems in this collection are as Poplavsky left them, since Tatishchev is known to have not only corrected but also *improved upon* Poplavsky's poems (see *S.*, 394-95).

130 N. Berdyaev, "Po povodu *Dnevnikov* B. Poplavskogo," in *Boris Poplavsky..., op. cit.*, pp. 150-55, here p. 150.

131 *Ibid.*, pp. 151-52, 152, 154 respectively.

friend Georgy Adamovich pointed to another problem when he spoke of him as being a child of two cultures.[132] Poplavsky seemed to be thinking along similar lines when he wrote of his rootlessness in a diary entry of August 4, 1933:

> But to some, life has given form and structure ... whereas I seethe under a terrifying pressure and find myself without a theme, without an audience, without a wife, without a country, without friends. And again my life is about to set out for somewhere, but then returns into its self and moves away from any realization. (*N.*, 111)

And, indeed, there were tragic aspects to Poplavsky's life that undermined his potential for involving himself with real life and deepened his sense of alienation over and above his social and cultural displacement. There was, for example, his feeling of emotional abandonment by his mother during his childhood years and later, his addiction to drugs, his mental illness and his loneliness. There were also, what Freud would have called, Poplavsky's sublimations to fill the inner emptiness – his search for God, his mystic quest, his huge thirst for knowledge, his surrealistic explorations of the subconscious and dreams, and perhaps even his compassionate concern for the individual and the future of European society.

But perhaps his greatest sublimation was his poetry. Nikolay Tatishchev, who knew him as well as anyone, made a very curious observation in 1974:

> Indeed, it was with music that Poplavsky defended himself against life, and it was the despair he felt before life that gave rise to the poet's power within him.[133]

Poplavsky's use of his poetry as a defense mechanism, as a way of coping with life, suggests that poetry may also have been a cover for his more personal and intimate experiences that he could only bring himself to touch upon metaphorically, if at all. Perhaps Adamovich came closest to expressing the reader's feeling of something left unsaid in Poplavsky's poetry, of a sense of incompleteness about Poplavsky's persona, when he wrote in 1955 that

> His poems are not he himself: they are a story about himself, more precisely, a commentary on him, an addendum to his dreams, thoughts, doubts and emotional impulses.[134]

Poplavsky himself may have given us a clue in a diary entry of July10, 1935, in which he spoke of the characters in his two novels:[135]

---

132 Adamovich, "Pamyati Poplavskogo," in *ibid.,* p. 21.
133 Tatishchev, "Dirizhabl' neizvestnogo napravleniya," *ibid.,* pp. 125-30, here p. 128.
134 Adamovich, "Poplavsky," *ibid.,* p. 14.

No, I found them [the characters] ready and waiting in my self, for they are my multiple personalities, and their struggle – the struggle in my heart between compassion and severity, between love of life and love of death – all of them are me, but who am I really? Among them I am a no one, a nothing, I am a field on which they do battle, a spectator. I am also a spectator because out of the dark of my soul all these personalities and many others have come out to meet the people who love me. (*N.*, 115-16)

There was much in Poplavsky that reminds one of Russian and European modernism: the same intensification of consciousness that Poe – who influenced Poplavsky's work (*N.*, 15, 21) – had already drawn attention to in 1843: "And have I not told you that what you mistake for madness is but over acuteness of the senses?",[136] the same "mystic need" in the absence of faith, and the same "unquenchable thirst for God," that the writer and religious thinker Dimitry Merezhkovsky, in an essay of 1893, believed characterized the whole of the 19th century,[137] and which Rimbaud, for example, gave voice to in his "Une Saison en Enfer" (A Season in Hell, 1873) when he wrote: "J'attends Dieu avec gourmandise" (Gluttonously I am waiting for God) and "J'ai soif, si soif!" (I am thirsty, so thirsty!),[138] the same pathological yearning for death and oblivion and, finally, the same alienation from life and repudiation of the real world outside, a state of mind that Joseph Frank in an essay of 1945 described as a flight from historical time.[139]

There was also a profound feeling of hopelessness in Poplavsky that he shared with Rimbaud. Thus, lines in Poplavsky's poem "Salome II" (*S.*, 78-80) written in 1929, bring the end of Rimbaud's "The Drunken Boat" to mind where a child, full of sadness, sails its little boat across a cold, black puddle, a boat as fragile as a butterfly in May.[140] Poplavsky's lines speak of a "pale-blue and droll sailor" (Goluboy i smeshnoy matros) searching in vain for his lost childhood:

---

135 Poplavsky's two novels were *Scandalous Apollo* (Apollon Bezobrazov, 1932) and *Homeward from Heaven* (Domoy s nebes, 1935). Some chapters appeared serially in Paris in the 1930s and in New York in the 1950s. The novels were finally published in full in St. Petersburg in 1993.

136 See Edgar Allan Poe, "The Tell-Tale Heart," in *Edgar Allan Poe,* Selected and Edited with an Introduction and Notes by Philip Van Doren Stern (New York, 1961), p. 293.

137 See D. S. Merezhkovsky, "O prichinakh upadka i o novykh techeniyakh sovremennoy russkoy literatury," in *Izbrannye stat'i. Simvolizm, Gogol, Lermontov,* Rpt. of vols. 10 and 15 of *The Complete Works,* St. Petersburg-Moscow, 1911-12 edition (Munich, 1972), pp. 207-305, here pp. 244-45, 296 respectively.

138 *Rimbaud. Complete Works, Selected Letters, op. cit.,* pp. 176, 184 (tr. pp. 177, 185).

139 See Joseph Frank, "Spatial Form in Modern Literature," in his *The Widening Gyre. Crisis and Mastery in Modern Literature* (Bloomington and London, 1963), pp. 3-62, here p.60.

140 Rimbaud, "Le Bateau ivre," *op. cit.,* p.120, tr. on p. 121.

Budet detstvo svoe iskat',
Nikogda ego ne naydet.
V okeane, gde spit toska,
Razob'etsya o vechnyy led. (*S.*, 79)
(He will look for his childhood,/ But will never find it./ In the ocean, where depression
sleeps,/ He'll be smashed against the eternal ice.)

Still, beyond all the anguish that assailed Poplavsky out of the dark of his
mental illness, one senses a heart-rending plea, a desperate need to be
remembered as a poet, which may explain the often outré and bizarre images
of his poetry. We get a hint of this in an article of 1932:

> Often, to escape all grief and distress, I go away to the library. I do this, because for a long
> time now I have come to understand the profound responsibility I owe to the dead writers of
> the past to read their works. For, I think they did not live for themselves or their
> contemporaries, but for me. It is as if they were beseeching me from their shelves to help
> them fulfill their purpose, to save their lives, which would otherwise remain so futile. (*N.*,
> 288)

His wish has come true, but for him the future looked bleak. In "Salome I"
(*S.*, 77-78), six years before his demise, he predicted his own death in the
figure of the droll sailor:

Goluboy i smeshnoy matros
otravilsya vinom iz roz,
...
Pozhaley, ego pozhaley!
Pomogi emu umiret'. (*S.*, 78)
(The pale-blue and droll sailor/ Has poisoned himself to death with a wine made from
roses,// ... Do have pity on him, have pity!/ Help him die.)

As these lines indicate, there was an innate contradictoriness in Poplavsky
that allowed him at the same time that he was accusing poetry of being a
potentially fatal activity to ask his readers for some kind of compassionate
understanding of his life as a poet. His distrust of poetry made for a tragic
ambivalence in Poplavsky towards his art.

The modernist revolution in aesthetic consciousness was, after all, an
intensified romanticism, which Poplavsky personified and lived to the full.
Modernism continued to move the poet into the centre of the universe in
which God could no longer be easily found and which, in turn, brought with
it a great loneliness for the poet coupled with a haunting sense of inner emptiness, a mystic hunger that no amount of spiritual yearning could still. Perhaps
it was living this spiritual crisis, whose psychological and intellectual

symptoms were inner discord, paradox and complexity, that made Poplavsky a poet both for his time and ours. His poetry is certainly living proof of that.

The Ebb of Joseph Brodsky's Poetic Inspiration

> But you don't dissect a bird to
> find the origins of its song.
>
> Joseph Brodsky: *Less Than One*

Poems 1965

In Brodsky's first collection of poems published in the U.S. in 1965, his metaphorical voice was full of promise:

V kazhdom iz nas
  Bog.[141]
(In every one of us/ there is a God.)

History might go its way, but a God's presence – the Source of universal energy – was in each genuine poem. Brodsky's poetic space had nothing to do with historical time, as horrifying as it might be. His poetic inspiration had its source elsewhere:

...
Sedaya noch',
i dremlyushchie ptitsy
kachayutsya ot siney tishiny. (*St.,* 29)
(The night is grey,/ and the slumbering birds/ are rocked by the blue stillness.)

In the larger, cosmic context, man was not dependent on the quirks of history, but had it in him to wait out the difficult times:

Ya khochu perezhdat', peregnat', perezhit' eto vremya, (*St.,* 41)
(I want to wait till this time is over, to overtake and survive it,)

It was in his power to do this, for even the dead in the Jewish cemetery near Leningrad had been in charge of their own lives:

---

141 Joseph Brodsky, *Stikhotvoreniya i poemy* (Washington D.C.-New York, 1965), p. 23. Further page references to this edition will be given in text or footnotes as *St.* All translations are mine.

Prosto sami lozhilis'
v kholodnuyu zemlyu, kak zerna.
I navek zasypali. (*St.,* 54)
(They simply lay down of themselves/ in the cold earth, like grains./ And fell asleep forever.)

Nor was he himself as a poet bound to the themes of time:

No chto-nibud' ostanetsya vo mne –
v zhivushchem ili v mertvom cheloveke –
i vyrvetsya iz mira
  i izvne
rasstanetsya, svobodnoe naveki. (*St.,* 57)
(But something will be left in me –/ in the living or the dead human being –/ and will break away from the world/ and from without/ it will depart, forever free.)

Being independent of time, however, made for a profound loneliness to which Brodsky gave powerful expression in his poem "You'll come home to your native land. So what." (Vorotish'sya na rodinu. Nu chto zh. *St.,* 58-59):

Kak khorosho na svete odnomu
idti peshkom s shumyashchego vokzala. (*St.,* 58)
(How good it feels in the whole wide world/ to leave a noisy railway station behind one, on foot and alone.)

The same feeling of loneliness was expressed in his beautiful, almost otherworldly, poem "The Garden" (Sad, *St.,* 64-65), or in his "Pilgrims" (Piligrimy, *St.,* 66-67). In the latter poem the pilgrim's eyes were full of sunset as they left the deserts of this world, with only the stars above worrying over them, and with the bitter knowledge that the world would always be the same:

i khriplo krichat im ptitsy,
chto mir ostanetsya prezhnim. (*St.,* 66)
(and the birds' hoarse cries tell them/ that the world won't change.)

Only lamentation and song could come close to capturing the ineffable essence of life (*St.,* 79). In his poem "Again I have visited" (Vot ya vnov' posetil, *St.,* 80-84), he tried to describe this eternal essence in terms of poetic existence:

Eto – vechnaya zhizn':
porazitel'nyy most, neumolchnoe slovo,
proplyvan'e barzhi,
ozhivlen'e lyubvi, ubivan'e bylogo,

parakhodov ogni (*St.,* 83)
(This is the eternal life:/ the astounding bridge, the never-silent word,/ a passing barge,/ the reviving of love, the killing of the past,/ the lights of the boats)

All this was enough for the poet. This was also why – over and above the ironic undertone – he was so relieved not to have to come back to anywhere:

Kak legko mne teper'
ottogo, chto ni s kem ne rasstalsya.
Slava Bogu, chto ya na zemle bez otchizny ostalsya.
(*St.,* 84)
(I'm so relieved/ that I haven't had to say farewell to anyone./ Thank God, that I've been left without a fatherland on earth.)

This was also why in the poem "I'm like Ulysses" (Ya kak Uliss, *St.,* 97-98), everything – his exile, his various destinations on earth, his losses on the road and in time – was but so much "rubbish" (erunda, *St.,* 97). And the reason for all this was that the poet had nothing in common with humankind:

"Neuzhto on byl voronoy?"
"Ptitsey, ptisey on byl." (*St.,* 107)
("Don't tell me he was a crow?"/ He was a bird, a bird.")

The Great Elegy to John Donne

"The Great Elegy to John Donne" (Bol'shaya elegiya Dzhonu Donnu)[142] was written in 1963, at a time when Brodsky knew very little of Donne and when his English was still at a rather "rudimentary" stage.[143] In this sense, the poem tells us more about Brodsky than it does about Donne, and gives us an almost prophetic insight, metaphorically speaking, – as if he had had a premonition himself – into the coming ebb of his creative inspiration. This elegy is probably Brodsky's finest poem, perhaps all the more overpowering precisely because of its foreshadowing nature.

When John Donne fell asleep, everything that had ever had any meaning for him, be it on earth or in the universe, fell asleep with him. Amid the hypnotic, repetitive flow of the poem, all light became extinguished and all sounds became mute, as Donne's eyes could no longer see or his ears hear – all, except the hoarse gurgling of water and snow somewhere, and the crunching or rustling of the snow that had fallen on earth out of the universe.

---

142 Joseph Brodsky, *Ostanovka v pustyne* (Ann Arbor, 1988), pp. 21-26. Page references to this edition will be given as *Ost.* All translations are mine.
143 See David M. Bethea, *Joseph Brodsky and the Creation of Exile* (Princeton, 1994), p. 84.

Some forty lines into the poem, the realization dawns on us that Donne's death and the Angst associated with it in Brodsky's mind, was the shadow of Brodsky's own anticipated death. The worst of it, however, was not death itself but the fact that with it also came the death of *poetry*. We can be fairly certain of the analogy that Brodsky drew between Donne and himself as a poet, by looking at the bird images that were to become so central to Brodsky's own creative process, especially as it ebbed over time:

> I ptitsy spyat. Ne slyshno pen'ya ikh.
> Voroniy krik ne slyshen, noch' ... (*Ost.*, 22)
> (And the birds are asleep. You cannot hear their singing./ You cannot hear the crows, it's night ...)

With the demise of the inspired creative process even God was asleep and earth had become an alien realm. The poet's death put to death all images, rhymes and lines of poetry which were now so very far from the "gates of paradise" (*Ost.*, 23). But, suddenly, someone was heard weeping in the dark. It turned out to be Donne's poetic soul, universal sister to Brodsky's, weeping in a thin, thin voice. At this crucial moment, another image, that would become associated with Brodsky's poetic impasse, surfaced:

> Tak tonok golos. Tonok, vpryam' igla.
> A niti net ... (*Ost.*, 23)
> (Such a thin voice. Thin as a needle./ But the thread is missing ...)

It was at this juncture that Brodsky, speaking in the first person, revealed his association with and his presence in the poem:

> ... lish' ya odin glaza otkryl, (*Ost.*, 24)
> (... I alone opened my eyes,)

Then the soul told Donne/Brodsky that he "used to be a bird" (Ty ptitsey byl, *Ost.*, 24) and that even God was defined by the work of the poet at night:

> Gospod' ottuda – tol'ko svet v okne
> tumannoy noch'yu v samom dal'nem dome. (*Ost.*, 24)
> (And God up there is but the light in the window/ of the house at the very outskirts during a foggy night.)

While time and fate still smiled upon the poet's work, his life was being spun by the shuttle:

> i vzad – vpered igla, igla letaet. (*Ost.*, 25)
> (and the needle, the needle shuttles back and forth.)

Donne/Brodsky slept in his nest like a bird and, like a bird's, his soul was pure even though he had lived a worldly, sinful life, a life that was nevertheless transformed through poetry be it in a world where the starling-houses were empty:

> estestvenney voron'ego gnezda
> nad seroyu tolpoy pustykh skvoreshen.
> Podob'e ptits, ... (*Ost.,* 25-26)
> ([a life] more genuine than a crow's nest/ above the greyish crowd of empty starling-houses./ Like a bird, ...)

The end of the poem was a poignant evocation of the creative life and death of a poet, indeed of all poets:

> Ved' esli mozhno s kem-to zhizn' delit',
> to kto zhe s nami nashu smert' razdelit?
> Dyra v sey tkani. Vsyak, kto khochet, rvet.
> So vsekh kontsov. Uydet. Vernetsya snova.
> Eshche ryvok! I tol'ko nebosvod
> vo mrake inogda beret iglu portnogo.
> Spi, spi, Dzhon Donn. Usni, sebya ne much'.
> Kaftan dyryav, dyryav. Visit unylo.
> Togo glyadi i vyglyanet iz tuch
> Zvezda, chto stol'ko let tvoy mir khranila. (*Ost.,* 26)
> (For if one can share one's life with someone,/ who then will share our death with us?/ This fabric has a tear. And all who wish can tear it./ At all ends. They'll leave and then return again./ Another rip! And only the firmament/ out there in the dark will sometimes take up the tailor's needle./ Sleep, sleep John Donne. Sleep deep, do not torment yourself./ Your coat is full of holes. Hangs there despondent./ You'll see, the Star that for so many years watched over your world/ will come out from behind the clouds and look at you.)

A Stop in the Desert

A Stop in the Desert (Ostanovka v pustyne) was first published in the U.S. in 1970. About one third of the lyrical poems in this collection had already been published in 1965. It was in the third cycle of poems *The Fountain* (Fontan, *Ost.,* 101-36) – with the exception of the portraits of Brodsky's school chums in "From the 'School Anthology'" (Iz 'shkol'noy antologii', *Ost.,* 119-27) – that Brodsky returned to the theme of his poetic identity.

The Fountain

The poems of this cycle were, for the most part, written during the period of Brodsky's hard labour. It is noteworthy for an exploration of the development of his poetic imagery that in almost every poem, including even the later poems of this cycle written up to 1969, the poet figured as a bird.

In this context, the poems continued where he had left off in 1965, identifying himself with the crow. As such the poems were meant to confirm his identity as a poet in a gallery of birds that was as varied as the poems which, on the realistic level, were filled with the details of the rural environment of a state farm.

Thus, the very first poem of the cycle raised the image of singing thrushes (*Ost.,* 103). Then came birds (*Ost.,* 104), cranes (*Ost.,* 107), a woodgrouse (*Ost.,* 108), a duck (*Ost.,* 110), a starling-house (*Ost.,* 111), a woodpecker (*Ost.,* 114), starlings (*Ost.,* 128) and doves (*Ost.,* 133). At times there could be heard the chirping, the whistles and the cries of birds (*Ost.,* 110, 117, 132) associated with the world of trees, forests and birches (*Ost.,* 104, 112, 113, 129). There was even a lone , distant cousin of the flying family in the live moth that the poet found in a warm hay-loft in winter (*Ost.,* 116). Again, as before, the poet became one of the birds:

> i dvadtsati pyati
> ot rodu,
> poyu na polputi
> v prirodu. (*Ost.,* 107, 1964)
> (And at/ twenty-five,/ I sing/ already halfway to nature.)

And

> ya prevrashchus' v glukharya, (*Ost.,* 108, 1964)
> (I'll turn into a woodgrouse,)

A Stop in the Desert

This cycle of poems was comparatively short – eight longer poems in all – but its focus on the connection of the poet and of the creative process with nature and the universe, made up for its brevity.

Brodsky had already written a poem on T. S. Eliot's death in the *The Fountain*: "January 1, 1965" (1 yanvarya 1965 goda, *Ost.,* 115; Eliot actually died on January 4). The poem addressed both Eliot's poetic fate and no doubt his own, since the prospect of five years of forced labour could not have augured too well for Brodsky's own future:

> Volkhvy zabudut adres tvoy.
> Ne budet zvezd nad golovoy.
> I tol'ko vetra siplyy voy
> rasslyshish' ty, kak vstar'.
> Ty sbrosish' ten' s ustalykh plech,
> zaduv svechu pred tem, kak lech',
> poskol'ku bol'she dney, chem svech
> sulit nam kalendar'. (1965)
> (The soothsayers will forget your address./ There will be no stars above your head./ And, as in olden times, you'll make out/ only the wind's husky howl./ You'll cast your shadow from your tired shoulders,/ blow out the candle before lying down,/ seeing as how the calendar promises us/ more days than candles.)

The three poems that opened *A Stop in theDesert* were also written on Eliot's death. "Poems on the Death of T. S. Eliot" (Stikhi na smert' T. S. Eliota, *Ost.,* 139-41, January 12, 1965) were central to the whole cycle in that they elevated the poet's significance to the level of natural phenomena. It is interesting to note that, in doing so, Brodsky did not celebrate Eliot's poetic achievements which were left behind, as much as the *power* of his poetic spirit which he merged with the ebb and flow of the sea. Only the sea's tides, their rise and fall, could do justice to the greatness of Eliot's poetic self and suggest the immensity of the loss:

> Na pustyryakh uzhe pylali elki,
> i vymetalis' za porog oskolki,
> i vodvoryalis' angely na polke.
> Katolik, on dozhil do Rozhdestva.
> No, slovno more v shumnyy chas priliva,
> za volnolom plesnuvshi, spravedlivo
> nazad vbiraet volny – toroplivo
> ot svoego ushel on torzhestva.
>
> Uzhe ne Bog, a tol'ko vremya, Vremya
> zovet ego. I molodoe plemya
> ogromnykh voln ego dvizhen'ya bremya
> na samyy kray tsvetushchey bakhromy
> legko voznosit i, prostivshis', b'etsya
> o kray zemli. V izbytke sil smeetsya.
> I yanvarem ego zaliv vdaetsya
> v tu sushu dney, gde ostaemsya my. (*Ost.,* 140)

(The Christmas trees were already ablaze in the waste lands of empty lots,/ and broken splinters were swept out beyond the threshold,/ and angels were put back upon the shelf./ A Catholic, he lived to see Christmas./ But, hurriedly he left the celebration of his triumph,/ the way the sea, at the noisy hour of high tide,/ having splashed beyond the breakwater, / will justly take back its waves.// It was not God, but time, Time/ that called him. And the young tribe/ of towering waves lightly carried and lifted up the burden of his movements/ to the very edge of the flowering fringe/ and, having said farewell, beat against the edge of earth./ And laughed amid the over-abundance of their strength./ And his high January tide floods/ the dry land of days, where we are left behind.)

The celebration of a poet's going, bathed the whole cycle in a nostalgic light. But it was a nostalgia with an edge. Thus, the two somewhat sarcastic poems to the Muse, which remind one of Blok's irreverence towards his Beautiful Lady, marred the celebratory tone of the whole. In the one, "To a Poetess" (Odnoy poetesse, *Ost.,* 142-43, 1965), a depreciative reference to the Muse, he saw himself as an "epigone and parrot," a mere "classicist," and addressed his Muse as "madam". In the other, "Farewell Miss Veronica" (Proshchayte, Madmuazel' Veronika, *Ost.,* 169-74, 1967), – mindful of its biblical associations, – he lamented Her absence, symbolized in the empty arm-chair she had once sat in (*Ost.,* 171), demoted Her to the crow that had now re-placed the eagle (*Ost.,* 173) and reduced Her universal home to a mere postal address (*Ost., 174*).

The chirping of birds suggested the coming of poetic inspiration but, instead, the Blokian deformation of the Muse and the decline in poetic inspiration continued in the mistaking of a fatted fowl for a rook (*Ost.,* 147), of a crow's nest turning out to be a lookout on a ship (*Ost.,* 149); in the "chirping titmouse and rustling grass" being only dreamed by the poet (*Ost.,* 152); in the roads that led "only into the forest" but under an empty heaven (*Ost.,* 158); and in his "New Stanzas to Augusta" (Novye stansy k Avguste, *Ost.,* 156-60, 1964), where it was now September and "all the birds had flown away" (*Ost.,* 156).

The waves, too, instead of being used in a major key, as in the Eliot poem, were now expressed in a minor, plaintive mode. Threateningly, the water was already at the level of his chest as he, the poet, was leaving on his last voyage (*Ost.,* 151); he, the poet, preferred to *drown* in the waves (*Ost.,* 154); and in "A Letter in a Bottle" (Pis'mo v butylke, *Ost.,* 148-55, 1965), – in itself a cry for help – he again addressed his Muse in a sarcastic, irreverent and ambivalent way:

Tak vspominayte zh menya, madam,
pri vide voln, stremyashchikhsya k Vam,
pri vide stremyashchikhsya k Vam valov
v bege strok i v guden'i slov. ... (*Ost.,* 155)
(So, madam, do please remember me,/ in the sight of the waves rushing towards You,/ in the sight of the billows rushing towards You,/ in the running of the poetic lines and in the hum of words. ...)

From a full gallop he had dropped into a trot, and even Euterpe, the Muse of music and lyrical poetry, or Calliope, the Muse of eloquence and epic poetry, could no longer help him (*Ost.*, 160). In fact, even he himself felt as if he no longer existed:

> Da zdes' kak budto vpravdu net menya. (*Ost.*, 159)
> (And, indeed, it is as if I weren't here at all.)

The End of a Beautiful Epoch

The End of a Beautiful Epoch (Konets prekrasnoy epokhi) was published in 1977. In essence, this collection of poems continued the theme of the loss of poetic empowerment and the deformation of his Muse.

He saw the Muse as his fiancée, who now drank, and the poet cursed his craft because he had no longer anything to give: for he came to the celebration of Christmas – Brodsky's favorite festive occasion perhaps because, metaphorically speaking, Christ's birth was the equivalent of the miraculous birth of poetry – with empty pockets.[144] He was now "totally in the power of hallucinations" (*Kon.*, 8). In the deranged world of the 20th century the sanctity of poetry and its creative inspiration had been replaced by artificial drugs:

> Shprits povesyat vmesto ikony
> Spasitelya i Svyatoy Marii. (*Kon.*, 12)
> (In place of the icon of the Saviour and of Holy Mary/ they'll hang a syringe.)

The empty arm-chair of the previous collection was now just a chair on which sat the poet himself "shaking with rage" and "not wishing to look for pearls in the compost!" (*Kon.*, 15). It was probably the poet who wandered "among the ruins, stirring up the leaves of yesteryear" (*Kon.*, 18)

The poem "To the memory of T. B." (Pamyati T. B., *Kon.*, 19-28, 1968) [Tatyana Borovkova] was an elegy to a friend who drowned in a boating accident. And just as Marina Basmanova could become a "concrete point of departure for metaphysical flights,"[145] so the Tanya of this poem became a concrete starting point for expressing Brodsky's increasing creative unease. Using his by now familiar images, he wrote:

---

144 Joseph Brodsky, *Konets prekrasnoy epokhi.stikhotvoreniya 1964-1971* (Ann Arbor, 1977), p. 6. Further page references to this edition in text or footnotes will be given as *Kon.*

145 Bethea, *Joseph Brodsky and the Creation of Exile, op. cit.*, pp. 89, 271 n. 45.

12
Chaek ne sprosish', i tuchi skrylis'.
Chto by smogli my uvidet', silyas'
glyanut' na vse eto ptich'im vzglyadom?
Kak ty kachalas' na volnakh ryadom
s lodkoy, ne vnemlya ikh rezkim krikam,.....

14
Chaek ne sprosish', i netu tolka
v gomone voln. ... (*Kon.,* 21, 22)

(12: You can't ask the seagulls, and the clouds are gone./ What could we see if we strained/ to look at all of this through the eyes of a bird?/ How you bobbed up and down on the waves/ right next to the boat, paying no heed to their shrill cries, ...// 14: You can't ask the seagulls, and there is no longer any sense in the hubbub of the waves. ...)

Communication between the poet and his Muse had stopped. Perhaps it explained the title of this collection. Poem after poem reiterated the poet's creative impasse in many different metaphorical contexts. To give just one example. In the poem "A Letter to General Z." (Pis'mo generalu Z, *Kon.,* 30-34, 1968), the poet made sure to tell us that this general did not really exist and had been selected only because "general" rhymed with "umiral" (was dying, m., *Kon.,* 33). Equally clear was the fact that the general's military campaign was synonymous with the poet's state of mind: the altar to Minerva, the goddess of arts and handicrafts, had been befouled; the gun barrels had turned soft and pointed downward, and the buglers who had taken their instruments out of their cases, both suggested masturbation (*Kon.,* 30); the lances were rusty, the wagons were rotting (*Kon.,* 31, 33) and the poet himself was worn out and tired of his "crusade" (*Kon.,* 32); the poet, a knight on horseback, found himself in an empty desert, still drawn to a hidden oasis, his thoughts filled with the image of a lovely woman, but his horse wouldn't budge (*Kon.,* 34); and the birds could only be heard, but not seen (*Kon.,* 32). It was simply impossible to write:

Dlya posledney stroki, ekh, ne vyrvat' u ptitsy pera. (*Kon.,* 60)
(Alas, can't tear out the bird's feather to write the last line.)

Crows' nests looked like caverns in the bronchial tubes (*Kon.,* 67) and ships' masts resembled naked trees:

V glubinakh rostra –
voroniy kashel'. Golye derev'ya. (*Kon.,* 69)
(In the depths of the boom –/ a crow's cough. Naked trees.)

The poet was not well.

A Part of Speech

A Part of Speech (Chast' rechi) was also first published in 1977.[146] It was dedicated to his parents. The poems preceding the title section of the book dealt mostly with social and historical reflections on Soviet life, with his impressions of Europe and the United States, and included more philosophical poems on life and death, on the afterlife and on nothingness (*Ch.,* 5-48, 97-113). Of these, two longer poems dealt with death by execution, and can be metaphorically related to his own poetic plight and to thoughts of suicide: "Twenty Sonnets to Mary, Queen of Scots," (Dvadtsat' sonetov k Marii Stuart, *Ch.,* 49-60, 1974), and "The Mexican Variety Show," (Meksikanskiy divertisment, *Ch.,* 61-72, 1975), which focussed on the execution of Maximilian, Emperor of Mexico. What made these two poems also relevant to Brodsky's creative dilemma were the associations in each poem to Pushkin and Mayakovsky.

Brodsky's title section "A Part of Speech" (*Ch.,* 75-96, 1975-76) was a moving paean to the Russian language, to Russia and to Russian poetry. But his poetic block was still there. He was still waiting for the poetic tide to rise, sitting in an "arm-chair" on a "bare verandah" (*Ch.,* 84). The poet's eyes roamed across the countryside but could only for a few, brief, almost nightmarish moments catch a fleeting sense of the poetic realm:

> I ulybka skol'znet, tochno ten' gracha
> po shcherbatoy izgorodi, pyshnyy kust
> shipovnika sderzhivaya, no kricha
> zhimolost'yu, ne razzhimaya ust. (*Ch.,* 90)
> (And a smile will slip across [the poet's face],/
> just like the shadow of a rook across a chipped
> fence,/ holding back the luxuriant dogrose shrub,/
> but crying out with closed beak through the honeysuckle.)

His poetry could no longer take him out of his dead end:

> Ty ne ptitsa, chtob uletat' otsyuda,
> potomu chto kak v poiskakh miloy vsyu-to
> ty proekhal vselennuyu, dal'she vrode
> net stranitsy podat'sya v zhivoy prirode. (*Ch.,* 91)
> (You're not a bird, to fly out of here again and again,/ because searching for your loved one/
> you've travelled across the whole universe,/ and there seems to be no more page left with
> which to plunge into live nature.)

---

146 Joseph Brodsky, *Chast' rechi stikhotvoreniya 1972-1976* (Ann Arbor, 1977). Page references to this edition in text or footnotes will be given as *Ch.*

In the end, Brodsky was only too conscious of it, all that was left of the poet for us, his readers, was not poetry but "a part of speech" (*Ch.,* 95).

New Stanzas to Augusta

New Stanzas to Augusta (Novye stansy k Avguste) were intended as love poems to Marina Basmanova and were published in 1983.[147] It must be noted again that almost half of the sixty poems in this collection had already been published in previous books of poetry.

There was still no ascertainable break in Brodsky's poetic impasse, although his hand continued to write poems (see for example, *No.,* 35, 36, 43, 76, 104, 133 and *passim.).* The poet now saw himself dressed in a joker's costume (*No.,* 77), the goldfinch (shchegol) who once used to chirp was gone [a possible play on words, because "shchegol'" with a soft sign, is a dandy and fop], and the fire in the stove was out (*No.,* 96). He was in fact trying to hide from this new bankrupt poetic reality:

> ot grammatiki novoy na serdtse pryacha
> okonchaniya shepota, krika, placha. (*No.,* 106)
> ([I'm] hiding the endings of whispers, cries and
> weeping/ from this new grammar).

He, the poet, was growing cold inside, he wrote in 1982 in his longer poem "Kellomyaki" (*No.,* 137-43) and was in fact *imitating* the once inspired creative process:

> ... kholodeya vnutri, ...
> ...
> imitiruya – chasto udachno – tot svet vo sne? (*No.,* 139)
> (... growing cold inside, ...// imitating – often
> successfully – that light of yore in my sleep?)

The "starling-house had outlived the starling," (*No.,* 140), and the poet's speech had become the "monologue of a parrot" (*No.,* 142). Addressing his Muse, who had once gifted him with poetic sight (*No.,* 145), he wrote poignantly:

---

147 Joseph Brodsky, *Novye Stansy k Avguste* (*Stikhi k M. B.,*[Marina Basmanova] *1962-1982)* (Ann Arbor, 1983). Page references to this edition in text or footnotes will be given as *No.* The title of this collection was inspired by Byron's *Stanzas to Augusta* (1816). See David MacFadyen, *Joseph Brodsky and the Soviet Muse* (Montreal-Kingston *et al.,* 2000), pp. 164-72.

Navsegda rasstaemsya s toboy, druzhok.
Narisuy na bumage prostoy kruzhok.
Eto budu ya: nichego vnutri.
Posmotri na nego – i potom sotri. (*No.,* 144)
(Let's part forever, friend./ Draw a simple circle on paper./ That will be me: nothing inside./
Look at it and then erase it.)

Urania

Urania was published in 1987.[148] In the first cycle of poems called
"Autumnal Cry of the Hawk" (Osenniy krik yastreba), Brodsky's poetic
landscape continued to express his poetic frustration. The arm-chair in which,
once upon a time, his Muse had sat and inspired him was now abandoned and
empty. In his poem "Dedicated to the Chair" (Posvyashchaetsya stulu, *Ur.,*
11-14, [1987]), the chair stood all alone, naked and unoccupied, in a room.
No one had sat in it that day, and it looked as if it wasn't there at all (*Ur.,* 12).
It had to be held together by nails, was "composed of a feeling of emptiness,"
stood in a bare room, with only this one chair in it, which would outlive the
poet (*Ur.,* 13). In other poems, it was the capital cities that stood empty in
summer (*Ur.,* 15), the grove was bare and naked as was "a huge naked grass-
hopper" (*Ur.,* 16). Outside lay the October boulevards and gardens, the birds'
nests were destroyed, their feathery dwellers gone, the money was spent,
chair after chair stood frozen in the October air (*Ur.,* 18). Nothing was left of
poetic inspiration:

ot velikoy lyubvi ostaetsya lish ravenstva znak
kostenet' v perekladinakh golykh sadovykh skameek. (*Ur.,* 18)
(of the great love only the equals sign remains/ to grow stiff and numb in-between the cross-
pieces of the naked garden benches.)

A monster, half human half beast, had taken his Muse's place in the chair:

Telo zastyv, prodlevaet stul.
Vyglyadit, kak kentavr. (*Ur.,* 20)
(The body, grown stiff, prolongs the chair./ Looks like a centaur.)

The poet confessed that he was now more like a sound impersonating a rook
and, having lost his speech, it was now more natural for him to turn to stone
(*Ur.,* 24). His head was in pain and ailing (*Ur.,* 28), and his previous "monologue of a parrot" (*No.,* 142) had stopped:

---

148 Joseph Brodsky, *Urania* (Ann Arbor, 1987). Page references to this edition in text or footnotes will be given as *Ur.*

... Tishina
molchaniem popugaya
bukval'no zavershena. (*Ur.,* 30)
(... The silence/ is literally finalized/ by the silence of the parrot.)

As a poet he had immortalized what he could not hold, and his Muse had forgiven him, as much as She could, for everything he had been up to, and all he was left with was to satirize and ape the creative process:

V obshchem, pesnya satira
vtorit shelestu kryl. (*Ur.,* 34)
(Generaly speaking, the song of the satyr
[or, the satirical song] / echoes and imitates the rustle of wings.)

His poetry had become the "idle talk and babble of an old man" (boltovnya starika, *Ur.,* 36) with "nothing" following in its wake (*Ur.,* 37).

Brodsky's imagery of himself as half man and half beast, centaur and satyr, had already been expressed at the beginning of the cycle in the monkey or ape that slumbered inside of him (*Ur.,* 8) and that, naked and crying out, came rushing out of a naturalist's ship's cabin (*Ur.,* 40). And the birds that had once inspired him had turned to wood:

... korabl'
vyglyadit odnovremenno kak derevo i zhuravl', (*Ur.,* 41)
(... the ship/ looks both like a tree [like wood] and a crane,)

The imagery of poetic bankruptcy was repeated in the ship going down – about which you could not question the seagull – and in the life preserver floating in the water without anyone hanging on to it (*Ur.,* 45, 46).

Finally, Brodsky's title poem of the cycle (*Ur.,* 49-52, 1975), re-capitulated metaphorically the poet's end in airless space: the lone hawk had been carried up far too high by the air currents into the ionosphere and on into the airless void where the distant stars took the place of millet, – of sustenance and survival, – a void, from where the hawk's final cry was like an "apotheosis of sound" before death (*Ur.,* 50-51).

It was not surprising, therefore, if the second, and longest, cycle of the collection "To Urania" (K Uranii) should have been addressed not to the Muse of poetry but to the Muse of astronomy.

"To Urania" had large descriptive sections of England and Italy, in particular. The shift towards descriptiveness in itself suggested what the overpowering number of images of poetic drought signified. Brodsky, the poet, said as much:

... I vakuum postepenno
zapolnyaet mestnyy landshaft. ... (*Ur.,* 79)
(and, gradually, the vacuum/ fills the local landscape.)

He could still, occasionally, hear his Muse's idle chatter (lepet, *Ur.,* 73) which was probably echoed by all the occasional bird cries throughout the cycle: a linnet in a thicket (*Ur.,* 74), a frightened starling (*Ur.,* 79), a turtle-dove (*Ur.,* 83). But these images of birds heard but not seen, were countered by their lifeless counterparts: a stuffed female quail (*Ur.,* 76), airy shapes of doves and seagulls that dissolved (*Ur.,* 83) and, again, silence staring at the parrot (*Ur.,* 74).

Metaphorically speaking, all these images suggested the poet's poetic impasse. And Brodsky did not mince his words: his poetry had become cheapened, he wrote, like the monkey who – not having enough time to become a human being – turned into a prostitute (*Ur.,* 85). His poems had become the "notes of a naturalist" (*Ur.,* 87); the nightingale had fled its cage and flown away, leaving the poet behind looking "Deformed and frightening, like a hieroglyph" (*Ur.,* 88), half man and half beast (*Ur.,* 89).

The descriptive penchant continued in his poems on Venice and Rome, as did the *descending mode* of his imagery which moved poetic expression towards a state of lifelessness. Thus, though he hoped that Euterpe might still look into his writing (*Ur.,* 94), in her absence there was only a predominating imagery of ruins (razvalin) (*Ur.,* 94, 95, 98, 111, 114, 116, 135, 137, 147), a sense of emptiness and silence that pursued him (*Ur.,* 98,102, 103, 111, 114, 116, 119,134, 156, 158), and the overpowering feeling of a creative vacuum (*Ur.,* 136). The poet's work became like the buzzing of a drone or the "aria of a parrot" (*Ur.,* 98), it was like the buzzing of a fly caught in a fly-trap (*Ur.,* 126, 155).

In his "Roman Elegies" (Rimskie elegii, *Ur.,* 111-17, [1981]), his eye caught the ruins, an "empty square without a fountain" (*Ur.,* 111), and he, the poet, saw himself as a "singer of rubbish" (Ya, pevets drebedeni, *Ur.,* 112). The jays were leaving the clump of Italian pines (*Ur.,* 115), and he wondered how a "wreck" (oblomok) like himself could even think of writing poetry (*Ur.,* 117). In his 4th (winter, [1980]) and 5th (summer, 1981) eclogues (*Ur.,* 118-31), he repeatedly mourned the fact that his life was dragging on to no effect (Zhizn' moya zatyanulas', *Ur.,* 118, 119, 120). The stars looked like a broken thermometer (*Ur.,* 121), it was impossible to catch Time in its pure form, for it was but the "meat of a mute universe" (*Ur.,* 122). The summer eclogue expressed a similar state of mind by way of images of useless, undesired and fruitless plants, such as the prickly burdock, tall weeds, the cockle weed, nestles, a dry blade of grass (*Ur.,* 124-25). The arm-chair of his

Muse that had turned into an empty chair earlier was now merely a stool (taburet) with dried up grooves (*Ur.,* 130).

There was only a momentary reprieve in his poem "The Rising Tide" (Priliv, *Ur.,* 132-34, [1981]):

> V severnoy chasti mira ya otyskal priyut, (*Ur.,* 132)
> (In the northern part of the world I have found a refuge)

But the relief was short-lived:

> Mozhno vydernut' nitku, no ne naydesh' igly. (*Ur.,* 134)
> (You can pull out the thread, but not find the needle.)

Indeed, the view of his future as a poet looked very gloomy, as he put it in his longer poem "Sitting in the Shade" (Sidya v teni, *Ur.,* 150-56, June 1983). Poetic thought had become paralyzed (*Ur.,* 150), only "forms of emptiness" and the "buzzing of flies" regaled the poetic eye (*Ur.,* 151); the smell of garbage was everywhere, the birds were pecking refuse instead of millet, out of urns (*Ur.,* 152), and a little terror of a kid was aiming his catapult at a sparrow intending to kill it (*Ur.,* 153-54).

All that was left after his Muse's departure, he wrote in a poem of 1981, was –

> ... zola,
> tusklye ugol'ya, (*Ur.,* 147)
> (...ashes,/ dull pieces of coal,)

His Muse had given him poetic sight, a voice with which to call Her, an ear with which to hear, but he had somehow *wasted* these gifts and was now thrown into fever or cold, into light or darkness – the rise and fall of poetic inspiration – and left turning like a planet, lost in the universe (*Ur.,* 149). There was no longer anywhere to go:

> Dal'she ekhat' nekuda. (Ur., 157)

His poem "To Urania" (*Ur.,* 158, [1982]) only echoed the hopeless tone of the whole.

The last cycle of poems "Life in a Scattered World [or, Life in a Diffused Light]" (Zhizn' v rasseyannom svete, *Ur.,* 159-89) only corroborated the generally mournful tone by reiterating the by now more than familiar images of Brodsky's creative distress. The title poem of the cycle (*Ur.,* 178-179) written in [1987][149] can stand for the rest of the poems which were , for the most part, put to paper between [1985 and 1987]. The Muse's nondescript voice, though it could still be heard, resembled the singing (!) of a hibernating fly, and was now whispering words which had no meaning. The poet's eye had become shortsighted "burning the naked mirror as would a nestle" (*Ur.,* 178).

Post-Nobel Poems, 1988-94[150]

Brodsky's post-Nobel poems (*So.,* III, 159-268, IV, 12-38) showed no fundamental shift from the despondent tone and imagery of his previous books of poetry. Indeed, if anything, the tone grew more inconsolable and desperate. His elegies to friends, his sensitivity to the passage of time and to the prospect of death, cast his poems into an even more palpable tragic mode. It was, perhaps, no accident either that an increasing tendency towards the prosaic and descriptive mode, and towards monotony, suggested a *poetic* petering out.

On Creative Ebb

I have tried in this essay to trace in Brodsky's poetry the diminishing curve of his poetic inspiration over time, a progressive decline in *emotional* power to which, in my view, his images bear more than sufficient witness. This, of course, is not to suggest that Brodsky, like Khodasevich for example, gave up on poetry – he did not. But, if we are to believe his imagery, he *knew* deep inside of himself that his creative days were numbered, that the emotional, spontaneous poetic flow of his creative inspiration was being swept out to sea leaving only the *intellectual* side of his creative personality behind.

Others have commented on Brodsky's tendency towards intellectualization or rationalization. Thus, David Bethea, though he was primarily interested in studying Brodsky's exile state of mind, touched on this problem a number of times. At one point, he had this to say about Brodsky's connection to Donne:

---

149 Brodsky had a cavalier attitude to the dating of poems in *Urania* – the majority were not dated. Dates in square brackets in this essay were taken from G. F. Komarov, ed., *Sochineniya Iosifa Brodskogo* (St. Petersburg, 1994). Henceforth cited as *So.*
150 Brodsky's last poems have been taken from *So.,* vols. III and IV.

This may explain some of the resistance to Brodsky's poetry as excessively cerebral, self-reflexive, overwrought, "un-Russian." These, after all, are the very reasons why Donne himself, under the cloud of Dr. Johnson's stricture, was neglected in his own tradition for centuries until his revival by Grierson and Eliot as a proto-modern. Brodsky has many connections with Donne and his epoch; some of these are consciously cultivated, others are simply "typological," part of larger *Gestalt* patterns that are intriguing and meaningful in their own right.[151]

At another, he suggested that Brodsky's intellectual handling of poems made him gravitate "as far away as possible from pure 'feeling' in the direction of pure 'mind'.[152] Brodsky's tendency towards the rational, undermining the emotional in the process, was intentional, Bethea argued, because Brodsky wanted to counter the more emotionally charged Russian poetic tradition: "The 'destructive rationalism' that Brodsky ascribes to Tsvetaeva and that he sees, with characteristic contrariness, as expanding the Russian poetic tradition *precisely by falling outside it* is, therefore, his own"[153] (his italics).

Reviewers of some of Brodsky's collections of poems, be it in English translation, also noted the lack of emotion in his poetry. Thus, John Simon, a cultural journalist, reviewing Brodsky's *Urania*, spoke of his "intellectually engaged but emotionally dry versifying"; and the American poet Robert Hass, Czeslaw Milosz's translator had, in 1983, expressed "perplexity that [Brodsky's] reputation seemed so in excess of the accomplishment," and that "'for the most part reading *A Part of Speech* is like wandering through the ruins of what has been reported to be a noble building.'"[154] But when speaking of Brodsky's elegy on T. S. Eliot, David Rigsbee himself seemed to confirm Brodsky's distancing himself from emotional expression:

In this elegy [he wrote], Brodsky begins to assign Auden's triad of making, knowing, and judging to poetry proper and so turns away from – or at the very least assigns an inferior place to – the human sovereingnty of emotion, ...[155]

Valentina Polukhina interviewing Elena Shvarts, in her view "one of the best known of present-day Leningrad poets" on May 3, 1990, recorded the following exchange:

---

151 Bethea, *Joseph Brodsky and the Creation of Exile, op. cit.,* pp. 83-84.

152 *Ibid.,* p. 95.

153 *Ibid.,* p. 106; see also pp. 109, 115.

154 See these critical references by David Rigsbee in his *Styles of Ruin. Joseph Brodsky and the Postmodernist Elegy* (Westport, Connecticut/London, 1999), pp. 2 and 17, fn. 5, respectively.

155 *Ibid.,* p. 35.

Q: What is it about Brodsky you find particularly unacceptable?
A: His coldness and rationality. At the same time, of course, I see what a great poet he is. It's just impossible not to see that.
Q: His coldness and rationality – that is just his way of dealing with tragedy.
A: I see that, but none the less it amounts to the same thing.[156]

Finally, Valentina Polukhina herself, in her study of Brodsky, said something to the same effect. Speaking of his early elegies, she made the following observations:

> Gradually he removes personal lyricism to the periphery. The degree to which philosophical speculation grows and the emotional field is narrowed – that is, a change in the *dominanta* – may be traced in the elegies considered below. Self-reflexion gives way to analysis of the very phenomenon of language and poetry. Alienation is transferred into the sphere of the most inalienable categories of the "I"; intimacy is replaced by abstraction. All this leads to an erosion of the traditional markers of the elegy.[157]

Vertumn

The waning of the emotional centre in Brodsky's poetry was most poignantly expressed in his elegiac longer poem "Vertumn", – Vertumnus, the god of change, protector of vegetation and fruit trees, a perfect metaphor for the protean and organic nature of poetry, – written in December of 1990 in Milan:

> ... Ya ovladel iskusstvom
> slivat'sya s landshaftom, kak s mebel'yu ili shtoroy (*So.,* III, 200)
> (... I have mastered the art/ of merging with the landscape, Just as I would with furniture or a blind)

This *dehumanization* of the poetic self was evident as well in his Nobel Prize speech of 1987: for, the *romantic idealization* of the poetic word – reminiscent of Russian Symbolist aesthetics – allowed him to bypass all the systems of belief and the philosophical and ethical doctrines that human beings live by, all the human suffering of the 20th century, leaving only poetic language as an eternal substitute for mortality, humanity and love. Such romanticization of poetry as – in his view – man's *only* future, left a lonely vacuum for the human race.[158]

---

156 Elena Shvarts, "Coldness and Rationality," in Valentina Polukhina, *Brodsky through the Eyes of his Contemporaries* (New York, 1992), pp. 215-36, here p. 219.
157 Valentina Polukhina, *Joseph Brodsky a poet for our time* (Cambridge *et al.,* 1989), p. 74.
158 See his "Nobel Lecture" in *So.,* I, 5-16.

It may very well be that Brodsky tried to *mask* his growing emotional vacuum with his intellectuality. This may explain why he was so powerfully drawn to Robert Frost's poetry which, he believed – in his 1994 essay on the poet – masked a tragic inner self with a deceptive pastoral poetic surface.[159] Though we may argue with Brodsky on the "absence of emotion" in Frost's poetry,[160] we can perhaps appreciate that Frost's poetic method – if Brodsky was right – may have been a useful model for his own creative dilemma. As he put it: "You can snivel at every turn, or you can bury your disasters deep down, that is, behave as Frost did."[161]

David MacFadyen has reminded us that Brodsky's one and only raison d'être, his justification for living and writing was to discover and chase after his immortal "feminine Muse,"[162] something that brings to mind Blok's poetic pining for his Beautiful Lady. It is also possible that Brodsky's obsession with death[163] was a symptom of an underlying anxiety – again reminiscent of Blok – that he might not have enough time left and fail to reach his Beloved. This anxiety over poetic failure was all the more disturbing since he himself did not seem to have any belief in an afterlife and, therefore, could not hope for a meeting beyond the grave. As he admitted to an interviewer in 1982:

> I read the Bible for the first time when I was twenty-three. It leaves me somewhat shepherdless, you see. I wouldn't really know what to return to. I don't have any notion of paradise. ... I went through the severe antireligious schooling in Russia which doesn't leave any kind of notion about afterlife.[164]

It seems clear that poetry and the poetic life became, for Brodsky, "an alternate form of existence,"[165] as he observed in connection with the Greek poet Constantine Cavafy, and that poetry for Brodsky was at the same time "a self-portrait of its author," as he remarked in a lecture on W. H. Auden in 1984.[166] It is for the same reason that he believed that a poet's work could not be broken up into stages because, in the end, "all creativity" was an organic, "linear process."[167]

---

159 See Joseph Brodsky, *On Grief and Reason. Essays* (New York, 1995), pp. 223-66.
160 See "Robert Frost," (1979-1982) in Volkov, *Conversations with Joseph Brodsky, op. cit.,* pp. 85-102, here p. 94.
161 *Ibid.,* p. 95.
162 See MacFadyen, *Joseph Brodsky and the Soviet Muse, op. cit.,* p. 9.
163 See Bethea, *Joseph Brodsky and the Creation of Exile, op. cit.,* pp. 93, 165-66.
164 Quoted in *ibid.,* p. 161.
165 Joseph Brodsky, "Pendulum's Song," in his *Less than One, op. cit.,* pp. 53-68, here p. 60.
166 Joseph Brodsky, " On 'September 1, 1939' by W. H. Auden," in *ibid.,* pp. 304-56, here p. 304.
167 See "W. H. Auden," (1978-83) in Volkov, *Conversations with Joseph Brodsky, op. cit.,* pp. 125-52, here p. 143.

But as the emotional energy of his poetic inspiration subsided, he must have realized that his creative existence *as a poet* was coming to an end. He said as much in his poem "Vertumn", when he reminded himself that –

... chto zavtra, v luchshem sluchae – poslezavtra
vse eto konchitsya. ... (*So.,* III, 201)
(... that tomorrow, at best, the day after tomorrow,/ all this will come to an end. ...)

Poignantly he wrote of his coming "ice age":

... Ibo oledenen'e
est' kategoriya budushchego, kotoroe est' pora,
kogda bol'she uzhe nikogo ne lyubish',
dazhe sebya. (*So.,* III, 203)
(... For, the turning to ice/ is a category of the future, a time/ when one doesn't love anyone anymore/ not even oneself.)

In the final two lines of the poem he expressed what his poetry had been telling him all along, namely that the poetic tide was receding and taking his creative inspiration with it:

"Vertumn, – ya shepchu, prizhimayas' k korichnevoy polovitse
mokroy shchekoyu, – Vertumn, vernis'". (*So.,* III, 204)
("Vertumn," I whisper, pressing my wet cheek/ against the brown floorboard, "Vertumn, come back".)

It is curious that this poem should remind us of T. S. Eliot, one of Brodsky's favorite poets, and of three lines in "The Waste Land" (1922) in particular:

And upside down in air were towers
Tolling reminiscent bells, that kept the hours
And voices singing out of empty cisterns and exhausted
wells.[168]

Eliot was, of course, recording a social and cultural trauma in metaphorical terms. But to the extent that he was himself a part of Western European spiritual bankruptcy, his lines spoke equally to his own inner devastated self. Brodsky wrote in the wake of even more unspeakable acts of inhumanity. He no longer possessed Eliot's idealism that there was still a spiritual centre to which man might turn. What Brodsky would have needed, above all, – if we recall his elegy to Donne – would have been a very special tailor who could have mended all the rips and tears in his emotional life as a poet. Failing this, there was only his poetry.

---

168 T. S. Eliot, *Collected Poems 1909-1962* (London/Boston, 1974), p. 78.

The Search for the Cosmic Connection
in Twentieth-Century Russian Poetry

Introduction

1

In twentieth-century Russian poetry we can discern two significant psychological trends: the one was *away from life,* bringing with it a growing dehumanization in poetic consciousness and expression, which reflected a like dehumanization in Russian society at large. The other was an attempt to revivify the *human* poetic experience by reconnecting it to life and to the cosmic source of *spiritual* being.

In the trend away from life, Russian symbolism played an influential role, for, its impact, as Osip Mandelshtam reminded us in the mid-twenties, reached far beyond the Bolshevik revolution of 1917. The symbolists' romantic intensification of poetic experience, removing life as we know it into abstract, transcendental spheres, the pathological destruction and fragmentation of personality and normality as we find it in Fedor Sologub's and Andrey Bely's work, the defilement of the ideal and its consequent spiritual stress and frustration as we see it gather force in Alexander Blok's poetry, the obsession with poetic craft as reflected in Valery Bryusov's poetic work, and ultimately, the symbolist idealization of the poet and the poetic word to the exclusion of any divine source, moved the great majority of Russian symbolist poets further and further away from real life experience, replacing it with poetic phantasms. Blok's creative impasse, Sologub's and Bryusov's intense solipsism and Bely's visions of chaos bore witness to the fact that there was a heavy price to pay for a poetic sensibility raised to a higher power, for that overacuteness of the senses (Poe) which carried within it the seed of emotional bankruptcy and spiritual crisis.

2

The trend towards dehumanization and lifelessness in Russian poetry (and literature) continued in the theory and practice of a number of literary groups whose influence reached into the twenties and early thirties. The transrational strain of Russian futurism for example (Aleksey Kruchenykh and Velimir Khlebnikov) – both dadaist precursors – turned poetic language into meaningless sequences of words. The Russian formalists (Viktor Shklovsky, Yury Tynyanov and Boris Eikhenbaum) focussed on literary text to the exclusion of authorial intent and of any psychological, historical or social context. The Russian imagists (Vadim Shershenevich, Anatoly Mariengof and Sergey Esenin) shared an exaggerated view of the social potency of poetic images conceived as entities in themselves. The Proletarian poets of the twenties (for example Vladimir Kirillov and Mikhail Gerasimov) romanticized the power of iron and the machine to the point of pathetic fallacy. And, finally, when in the 1930s socialist realism became an imperative fact in literary theory and practice, human beings in art turned into lifeless models of communist doctrine (for instance Nikolay Ostrovsky and others).

3

In retrospect, there is no doubt that Russian poetry and literature in the first quarter of the twentieth century and beyond, caught something of that dehumanization in life that reached its apex in the Stalinist years. The search for the lost cosmic connection, for that sacred source of spirituality in the universe with which to revivify Russian poetic experience was, therefore, an important counter-trend not only to the shift away from life, but also to the nineteenth-century materialism and nihilism, the mystic hunger and the thirst for God, that had clearly spilled over into the twentieth century bringing with it a spiritual crisis which Fedor Dostoevsky and Friedrich Nietzsche, as well as Dmitry Merezhkovsky and Arthur Rimbaud had foreseen.

What binds the four poets of this essay together is their religious impulse which, in each individual case, outstripped the particular aesthetic and ideological orientations of the literary groups to which they belonged. Thus Vyacheslav Ivanov's (1866-1949) religious humility, his *certitude* that sacred beginnings existed, could neither be contained nor satisfied by the megalomanic, arrogant and self-obsessed symbolist aesthetics. For Mayakovsky (1893-1930) and Esenin (1895-1925) likewise, the aesthetic iconoclastic confines of futurism and imagism respectively, did not prevent them from reaching out for the Sacred. As for Pasternak (1890-1960), after his early flirtation with futurism, he had to overcome the limitations of his own highly metaphorical, at times even abstruse, early poetic output, in order to be able finally to arrive at his Zhivago poems with their pure and intuitive spirituality.

Vyacheslav Ivanov's Sonnets, 1919-24

> Out of the depths have I called to thee, O Lord;
> Lord, hear my cry.
>
> Psalm 130

Winter Sonnets (Dec. 1919- Feb. 1920)

Renato Poggioli regarded Vyacheslav Ivanov – a major figure in the Russian symbolist movement – as "the keeper of ... a mystical wisdom," and his poetry as "essentially a religious search."[169] Maurice Bowra also noted that, for Ivanov, poetry was "a mystical activity," linked to a divine source in the universe that could heal and restore man's spirituality.[170] Vladimir Markov put it this way: "If I were forced to do the impossible and to sum up in a short phrase what Vyacheslav Ivanov is about, I would say: the language of the gods."[171]

One could already sense Ivanov's mystical feeling for the universe in one of his earliest collections of poetry, *Pilot Stars* (Kormchie zvezdy, 1903).[172] By the time he wrote his *Winter Sonnets* (Zimnie sonety), which mark one of the high points of his poetry, this mystical feeling had taken deep root in his being. Bowra suggests that Ivanov tended to choose the sonnet form in response to disastrous circumstances, because the sonnet allowed him to control emotions that otherwise would have overpowered him.[173] This reminds us of Günter Grass's method of undercutting pain by objectifying it in his writing. And, in actual fact, the *Winter Sonnets* were written when Ivanov's third wife, Vera Shvarsalon, and their children – a daughter, Lidiya and a son, Dimitry – lay ill in a hospital some forty kilometers outside of Moscow and

---

169 Renato Poggioli, *The Poets of Russia 1890-1930, op. cit.,* pp. 161-70, here pp. 161, 166-67. See also Michael Wachtel, "Vyacheslav Ivanov: From Aesthetic Theory to Biographical Practice," in *Creating Life. The Aesthetic Utopia of Russian Modernism,* edited by Irina Paperno and Joan Delaney Grossman (Stanford, 1994), pp. 151-66, here pp. 158, 163, 165.

170 See *Svet vecherniy. Poems by Vyacheslav Ivanov,* edited by Dmitri Ivanov, with an introduction by Sir Maurice Bowra and commentary by O. Deschartes (Oxford, 1962), pp. xix,xvii respectively. This collection of poems will be cited hereafter as *Svet.* See also V. Zhirmunsky, "Symbolism's Successors," in *The Noise of Change: Russian Literature and the Critics (1891-1917),* Edited and Translated by Stanley Rabinowitz (Ann Arbor, 1966), pp. 217-47, here p. 219.

171 Vladimir Markov, "Vyacheslav Ivanov the Poet: A Tribute and a Reappraisal," in *Vyacheslav Ivanov: Poet, Critic and Philosopher,* edited by Robert Louis Jackson and Lowry Nelson, Jr. (New Haven, 1986), pp. 49-58, here p. 53.

172 See Sergey Averintsev, "The Poetry of Vyacheslav Ivanov," in *ibid.,* pp. 25-48, here p. 32.

173 Bowra in *Svet,* pp. xviii, xix.

he would visit them in an open sleigh in the dead of winter along almost impassable roads, himself barely hanging on to life in a Russia still torn by civil war.

A poetic commentary on each of the twelve sonnets of this cycle could easily run into many pages because of Ivanov's highly compressed and associative metaphorical language. But we can shorten our poetic foray into his winter sonnets[174] by singling out certain recurring features and themes of the cycle that give it a more permanent structure.

For one, the poetic chemistry of the sonnets is contrapuntal, so that in each poem a sometimes elusive though ever present transcendental reality, with its promise of warmth and refuge, is set against the lifeless world of winter with its bitter cold through which the poet travels. The contrapuntal motif is also picked up by the theme of the poet's earthly double who must needs drag his own coffin behind him in the horse-drawn sleigh, while the poet, having betrayed his mortality, his flesh and blood, builds his other-worldly place of worship (khram nerukotvornyy, Sonnet 3). There are therefore two simultaneous journeys in the sonnets, one earth-bound, the other on its way towards heaven (Sonnet 7). Again, in contrast to the horse-drawn sleigh, the poet's sleigh is drawn by reindeer (Sonnets 1 and 10), a fitting symbol for the soul, for beauty and for salvation.[175] Small wonder then, if the poet's lodging for the night in a warm hut, the wood crackling in the stove, or in the warmth of a dense gully (Sonnets 1, 9 and 10), likened to the "warmth in the confines of a magic circle" (Teplo v cherte magicheskogo kruga, Sonnet 8), is, in its double meaning, so central to the cycle as a whole.

De Profundis Amavi

The nine sonnets of this cycle inspired by Psalm 130, calling to God out of the deepest sorrow and misery, were written between June and August of 1920 when Ivanov was recuperating from the hardships of civil war in a sanatorium outside of Moscow. It was during this time too, in June and July, that he engaged in that now famous *Corner-to-Corner Correspondence* with Mikhail Gershenzon, a philosopher and literary critic, who had happened to be put into the same room with him.

---

174 *Svet,* pp. 96-101. Poggioli thought these sonnets were Ivanov's "perhaps... most human and poignant lyrical masterpiece." See Renato Poggioli, "A Correspondence from Opposite Corners," in his *The Phoenix and the Spider. A Book of Essays about some Russian Writers and Their View of the Self* (Cambridge, Mass., 1957), pp. 208-28, here p. 211.

175 See *Entsyklopedicheskiy slovar',* edited by F. A. Brokgauz and I. A. Efron, Volume 42 (St. Petersburg, 1897), pp. 873-74.

The sonnets[176] in part reiterated the otherworldly sensibility of the *Winter Sonnets* (e.g. Sonnets 1, 3, 4, 6, 7, 8, and 9). But what was more explicit in these poems than it had been in the *Winter Sonnets* was his worry about his wife and children expressed in his sense of the precariousness of human relationships and of love in particular:

I molot po serdtsu udarit vdrug. (Sonnet 5)
(For suddenly a hammer might strike the heart.)

It seemed that the only way for him to escape his tragic sense of foreboding would be to bid farewell to earth's sickly and delirious life's dream (Sonnets 1 and 2):

S glavy stryakhnut, ya silyus' volny sna: (Sonnet 6)
(I try to shake off the waves of dream from my brow)

Ivanov's prophetic intuition was to prove itself a second time in his life. For, just as in October of 1907 he had stopped short from finishing a sonnet because he suddenly had had a premonition of his second wife's, Lidiya Zinovieva-Annibal's, imminent death, – he was to publish one of his finest collections of poems, *Cor Ardens* (The Burning Heart) in 1911 in the wake of this personal tragedy – so now too he left the ninth sonnet unfinished, haunted by a similar premonition, just a few days before Vera's death on August the 8th.[177]

Roman Sonnets

After Vera's death, Ivanov and his two children were allowed to leave Moscow. After a six-week stay in a sanatorium in Kislovodsk in the North Caucasus, Ivanov chose to go to Baku on the Caspian Sea arriving there in October of 1920. He became a full professor of classical philology and poetics at the newly-founded university there. He hoped he would somehow manage to get out of the USSR and reach Italy. But it was to be only at the end of August 1924 – with the help of Anatoly Lunacharsky, the then Soviet minister of culture – that he was finally allowed to leave with his family for a six-week stay in Venice for the opening of a Soviet Pavillion. He never went back. In the spring of 1926 he converted to Catholicism, and in the autumn of

---

176 *Svet,* pp. 102-6. The translations are mine.

177 See Olga Deschartes' introduction to Vyacheslav Ivanov, *Sobranie sochineniy,* edited by D. V. Ivanov and O. Deschartes (3 vols.; Brussells, 1971-79), I, 7-227, here pp. 119-20, 169-70. This edition will be cited hereafter as *Sobranie.* See also *Svet,* pp. 204-6.

that year he was offered a tenured professor position in Pavia, teaching students enrolled in French, German and English literatures. Ten years later he settled permanently in Rome. He spent the rest of his life in Italy until his demise in the summer of 1949, which he foresaw in a sonnet that he finished one day before his death.[178]

It was thus in September of 1924 that Ivanov saw his beloved Rome again – the city where he had first met Lidiya in 1893 – and began to write his nine Roman sonnets[179] which he finished by early January of 1925. These beautiful poems seem to have been written at the height of Ivanov's poetic power. Very probably, the sudden sense of freedom in having escaped revolutionary Russia with his children, and the happy memories associated with Rome, contributed to this release of creative inspiration.

In this ancient spiritual centre it was natural for Ivanov to speak of eternity and immortality that he felt were reflected in the fountains and sculptures of Rome, and especially in the mountain sources of pure water that fed the fountains of this holy city.

The juxtaposition of immortal stone and eternal water in this cycle connected especially well with the contrapuntal thrust of his *Winter Sonnets.*

In Sonnet 1 Ivanov saw eternal Rome as a refuge for all homeless wanderers of the earth and found its immortality expressed in its paradoxical Phoenix-like history:

> I pomnit v laske zolotogo sna,
> Tvoy vratar' kiparis, kak Troya krepla,
> Kogda lezhala Troya sozhzhena. (Sonnet 1)
> (And your gate-keeper, the cypress/ Caressed by its golden dreams,/ Remembers how Troy grew strong/ When Troy lay in its ashes.)

The word "pristan'" (pier, harbour) in the sonnet was the perfect word for suggesting not only a haven and refuge, but also the point where the incoming sea brought its wanderers and refugees to land, water and land echoing the interaction in the city, of water and stone.

Again, a sculpture of the Dioscuri Castor and Pollux, patrons of mariners, watering their horses at the well of the nymph Juturna (in Sonnet 2), made for a similar contrapuntal connection with Sonnet 3 through which flowed the blissful water from the mountains to feed the aqueducts of Rome.

The sounds of murmuring water again resounded in Sonnet 4 and linked up with images in Sonnet 5 that were associated with sea and fountains (e. g. dolphins, a Triton blowing into a conch-shell, Bernini's four fountains).

---

178 *Svet,* p. 205.
179 *Ibid.,* pp. 106-10.

Then, in Sonnets 6 and 7, the sixteenth-century Florentine fountain of Tartarughe with its sculpture of Asclepius, the Greek god of medicine and healing, was associated with the crystal sounds of the fountain's water reaching out for the light. The last two lines of Sonnet 7 summed up well the mingling of the material and incorporeal, of the heavenly and earthly dimensions that inspired the whole cycle:

> I v gladi oprokinuty zerkal'noy
> Asklepiy, klen, i nebo, i fontan.
> (And the smooth surface of the water mirrors upside-down/ Asclepius, the maple, sky and fountain.)

In Sonnet 8 Ivanov celebrated his return to Rome, with sea horses, goddesses and Neptune, the god of the sea himself, in attendance, as the fountain of Trevi, the goddess of all fountains, fed by a virginal water source, the Aqua Virgo, became a "magical fountain" that returned Ivanov, the pilgrim, to his sacred haunts.

In the last sonnet, originally entitled "Aqua Virgo", the poet asked the obvious question:

> Ne Vechnost' li svoy persten' obruchal'nyy
> Prosterla Dnyu za gran'yu zrimykh met?
> (Is it not Eternity beyond the visible realm/ Who has reached out Her wedding ring to Day?)

Of the Divine Dimension

Ivanov remained a mystic all his life, in the sense that he harboured an all-embracing profound intuition of the existence of a "divine expanse"; and this is also why he called Goethe – and we might add Novalis – "the distant father of our Symbolism."[180] And Gershenzon, in his *Corner-to-Corner Correspondence* with Ivanov could not hide his sneaking admiration for Ivanov's wholeness: "Your spirit is not divided," he wrote in his last letter, "and this wholeness charms me ...".[181] But as Sergey Makovsky – poet, literary critic, memoirist, a contemporary of the Silver Age – has noted, there was also a spiritual turmoil in Ivanov: "He too was parched with religious thirst ..."

---

180 See Ivanov's "Thoughts on Symbolism," (1912) in Vyacheslav Ivanov, *Selected Essays*, Translated from the Russian and with notes by Robert Bird, Edited and with an introduction by Michael Wachtel (Evanston, Illinois, 2001), pp. 50-58, here p. 56. See also Ivanov's "The Testaments of Symbolism," (1910) in *ibid.*, pp. 36-49.

181 See Vyacheslav Ivanovich Ivanov and Mikhail Osipovich Gershenzon, "A Corner-to-Corner Correspondence," in Marc Raeff, ed., *Russian Intellectual History an Anthology*, with an Introduction by Isaiah Berlin (New York , *et al.*, 1966), pp. 373-401, here p401.

(religioznoy zhazhdoy tomilsya i on).[182] This is reminiscent of Dostoevsky and Rimbaud.

If poetry for Ivanov was a bridge to the Divine, it is a curious fact that for some twenty years after the completion of his *Roman Sonnets* he wrote only twelve poems.[183] Was this a recurrence of his bout of atheism in the 1880s? In this context, the 118 poems of his *Roman Diary for 1944* – once again followed by a sharp decline in poetic productivity – must be seen as a return of his poetic inspiration and as a spiritual breakthrough. It is perhaps equally noteworthy that towards the end of his life – not unlike Pasternak's poems in *Doctor Zhivago* – Ivanov's poems of the *Roman Diary* had also gained in simplicity and straightforwardness.[184]

Vladimir Mayakovsky's Prerevolutionary Longer Poems, 1913-15

Vladimir Mayakovsky (A Tragedy)

There are at least two Mayakovskys: the pre- and post-revolutionary ones. And though, unlike his contemporary poet Sergey Esenin, Mayakovsky had fully commited his poetry to the atheist Bolshevik state after the Revolution of 1917, in the poem *VO VES' GOLOS* (At the Top of My Voice), which Mayakovsky wrote in the beginning of 1930, shortly before his suicide, he judged his post-revolutionary poetry as a betrayal of his poetic calling:

> No ya
>   sebya
>   smiryal,
>   stanovyas'
> na gorlo
> sobstvennoy pesne.[185]
> (But I / tamed / myself, / stepping on / the throat /of my own song.)

It is in his prerevolutionary poetry therefore, that we get closer to the poet, to the full force of his poetic voice, its iconoclasm, its revolutionary poetics, its emotional power and its genuine humanism. What has not always been

---

182 Sergey Makovsky, "Vyacheslav Ivanov," in his *Portrety sovremennikov* (New York, 1955), pp. 269- 310, here p. 283.

183 *Sobranie,* I, 206.

184 See also Makovsky, p. 292.

185 See V. Mayakovsky, *Sobranie sochineniy v chetyrekh tomakh,* edited by L. Yu. Brik and P. K. Luppol (4 vols.; Moscow, 1936), IV, 356-63, here p. 358. References to this edition will be cited hereafter in the text. The translations are mine.

brought into view, however, was Mayakovsky's unadulterated spiritual and religious perspective.

His longer poem *Vladimir Mayakovsky (A Tragedy, 1913)* was a case in point. It was full of Mayakovsky's spiritual yearning *to have contact with God,* even though this God seemed to be the traditional Old Testament God. Mayakovsky's "soul" was "taut with tension" (I, 76) he told us, it needed to be darned (I, 77), in fact he was still looking for his lost, invisible soul (I, 82). And no one was really aware of his spiritual hunger (I, 84), his exhaustion or his pain (I, 92), or of the shreds of his soul left hanging on the spears of houses (I, 93). The old man with the cats was not fooled by Mayakovsky's risible exterior:

> I vizhu – v tebe na kreste iz smekha
> raspyat zamuchennyy krik. (I, 78)
> (And I see how your tortured scream/ is crucified on a cross of laughter.)

This analogy with the suffering Christ was reemphasized at the end of the poem in the image of Mayakovsky being "in the grip of an infinite yearning" (gde v tiskakh beskonechnoy toski, I, 94), and in his vow, at no matter what cost, to reach that merciless Jewish-Christian God – that "dark god of terror and calamity" (temnomu bogu groz) – in order to bring him all those tears he had been collecting in compassion for suffering humanity (I, 94).

A Cloud in Trousers

A Cloud in Trousers (Oblako v shtanakh, 1915) – as well as *The Backbone Flute* (Fleyta-Pozvonochnik, 1915) – was inspired by Mayakovsky's meeting the married Lili Brik, who was to remain the love of his life.[186] The poem was at the surface a critique of prerevolutionary Russian society in toto (I, 389), yet behind its social invective and love theme, the poem spoke intensely of his spiritual need to have contact with the Divine, in this case in its feminine guise.

The poem had originally been entitled by Mayakovsky *The Thirteenth Apostle* (I, 388). Its spiritual theme of contact with the Divine was expressed metaphorically in the poet's impatient and increasingly desperate wait for *Maria's* arrival.The realization that she would not come, i. e. that the Virgin Mary was not about to appear, only added to his torments and pain which were suddenly raised to a metaphysical level:

---

186 See Hugo Huppert, *Erinnerungen an Majakowskij* (Frankfurt a. Main, 1966), pp. 50-53.

Ya – gde bol', vezde;
na kazhdoy kaple slezovoy techi
raspyal sebya na kreste. (I, 107)
(I am wherever pain is;/ in every drop of tears flowing/ I've crucified myself on the cross.)

The religious imagery once again signalled the presence of the spiritual realm. For, at a pub, trying to soothe his pain with liquor, he saw himself as the Mother of God's most beautiful son (I, 112), and as the thirteenth apostle (I, 113). In the end, quite apart from his outright attack on the Christian God (I, 118-19), his fear of forgetting Her name was equivalent to the poet's fear that he might forget "a poetic word born in the torments of night / its greatness equal to God's" (I, 116). Still, his poetry would find its way to the house of his Father:

millionom krovinok usteletsya sled
k domu moego ottsa. (I, 117)
(and the path to the house of my Father/ will be covered with millions of droplets of my blood.)

The Backbone Flute

In this poem, Mayakovsky's love-sick suffering over Lili Brik became so unendurable that, on the one hand, he was pushed to thoughts of suicide, but on the other, he was ready to atone for his blasphemies against God (I, 121), by offering himself up to be sacrificed at the hands of God himself, if only this would end his emotional suffering (I, 122-23).

Hence, again, Mayakovsky raised his earthly travails to a higher spiritual dimension, where ultimately, the agony associated with the act of writing poetry was equated to the Crucifixion:

Vidite –
gvozdyami slov
pribit k bumage ya. (I, 130)
(You see – / I'm nailed to the paper/ with the nails of my words.)

The Diapason of Love

Victor Erlich has remarked on Mayakovsky's surprising use of religious imagery in his prerevolutionary longer poems:

The pervasive theme of martyrdom occasions here a wealth of religious imagery striking in a poet so militantly secular and so blatantly materialistic.[187]

But our look at three of Mayakovsky's prerevolutionary longer poems, which have generally been considered to be his best work, suggests, on the contrary, a spiritual and religious sensibility that ran deep in his poetry in its repeated attempts to connect to the spiritual realm.

Sergey Esenin's Upside Down Paradise

Esenin's Inoniya

In Esenin's poetic work, the balance between life and death was, at best, always precarious. It would seem that, in the end, death won out not only in his poetry,[188] but also in his life when he committed suicide in 1925.

Esenin's longer poem *Inoniya* (1918) was written in the wake of the revolutionary euphoria of 1917. A number of influences shaped the poem: the Christian Marxist idealism of the Scythian movement of the time; Esenin's innate hostility to the industrialization of his rural world and to the West; the social phantasies of imagism and, of course, the traditional Christian perspective combined with a pagan sense of nature that imbued so much of his prerevolutionary poetry. Having said this, one has to add what was to Esenin perhaps the most important aspect of the poem which was inspired by the ancient millennial dream of a Russian peasant paradise on earth.

But his peasant paradise was an upside-down paradise grounded in heaven rather than on earth. One of his images tells us as much:

Po tucham idu, kak po nive, ya,
Svesyas' golovoyu vniz.[189]
(I'm walking on the clouds as on a field,/ With my head upside down.)

Notwithstanding his blasphemies against the traditional Christian God and against Christ (II, 36, 37, 38, 39), the poetic inspiration for his peasant paradise was fuelled not only by his readings in Russian mythology and folk

---

187 See Victor Erlich "The Dead Hand of the Future: Vladimir Maiakovskii," in his *The Double Image. Concepts of the Poet in Slavic Literatures* (Baltimore, Maryland, 1964), pp. 120-32, here p. 123.

188 See Constantin V. Ponomareff, "The Metaphysics of Vision," in his *Sergey Esenin* (Boston, 1978), pp. 88-101.

189 See "Inoniya," in Sergey Esenin, *Sobranie sochineniy* (5 vols.; Moscow, 1961-62), II, 36-44, here p. 43. References to this edition will be cited hereafter in the text. The translations are mine.

poetry,[190] but by a spiritual and religious sensibility intent on replacing the sombre otherworldly Christianity with a new spiritual faith that retained its otherworldly focus:

> Ne khochu vospriyat' spaseniya
> Cherez muki ego i krest:
> Ya inoe postig uchenie
> Probodayushchikh vechnost' zvezd. (II, 36)
> (I don't want to accept salvation/ Through his torments and cross:/ I have come to know another teaching/ Of the stars butting through eternity.)

As can be seen from the above, the locus of his paradise was *not* on earth but in the infinite reaches of space:

> Ya khochu, chtob na bezdonnom vytyazhe
> My vozdvigli sebe chertog. (II, 38; see also II, 55-56)
> (I want us to raise our mansion/ On the bottomless stretches of space.)

His rejection of traditional Christianity was also based on his view that it provided *no access* to heaven:

> Ne khochu ya nebes bez lestnitsy, (II, 37)
> (I don't want a heaven without a ladder,)

To leave us in no doubt as to the future site of his paradise, he, the new prophet, thundered in an apocalyptic spasm:

> Kolenom pridavlyu ekvator
> I pod buri i vikhrya plach
> Popolam nashu zemlyu-mater'
> Razlomlyu, kak zlatoy kalach.
>
> I v proval, otenennyy bezdnoyu,
> Chtoby mir ves' slyshal tot tresk,
> Ya glavu svoyu vlasozvezdnuyu
> Prosunu, kak solnechnyy blesk. (II, 40)
> (I'll pin down the equator with my knee/ And to the wailing of storms and whirlwinds/ I'll break our mother earth in half/ As I would a golden loaf of bread.// And into the gap overshadowed by the abyss,/ I shall stick my starlit head as bright as the sun/ So that the whole world hears this crack.)

---

190 See N. Kravtsov, "Esenin i narodnoe tvorchestvo," and B. V. Neyman, "Istochniki eydologii Esenina," in *Khudozhestvennyy fol'klor,* edited by Yury Sokolov, vols. IV-V (Moscow, 1929), pp. 193-203 and 204-17 respectively.

Esenin's neologistic title of the poem – *Inoniya,* a land in elsewhere – was certainly suggestive of a paradise that was not of this earth. Two other lines in this cosmic poem also give us a clue as to the *creative* motivation behind his religious vision:

> Ya inym tebya, gospodi, sdelayu,
> Chtoby zrel moy slovesnyy lug! (II, 38)
> (Lord, I shall make you into another,/ So that my poetic meadow might ripen!)

Boris Pasternak's Doctor Zhivago Poems

Pasternak's Poetic Sensibility

When one looks at Pasternak's novel *Doctor Zhivago* (first published in Italy in 1957), a novel that was inspired by the poems placed at the end of it, one realizes that Pasternak against all odds – after all the tribulations facing him as a writer and poet during the quarter century of Stalin's totalitarian rule – survived into the fifties as a post-symbolist poet.

Perhaps Nicola Chiaromonte, writing about Pasternak's spiritual survival, has put it best:

> It [the novel] is, in substance, a meditation on history, that is, on the infinite distance which separates the human conscience from the violence of history and permits a man to remain a man, to rediscover the track of truth that the whirlwind of events continually cancels and confuses. One might say that all of *Dr. Zhivago* is dedicated to a description of this distance, and to the insistent representation of the truth manifested in it.[191]

In a poem of 1936, Anna Akhmatova said all this in one line, when she described Pasternak making his way timidly over the needles of conifers,

> Chtob ne spugnut' prostranstva chutkiy son.[192]
> (In order not to frighten off the sensitive dream of space.)

The dissident literary critic and writer Andrey Sinyavsky also commented on Pasternak's "'intimacy with the universe'."[193] To Olga Hughes, Pasternak

---

191 Nicola Chiaromonte, "Pasternak's Message (1958)," in *Pasternak. Modern Judgements,* edited by Donald Davie and Angela Livingstone (London, *et al.,* 1969), pp. 231-39, here p. 232.

192 *Ibid.,* p. 152.

193 *Ibid.,* "Boris Pasternak," pp. 154-219, here p. 166.

seemed reminiscent of the mystic St. Seraphim of Sarov.[194] C. M. Bowra
meant approximately the same thing when he wrote that

> Pasternak's view of nature is central to his work and his poetry illustrates his belief that a
> creative force is at work in everything and that elements in the natural scene are as powerful
> as those in man and closely connected with them. His special interest is in his contact or
> conflict with such powers.[195]

The Poems of Doctor Zhivago

The poems of doctor Yury Zhivago were all about this spiritual contact with
the cosmic and divine creative forces in the universe. It is for this reason that
the poems were central to his writing the novel, in his words "preparatory
steps" to it,[196] and that he considered *Doctor Zhivago* the height of his creative achievement.[197] In an interview with Nils Ake Nilsson in 1958 he spoke
of the spiritual and the religious in man as "a vital feeling" of "travelers
between two stations."[198]

The twenty-five poems of doctor Zhivago (i. e. the doctor of everything
that is alive)[199] were centered around this "vital feeling," that is to say, they
were centered on our spiritual connection to the sacred source of our human
existence.

Pasternak's first poem "Hamlet," in which the addressee was God, set a
profound religious tone for the whole cycle of poems. Pasternak as Hamlet
and Christ playing out his fated role on the stage of life was not only being
watched by his contemporary audience but also by the still somewhat distant
divine realm as well:

> Na menya nastavlen sumrak nochi
> Tysyach'yu binokley na osi. (532)
> (The darkness of night is aimed at me/ Along the sights of a thousand opera-glasses.)

---

194 See Olga R. Hughes, *The Poetic World of Boris Pasternak* (Princeton and London, 1974),
   pp. 160, 162.

195 See "Boris Pasternak, 1917-1923," in C. M. Bowra, *The Creative Experiment* (New York,
   1948), pp. 128-58, here p. 147.

196 Boris Pasternak, *Proza 1915-1958. Povesti, rasskazy, avtobiograficheskie proizvedeniya,*
   edited by G. P. Struve and B. A. Filippov, introduction by Vladimir Weidlé (Ann Arbor,
   1961), p. 352.

197 *Ibid.,* p. 34.

198 Nils Ake Nilsson, "Pasternak: 'We are the Guests of Existence'," *The Reporter,* XIX (November 27, 1958), p. 35.

199 See Boris Pasternak, *Doktor Zhivago* (Ann Arbor, 1959), pp. 532-66. References to these
   poems will be cited hereafter in the text. The translations, unless otherwise indicated, are by
   Max Hayward and Manya Harari.

The third poem "In Holy Week" caught the same religious, cosmic sense of existence:

> Eshche krugom nochnaya mgla:
> Takaya ran' na svete,
> Chto ploshchad' vechnost'yu legla
> Ot perekrestka do ugla,
> I do rassveta i tepla
> Eshche tysyachelet'e. (533)
> (It is still the dark of night/ And still so early in the world/ That the square lies like an eternity/ Between the corner and the crossroads/ And dawn and warmth/ Are a thousand years away.)

The universe was far simpler than cunning people imagined, the poet tells us (541), and in the story of the birth of Jesus in Nazareth, the Sacred by way of the Christmas star finally entered human existence:

> Sred' tseloy vselennoy,
> Vstrevozhennoy etoyu novoy zvezdoy. (555)
> (The sight of the new star/ Startled the universe.)

Invisible angels walked among the shepherds, leaving their footprints in the sand (556), thereby confirming the reality of the miraculous and its connection with mankind (see also 560-61).

In the poem "The Earth" (No. 21), Pasternak expressed his belief in the spiritual function of the poet to bring together the sacred and earthly realms:

> Na to ved' i moe prizvan'e
> Chtob ne skuchali rasstoyan'ya,
> Chtoby za gorodskoyu graniyu
> Zemle ne toskovat' odnoy. (560)
> (Surely it is my calling/ To see that the distances should not lose heart [should not have to yearn],/ And that beyond the limits of the town / The earth should not feel lonely?

There followed the two Mary Magdalene poems (562-64) with their profound sense of the healing power of eternity. Then came the last poem, "The Garden of Gethsemane" (564-66) which, together with the Hamlet poem framed, as it were, the whole cycle of poems, sanctifying them the way the poems had initially sanctified the novel.

This final poem celebrated the overcoming of the astronomical distances separating the stars from man, bringing the Sacred so close to human habitation that one could practically reach out and touch the realm of the Divine:

Luzhayka obryvalas' s poloviny.
Za neyu nachinalsya Mlechnyy put'. (564)
(The field tailed off/ Into the Milky Way.)

Not surprisingly, this sacred moment of spiritual connection became associated with *Doctor Zhivago:*

'No kniga zhizni podoshla k stranitse,
Kotoraya dorozhe vsekh svyatyn'. (565)
('But the book of life has reached the page/ Which is the most precious of all holy things').

Pasternak's intuition of the Sacred, his poetic feeling that he was a humble part of a larger whole, was well expressed in his poem "Night" which belonged to his collection of poems entitled *When the Weather Clears* (Kogda razgulyaetsya, 1957):

Ne spi, ne spi, khudozhnik,
Ne predavaysya snu.
Ty – vechnosti zalozhnik
U vremeni v plenu.[200]
(Don't sleep, don't sleep, artist,/ Don't give in to sleep./ You are eternity's hostage/ A captive of time.)

The Sacred Link

In retrospect, it is interesting to note that of the four poets above, even Mayakovsky and Esenin who were blasphemers and iconoclasts were, at a deeper spiritual level, religious in the sense that their poetic vision did *not* rule out their deeper sense of an otherworldly divine presence. In Ivanov and Pasternak the religious feeling seemed much more securely anchored, more deeply rooted, without all the hyperbolic and iconoclastic bombast of futurist and imagist ideology and aesthetics.

In retrospect too, for Mayakovsky and Esenin, heaven, though present in their poetic consciousness, was a *problematic* presence. Not so for Ivanov and Pasternak. Indeed, Pasternak might have been speaking for the both of them, when he suggested that the universe was far simpler than subtle philosophers might imagine. I think, Isaiah Berlin, once again, put it well, when he spoke of the artist and of the function of his art:

---

200 Boris Pasternak, *Poeziya. Izbrannoe,* edited by N. Anatol'eva, N. Tarasova and G. Shishkina (Frankfurt a. Main, 1960), p. 374.

... and so creation is marvellous, because it is a form of being at one with the *anima mundi,* the spirit that for Neoplatonic Christianity informs and moves the universe. Dante, Tasso, Milton were seen by their admirers, and perhaps saw themselves, as divinely inspired seers; others were conceived as providers of delight – Boccaccio, Rabelais, Shakespeare probably saw themselves in this way. All art has a purpose beyond itself: to tell the truth, to instruct, to please, to heal, to transfigure men; or to serve God by embellishing his universe and by moving men's minds and hearts to fulfil his (or nature's) purposes.[201]

Rest in peace, poets, you have done your work.

---

201 See Isaiah Berlin, "Artistic Commitment. A Russian Legacy," in his *The Sense of Reality. Studies in Ideas and Their History,* Edited by Henry Hardy, With an Introduction by Patrick Gardiner (London *et al.,* 1996), pp. 194-231, here p. 196.

Nikolay Gumilev's *The Pillar of Fire*

It is generally accepted that Gumilev's (1886-1921) *The Pillar of Fire* (Ognennyy stolp, 1921), published shortly after his execution by a Bolshevik firing squad, was the height of his poetic achievement. Earl Sampson has pointed out that this collection of poems – coming in the wake of Gumilev's acmeist phase – was a return to Russian symbolism, but "on another higher level of the spiral."[202]

It was ironic that Gumilev, in his *Letters on Russian Poetry* (1923), a collection of earlier reviews and articles published between 1909 and 1916, should in his discussion of the symbolist poetry of Fedor Sologub (1910) have described a poetic personality that resembled his own:

> The images of Sologub ... but how can one speak of images, if in the poet's own eyes, there is only an "I", the only reality that has created the world. And it is not surprising that this world is only a desert in which there is nothing to love, because to love means to feel something that is higher and better than oneself ...[203]

Gumilev has usually been seen as a romantic poet in search of ideal love and exotic and dangerous adventures, but *The Pillar of Fire* shows us how very close he still was to the symbolist obsession with poetic self, almost God-like. In Renato Poggioli's words: "It is to poetry, not less than to religion, that Gumilev assigns the task of educating mankind, or, as he says, of 'raising man to the level of a higher type'."[204]

The poem that best expresses this side of Gumilev is "Memory" (Pamyat'). We see this in what one might describe as Gumilev's romantic replacement of God with himself, the poet, though this is done in an indirect way, purposely obscuring his meaning, but still in the end suggesting it.

Amid all his reincarnations as a poet in the flow of the forever changing forms of soul, the central focus of the poem was on his keeping *his body* intact, in other words, retaining the *immortality* not of his soul but of his body and, with it, of course, Gumilev's physical and poetic identity. But in telling us that the first two ancestors of his body were poets, he was less than honest when he chided the second poet for being obsessed with his poetic self:

---

202 Earl D. Sampson, *Nikolay Gumilev* (Boston, 1979), p. 148; see also p. 183, fn. 47.

203 N. Gumilev, *Sobranie sochineniy,* edited by G. P. Struve and B. A. Filippov (4 vols.; Washington, 1962-68), IV, 241. Further references to this edition will be given in the text. The translations are mine.

204 Poggioli, *The Poets of Russia 1890-1930, op. cit.,* pp. 226-27.

On sovsem ne nravitsya mne, eto
On khotel stat' bogom i tsarem,
On povesil vyvesku poeta
Nad dver'mi v moy molchalivyy dom. (II, 35)
(I don't like him at all,/ It was he who wanted to become god and emperor,/ And who put up the signboard of poet/ Over the doors into my silent house.)

But the first stanza of the poem had already given the lie to the cover-up in these lines, for there Gumilev expressed the infantile wish to remain in effect spiritually stunted in exchange for his dream of physical immortality in time:

Tol'ko zmei sbrasyvayut kozhi,
Chtob dusha starela i rosla.
My, uvy, so zmeyami ne skhozhi,
My menyaem dushi, ne tela. (II, 35)
(Only snakes shed their skins,/ So that their souls might age and grow./ We, alas, are not at all like snakes,/ We change souls, not bodies.)

And yet, in the same breath – there was here a glitch in his logic – he was also envious of God's spiritual glory, which brought him back to the real intent of his poetic vision in the first place:

Ya vozrevnoval o slave Otchey,
Kak na nebesakh, i na zemle. (II, 36)
(I became jealous of the Father's glory,/ Be it in heaven or on earth.)

Gumilev's poetic rivalry with God was expressed in other poems as well: in one, the word was equal to God (II, 39); in the poem "Soul and Body" (Dusha i telo), the line between God and Gumilev seemed intentionally blurred, thereby creating a kind of equivalence between the divine and the poetic consciousness (II, 41-42); and in "The Sixth Sense" (Shestoe chuvstvo, II, 46-47) it was high time for man to be elevated to a higher order of being.

But the premonition of disaster befalling the poet was already contained in his poem "Memory":

I togda poveet veter strannyy –
I prol'etsya s neba strashnyy svet, (II, 36)
(And then a strange wind will blow – / And a terrifying light will pour down from the heavens.)

The fulfilment of these ominous lines came in Gumilev's remarkable poem "The Streetcar Gone Astray" (Zabludivshiysya tramvay, II, 48-50) which revealed that more intuitive, darker side of his poetic consciousness.

In graphic, nightmarish images the poem made the point that Gumilev was, after all, mortal, and that it was love (II, 50) – not self-glorification – which, in the end, was most important to a human being's life. This poem took up a special place in Gumilev's oeuvre, for not only was it a reality check for him, but it had also come to him unbidden. Earl Sampson qoted Irina Odoevtseva – acmeist poet and later novelist, – who remembered Gumilev's description of how the poem had come into being. It seems clear that he felt the lines had come to him from elsewhere, and that the poem as it were had written itself quite apart from his own poetic intent:

> I don't understand [Gumilev told her] even now how it happened. ... And then it happened. I immediately found the first stanza, as though I received it complete, and didn't compose it myself. ... I continued walking and speaking line after line, as though I were reciting someone else's poem.[205]

The haunting and nightmarish quality of the poem suggests the traumatic shock with which it must have hit Gumilev's usually self-indulgent and self-absorbed poetic consciousness, pushing him to the realization that his part in creation was as humble as everyone else's:

> Ponyal teper' ya: nasha svoboda
> Tol'ko ottuda b'yushchiy svet,
> Lyudi i teni stoyat u vkhoda
> V zoologicheskiy sad planet. (II, 49)
> (Now I understand that our freedom/ Is only the light reaching us from the other world,/ People and shades stand at the entrance/ Into the zoological garden of the planets.)

What gave the poem also its own kind of unity was the repeated and terrified call of the poet for the vision to stop:

> Ostanovite, vogonovazhatyy,
> Ostanovite seychas vagon! (II, 48, 49)
> (Stop the streetcar, driver/ Stop it right now.)

But the streetcar went on and on into an otherworldly realm where the dead dwelled, where railway stations only sold tickets to spiritual destinations (II, 48, 49), and where the passengers were beheaded and their cut-off heads – like some heads of cabbages and turnips – were the price to be paid for the journey. Here, Gumilev's fate was like everyone else's:

> V krasnoy rubashke, s litsom kak vymya,
> Golovu srezal palach i mne,

---

205 Sampson, *op. cit.,* p. 135.

Ona lezhala vmeste s drugimi
Zdes', v yashchike skol'zkom, na samom dne. (II, 49)
(And the executioner in a blood-red shirt,/ With a face like an udder, cut off my head/ Which
lay together with others/ In the slippery bottom of a garbage bin.)

Of the End of a Romantic

Like so many romantic poets, Gumilev did not stand the test in clear daylight.
Typically too, as Khodasevich has pointed out, Gumilev was not a very
attractive moral human being.[206] Of course, Gumilev tried to counter his
everyday self by projecting a number of poetic selves between the years of
1905 to 1921. There was, for instance, the romantic poet in love, the poet
bent on proving himself in battle and conquests, or, like Rimbaud, following
the call to exotic lands and dangerous adventures, as we see it in Gumilev's
African poems published just before his death.

But it was in a poem of 1912 "I Believed, I Thought ..." (Ya veril, ya
dumal ...), written for Sergey Makovsky, which was in his fourth book of
poems *Foreign Heaven* (Chuzhoe nebo), a collection of poems dedicated to
Anna Akhmatova, that he had written in an almost prophetic vein of his
ultimate downfall:

I esli ya voley sebe pokoryayu lyudey,
I esli ya sletaet ko mne po nocham vdokhnovenie,
I esli ya vedayu tayny – poet, charodey,
Vlastitel' vselennoy – tem budet strashnee padenie.
(I, 168)
(And if I subjugate people to my will,/ And if inspiration comes to me at night,/ And if I
know of mysteries,/ Poet and wizard that I am, sovereign over the universe,/ My fall will be
all the more terrifying.)

Although, as an acmeist poet, he had striven for a depiction of life in all its
concrete details as over against the overpowering pull of Russian symbolism,
he never quite freed himself of the symbolist influence. And so, he too, like
the symbolists before him, allowed his poetry to replace his life. As Sergey
Makovsky put it: "Poems made up all his life,"[207] and he went on to say that
Gumilev never accepted life as it was:

---

206 See Khodasevich, "Gumilev i Blok," (1931), in his *Nekropol', op. cit.,* pp. 118-40.
207 Sergey Makovsky, "Nikolay Gumilev," in his *Na parnasse serebryanogo veka* (Munich,
1962), pp. 195-222, here p. 199, my tr.

... all his life he did not accept life as it was, he was forever running away from it into the past, into the grandeur of distant ages, into desert Africa, into the wizardry of knightly times, and into dreams of the orient's *A Thousand and One Nights*.[208]

Marc Slonim said essentially the same thing:

It is quite possible that Gumilev's idealization of strength, combativeness, and virility was a means of overcoming his own sensitivity and shyness: the intrepid conquistador was not the real Gumilev, but his romantic superego, what he wished and attempted to be.[209]

Gumilev, the romantic spirit, was not able to overcome the self that he was, – suffering probably from a chronic inferiority complex – nor to accommodate his life to his poetic vision of himself as God or superman. It was not the poet, but life which, in the end, caught up with him.

---

208 *Ibid.,* p. 201, my tr.
209 Slonim, *Modern Russian Literature. From Chekhov to the Present, op. cit.,* p. 215.

Alexander Blok's *The Twelve*[210]

Prerevolutionary Poems

Blok's spiritual biography, the pilgrimage of his soul, is contained in his poetry. And all his prerevolutionary poetry, prior to his writing *The Twelve* in the beginning of 1918, was an expression of an almost mystic yearning for a cosmic female presence who came to haunt his entire poetic output in the forever fleeting form of a beautiful woman, whom he called the Beautiful Lady.

His earliest work *Ante Lucem*[211] (1898-1900) was in search and anticipation of his Beautiful Lady, who was at first identified as a "Someone" (I, 29), but took on an increasingly feminine shape until, at one point in the cycle, Blok referred to her as "The Eternally Youthful One" (Vechno-yunnaya, I, 53).

His *Poems About the Beautiful Lady* (Stikhi o prekrasnoy dame, 1901-2), an outpouring of some 160 poems, continued his romantic adventure. But the lady of his poetic dreams remained a protean presence that haunted his restless nights as sounds and whispers, mocking laughter and tempting lights.

Her otherworldly and sacred nature was also suggested by her being associated with Christian symbolism, with churches and cathedrals, with burning candles, but also with nature, all of which made her into a ubiquitous presence.

A new and significant symbolization was her association with the snowy whirlwind (vikhor' snezhnyy, I, 154, 213). Sometimes she was presented as an empress wed to the cold of winter (I, 147), or appeared as a sorceress in the middle of a blizzard, becoming almost the blizzard itself:

Ty v beloy v'yuge, v snezhnom stone
Opyat' volshebnitsey vsplyla,
I v vechnom svete, v vechnom zvone
Tserkvey smeshalis' kupola. (I, 143)
(You have again surfaced as a sorceress/ in the white blizzard, in the snowy wailing,/ And in the eternal light, in the eternal ringing of the churches/ The cupolas have become merged.)

---

210 This essay is based on my article "Aleksandr Blok's *The Twelve:* A New Interpretation," in *Canadian Slavonic Papers,* Volume XIV, No. 3 (Autumn, 1972), pp. 465-88. It is much revised.

211 See Aleksandr Blok, *Sobranie sochineniy v vos'mi tomakh, op. cit.,* I, 3-73. Further page references to this edition will be given in the text. The translations are mine.

Towards the end of the cycle however, Blok's despair and disillusionment because of his failure to find and hold his Beautiful Lady, began to infiltrate his poems. With it came his anger and revenge by casting her into the figure of a prostitute.

The swamp, inhabited by little devils and imps, central to his cycle of poems *Earth's Bubbles* (Puzyri zemli, 1904-5), was a further symbolic expression of Blok's disenchantment. But even here, he tried to maintain his faith in Her (II, 7), for the swamp too had its own grandeur and majesty for being connected in its own way to the eternal realm of the Beautiful Lady [the word "eternity" in Russian is a feminine noun]:

Eto Vechnost' Sama snizoshla
I naveki zamknula usta. (II, 17)
(Eternity Herself has deigned to come down here/ And sealed her lips forever.)

Blok's cycle of poems *The City* (Gorod, 1904-8) was an even stronger expression of his disillusionment and his denunciation of the Beautiful Lady as the Ideal that she had once been to him. And he degraded and debased Her imagery. What had once been holy – cathedrals, churches, burning candles – was now turned into cheap rooming houses, unlighted gateways and dingy taverns. Poetic inspiration was replaced by drinking, the poet turning into a drunkard and his lovely lady a prostitute. Still, even in this city of the fallen, he felt Her presence, and she reappeared in the guise of a prophetic sibyl, a goddess, or as an ineffable shade resembling evening madonnas (II, 155, 157, 158, 177).

Although Blok's *The Snow Mask* (Snezhnaya maska, 1907) was dedicated to the actress Natal'ya Volkhova, the passionate relationship reenergized his poetic imagination so that he could once again devote himself to his Beautiful Lady.

In this cycle, the blizzard (metel') and the cold snows became associated with the starry abysses from whence blew the wind of his Lady's power. The Beautiful Lady, now the northern daughter of the snowy whirlwinds (vikhrey severnaya doch') drove the poet with Her intensely cold and cruel lashes of winter (II, 228). And out of Her starry and cosmic stretches she sang to him of their eventual reunion:

Rukavom moikh meteley
   Zadushu.
Serebrom moikh veseliy
   Oglushu.
Na vozdushnoy karuseli
   Zakruzhu.
Pryazhey sputannoy kudeli

Obov'yu.
　Legkoy bragoy snezhnykh khmeley
Napoyu. (II, 220)
(I shall choke you to death/ With the sleeve of my blizzards./ I shall stun you/ With the silver of my merry-making./ On my aerial merry-go-round/ I'll make you dizzy./ I shall wind myself around you/ Like some tangled spinning yarn of hemp./ And I'll give you to drink [also, possibly, sing to you]/ Of my snowy, intoxicating home brew.)

And Blok did not tarry with his answer:

I net moey zavidney doli –
V snegakh zabven'ya dogoret',
I na pribrezhnom snezhnom pole
Pod zvonkoy v'yugoy umeret'. (II, 224)
(And I long for nothing more/ Than to finish burning in the snows of oblivion,/ And on a coastal wintry field/ To die to the sounds of the blizzard.)

As Blok put it in his *A Terrifying World* (Strashnyy mir, 1909-16) collection of poems, the Beautiful Lady remained an ever present reality in his poetic consciousness:

Dlya inykh ty – Muza i chudo.
Dlya menya ty – muchen'e i ad. (III, 7)
(For others you are both a Muse and a wonder./ But for me you are torment and hell.)

The Twelve

Blok's poem *The Twelve* came into being in January and February of 1918.[212] In the process of writing it, Blok heard a din and rumbling around him which, at one point, grew into a terrifying noise, making him exclaim on that day that he felt himself to be a genius (III, 198-99). The poem itself was not a new departure, but an integral part of his previous poetic work, and expressed in its imagery one final invocation to the elusive Beautiful Lady.

From the very outset, She was the constant driving force of the poem, at first as a winter wind which gradually built up into a raging blizzard. The wind and the snowy flurries seemed to cover all creation (III, 347). And the revolutionary soldier Petka's relationship to Katia, the prostitute, the white officer whose mistress she was, and their deaths at the hands of Pet'ka and the revolutionaries (III, 352, 353), were all a metaphorical replay of Blok's long-standing relationship to the Beautiful Lady. Pet'ka's remorse (III, 354) was a tell-tale moment in the poem.

---

212 See P. N. Medvedev, ed., *Zapisnye knizhki Al. Bloka* (Leningrad, 1930), pp. 197-99.

After this murder, the blizzard gained in power as the twelve red revolutionary soldiers made their way through the storm. Suddenly, *someone* seemed to be waving a flag ahead of them (III, 358). It was then that the blizzard's laughter that had taunted and mocked the red soldiers (III, 359) took on the appearance of Christ, both protected by the blizzard and part of it (III, 359).

The Apparition of Christ

If one looks at the imagery of *The Twelve,* it is not too difficult to recognize Christ's apparition looming in the blizzard as yet another elemental incarnation of the Beautiful Lady. We have it from F. D. Reeve that the Christ figure according to Medvedev's study of Blok's manuscripts for the poem was far from accidendal, and that it was , in fact, endemic to all the stages associated with the writing of the poem.[213] Blok's preoccupation with Christ was also reflected in a draft for a drama about Jesus in Blok's diary for January 7, 1918, where Jesus was described as an artist with a feminine sensibility.[214] There was also Blok's Notebook entry of January 25, 1918, that he would like to settle down and write about Jesus, something that had relevance only to him: "a svoe by pisat' (Iisus)."[215]

In his diary entry for the 10th of March 1918, Blok also pointed to the *female* nature of both the blizzard and Jesus:

> Did I ever "extol" Christ? I only noted the fact that if you peer into the columns of the blizzard *on this road,* then you will see Jesus Christ. But sometimes I myself deeply hate this womanly phantom. (VII, 330, Blok's italics; my tr.)

And asked by Yury Annenkov, the illustrator of *The Twelve,* in the summer of 1918, as to how he saw the image of Christ, Blok said that Christ appeared to him as a white spot looming up ahead, white like snow, and hauntingly obsessive. And there too a red flag swirled: all this was annoying, teased, but drew him on to follow the spot which kept receding (III, 629).

Blok did not like the end of the poem and wanted Christ to be another. The problem worried him terribly.[216] But the unerring sense of the poet in him recognized the image as inevitable:

---

213 See F. D. Reeve, *Between Image and Idea* (New York, 1962), p. 211.
214 See P. N. Medvedev, ed., *Dnevnik Al. Bloka, 1917-1921* (Leningrad, 1928), pp. 95-96.
215 Medvedev, *Zapisnye knizhki Al. Bloka,* p. 198.
216 *Ibid.,* p. 199. see also VII, 326; VIII, 513-14.

> I do not like the end of *The Twelve* either. I would like its end to be different. When I finished the poem, I was amazed myself: why Christ? But the more I looked into it, the more clearly I saw Christ. And , then and there, I made an entry: 'Unfortunately it has to be Christ'. (III, 628, my tr.)

True to his poetic intuition, Blok could not help the appearance of the image of Christ because that image expressed and summed up Blok's lifelong journey in search of the Beautiful Lady.

In Retrospect

In its own time and later, *The Twelve* was variously interpreted. The Marxists especially read it from a political perspective. But it was also interpreted as a poem having a spiritual, moral and social regenerative function.[217] There were also psychoanalytical interpretations which bypassed both politics and ideology. Thus, Marina Tsvetaeva saw the poem as an inspired musical product of dream consciuosness,[218] and D. S. Mirsky compared it to Coleridge's "Kubla Khan" or the first part of Goethe's *Faust*.[219]

In the end, Blok the poet, was all of a piece. Perhaps this is what he meant in his Notebook entry for August 1918, when he wrote that whosoever wished the better to appreciate him and his poetry, should very attentively read *all* his work in sequence.[220]

In Blok's eyes, the lyrical poet was always sensitive to his times (VI, 83) and *The Twelve* was a famous case in point. But as Blok put it in his note on the poem, it was not a political poem, though it did reflect the revolutionary time with its impact on nature, life and art. Still, he hoped, it would remain a *poem* where he had simply given himself over to the elements (otdalsya stikhii), and this would in future keep the meaning of the poem alive (III, 474-75).

In the final analysis, *The Twelve* can be regarded as a telling example of the *organic* creative unity in a poet's work, which cannot be derailed by external political upheavals. Though Blok was confused by the image of Christ surfacing in his work, it is at least clear to us that the Christ figure in *The Twelve* was a continuation and development of the theme of the Beautiful Lady, and that, subconsciously, Blok was absolutely right when he re-

---

217 See My article, pp. 465-67.
218 Marina Tsvetaeva, "Iskusstvo pri svete sovesti," in *Izbrannaya proza, op. cit.,* pp. 381-406, here p. 389.
219 Mirsky, *A History of Russian Literature, op. cit.,* p. 462.
220 Medvedev, *Zapisnye knizhki,* p. 201.

marked, perhaps unwittingly, but true to his poetic imagination that, unfortunately, it had to be the image of Christ in the poem.

Alienation in Sergey Esenin's Poetry[221]

A Thematic Overview

Esenin's emotional and poetic appeal to a country that was still largely rural and half-illiterate, is all the more remarkable because so much of his poetry was an expression of *alienation* in a variety of thematic contexts.

The motifs of alienation were many in Esenin's poetic work.[222] There was, for instance, the outcast motif so poignantly expressed in his longer poem "Pugachev" (IV, 159-96, 1921), or in his *Tavern Moscow* poems (Moskva kabatskaya, II, 119-32, 149-52, 1922-23). Esenin's identification with the animal world was similarly an expression of his feeling of alienation. We see this in a number of earlier poems (in 1914 and 1915), in his longer poem "Mares' Ships," (Kobyl'i korabli, II, 87-90, 1919), and also in his moving poem "Wolf's End" (Volch'ya gibel', II, 111-12, 1922), where his identification with the wolf became a metaphor for the end of his beloved village world through urban development. Elsewhere, his innate wish to merge with nature was memorably given voice in a poem of 1919:

> Ya khotel by stoyat', kak derevo,
> Pri doroge na odnoy noge. (II, 91)
> (Like a tree I'd like to be standing,/ By the road on one leg alone).

There is no doubt, that one of Esenin's most painful, alienating experiences was the gradual disappearance of his familiar rural world, an experience that triggered an overpowering sense of his own uselessness and superfluousness. This state of mind was especially reflected in a series of 1924 poems such as "The Return Home" (Vozvrashchenie na rodinu, II, 159-63), "Soviet Russia" (Rus' sovetskaya, II, 168-71), and others. But the first line of a poem of 1920 had already predicted his disappearance as a poet:

> Ya posledniy poet derevni, (II, 97)
> (I am the last poet of the village).

---

221 This essay – much revised – is based on my article "Death and Decay: An Analysis of S. A. Esenin's Poetic Form," in *Canadian Slavonic Papers,* Vol. X, No. 2 (Summer, 1968), pp. 180-209.

222 See Sergey Esenin, *Sobranie sochineniy,* edited by A. T. Tvardovsky *et al.* (5 vols.; Moscow, 1961-62), Further references to this edition will be given in the text. The poetry translations are mine.

There were other alienation motifs. From his earliest poetry to his last, themes of deceit and betrayal in love, in happiness and in life, only fed his feeling of *rejection,* until a poem of 1925 summed it all up:

Glupoe serdtse ne beysya!
Vse my obmanuty schast'em. (III, 32)
(Foolish heart, stop beating!/ We are all deceived by happiness.)

Even on the spiritual plane, poems like "Inoniya" (II,36-44, 1918), signified his alienation from traditional Christianity.

The motif of *cold* – closely associated with the theme of death – was an especially tell-tale expression of alienation. Already in a poem of 1918 (II, 34), he had given notice that he was aware of the fatal cold within him. A few years later, in a poem of 1921, which anticipated his last nightmarish days, the cold inside distorted his view of the world outside to the point where even a street lantern reflected in a dark puddle and chilled to the bone, showed him a head without lips. To avoid seeing worse things, he wrote, he decided to squint at the world, in order to see less of it. It was, he said, a bit warmer and less painful that way (II, 107-8).

In the last three months of his life, from autumn to December of 1925, the theme of cold surfaced in the twelve poems he wrote on Russian winter (III, 99-113; see 249). This cycle of farewell poems was a moving dirge to loss and emptiness, to homelessness and disillusionment. Only a few flashes of childhood and of his village of long ago brought some momentary relief. The image of a lone, drunken maple, dancing on an empty and desolate wintry field, became a personal metaphor, a harbinger of Esenin's fast approaching end.

Death as the ultimate alienation from life was easily the most pervasive theme in Esenin's poetic work. Even lexically, death left an indelible imprint on his poetry.[223] In one of his *Tavern Moscow* poems of 1923 he had already given voice to his spiritual and creative exhaustion:

Ya ustalym takim eshche ne byl. (II, 151)
(Never before have I been this tired)

Persian Motifs

There was, however, a brief reprieve from the themes of alienation. In 1924-25 Esenin wrote a cycle of poems entitled *Persian Motifs* (III, 7-35), –

---

223 See my article (1968), pp. 180-83, 203-8.

influenced by the Persian poetry of Firdusi, Omar Khayyam and Saadi whose work dates back to the 10th to 13th centuries A.D. – which were an attempt at poetic therapy. Although Esenin never went to Persia, his imagined Persia became a land of healing for the ailing poet. The very first stanza of the cycle announced his intent:

> Uleglas' moya bylaya rana –
> P'yanyy bred ne glozhet serdtse mne.
> Sinimi tsvetami Tegerana
> Ya lechu ikh nynche v chaykhane. (III, 7)
> (My wound has stopped hurting – /And drunken delirium no longer gnaws at my heart./ I am healing myself in a teahouse/ With the blue flowers of Tehran.)

Much of the cycle was devoted to the theme of imaginary sexual encounters which, however, lacked the healing power that Esenin sought. And, in the end, these poems proved to be of no solace. In fact, in one of the poems, Esenin's farewell to his mistress Shagane sounded very much like his suicide poem:

> Do svidan'ya, peri, do svidan'ya. (III, 23, 1925)
> (Goodbye, peri, [a guardian angel or beautiful woman] goodbye.)

But he was, in effect, saying farewell to his poetic life, for, as it became clear in a later poem, his beloved Shagane was but a personification of his poetry:

> Ya ne znayu kak mne zhizn' prozhit'!
> Dogoret' li v laskakh miloy Shagi
> Il' pod starost' trepetno tuzhit'
> O proshedshey pesennoy otvage? (III, 28, 1925)
> (I don't know how to go on living!/ Should I finish burning in the caresses of my lovable Shagane/ Or should I wait until old age comes to me/ And anxiously grieve over my past poetic achievement?)

This was, of course, one of the existential problems that Esenin faced as a poet who did not really want – or who was *afraid* – to outlive his poetic fame.

In the last few poems of the cycle the Persian dream that had been intended to heal him, vanished and Soviet Russia suddenly reappeared and shattered the poetic illusion (III, 30). In the very last poem, in true symbolist fashion, Esenin confessed that, in effect, he had failed to *live* his life, and that instead he had sold his life for a song:

> Pust' vsya zhizn' za pesnyu prodana, (III,35, 1925)
> (So what if my whole life has been sold for a song).

Delirium Tremens

Like Dylan Thomas, with whom he had much in common, Esenin, in the end, drank himself to death.

The reasons for this and for his suicide were many. One we found in his poetry which reflected a profound alienation from the urbanization of his beloved village world. The prospect of being a displaced village bard did not much appeal to his poetic self-obsession. And what started with an estrangement from normal, everyday reality led, along with his growing alcoholism, to an eventual mental derangement and social isolation. For indeed, Esenin's profound sense of alienation lay in his basic incapacity for *human,* not poetic, communication. In time, this process of alienation led to the disintegration of personality, until he actually saw vultures sitting at the end of his bedstead.

Still, in retrospect, if one views Esenin in a wider context, he also drank because, like Blok before him, he felt muzzled as a poet by a political system that had no tolerance for lyrical poets who could not be politicized in Marxist fashion. As Leon Trotsky, the Commissar for War, who had much in common with the aesthetically sensitive commandants of Nazi extermination camps, said in his obituary of Esenin:

> Our epoch is a grim epoch, it is perhaps one of the grimmest in the history of so-called civilized humanity. The revolutionary born for these decades is possessed by the furious patriotism of his epoch, which is his fatherland in time. Esenin was not a revolutionary. The author of "Pugachev" and of "The Ballad about the Twenty-Six" was the most intimate of lyrical poets. Our epoch, however, is not a lyrical one. In this lies the *main* reason why Sergey Esenin left us and his epoch wilfully and so early. (Trotsky's italics)[224]

Nor was Esenin happy in love.[225] He was also aware of his limitations as a poet which he put into the mouth of his cynical Dark Man:

> Byl on izyashchen,
> K tomu zh poet,
> Khot' s nebol'shoy
> No ukhvatistoy siloyu. (III, 210)
> (He [Esenin] was elegant,/ And what's more, a poet,/ Of small / But effective power.)

It was this longer poem "The Dark Man" (Chernyy chelovek, III, 209-14) on which Esenin worked from 1923 to 1925, which became his testament to the road covered and to his tragic end. In its first stanza, repeated a second time further on in the poem, Esenin spoke in his own person:

---

224 L. Trotsky, "Pamyati Sergeya Esenina," *Pravda,* January 19, 1926, p.3. My tr.
225 See Gordon McVay, *Esenin. A Life* (Ann Arbor, 1976).

Drug moy, drug moy,
Ya ochen' i ochen' bolen.
Sam ne znayu, otkuda vzyalas' eta bol'.
To li veter svistit
Nad pustym i bezlyudnym polem,
Tol' kak roshchu v sentyabr',
Osypaet mozgi alkogol'. (III, 209)
(Friend, friend,/ I'm ill, very ill, my friend./ Don't know myself where this pain has come from./ Feels as if wind whistled over/ An empty and desolate plain,/ Or, as if alcohol stripped the brain,/ The way a grove is stripped of its leaves in September.)

Esenin had just left a psychiatric clinic in Leningrad when, on December 28, 1925, he hanged himself in the Hotel d'Angleterre, from the water pipes in the icon corner of his room, just across from St. Isaac's Cathedral.

Osip Mandelshtam's *Stone* and *Tristia*
Poet of Loneliness

> Whoever has a heart, must hear, oh time
> How your ship is going down to the bottom.
>
> O. Mandelshtam: *Tristia* (Spring, 1918)

Mandelshtam's On Poetry

Clarence Brown, in an insightful essay on Mandelshtam, wrote the following: "He was a master at describing emptiness, absence, vacancy, silence. I know of no equal to him in this regard, at least not in literature" (Ma, I, iv). Emptiness, absence, vacancy and silence are all metaphors of loneliness which marked his poetry from beginning to end.

But even his essays on poetry, most of them written in the 1920s, confirmed this sense of human solitude and isolation. The poet, he wrote, stood alone, having only his innate poetic sense to follow. This was why there was no need to belong to any poetic schools or established poetics (Ma, II, 225). The poet's only link in the universe was to God (Ma, II, 233-34) and it was perhaps because of this spiritual connection that the poet had that "teleological warmth" with which to humanize his environment (Ma, II, 253), and the strength to remain true to himself and to his poetic calling (Ma, II, 236). It was this creative sense of being that allowed him to keep that "consciousness of his poetic integrity" (Ma, II, 240), infuse his poetry with life (Ma, II, 259) and guard it against being infected by that fatal "peace of despair" (Ma, II, 276) that had characterized the spiritual climate of the 19th century.

In a crucial sense, Mandelshtam's essay on the French poet François Villon was, psychologically speaking, a parallel life to his own: "The 15th century was cruel to individual destinies" (Ma, II, 305). Their intensely felt loneliness and social isolation must have been like Rilke's, with nothing to fall back upon except poetry. This kind of loneliness has been said to have helped shape our modern literary consciousness,[226] a loneliness that Rilke described poignantly in his *Malte*: "... and I myself, yes, my God, have no roof over my head, and rain falls into my eyes." (... und ich selbst, ja, mein Gott, ich habe kein Dach über mir, und es regnet mir in die Augen).[227] Mandelshtam's wife, Nadezhda Mandelshtam, has ever so memorably written of the profound sense of nightmarish isolation and paranoia under Soviet Russian totalitarianism that took hold not just of individuals, but of the Russian nation as a whole.[228]

The Stone

When Mandelshtam died in a Soviet concentration camp in 1938, he was forty-seven years old and had left a relatively small poetic oeuvre behind, even smaller if we were to accept Nils Åke Nilsson's view of Mandelshtam's poems of the thirties as a shift away from his poetic development: "His poems preserved from this period are to be looked upon more as personal documents than as a real continuation of his earlier poetry."[229] That there was a drop in his poetic inspiration – no doubt due in part to the stresses of Soviet life – was also suggested by his 1928 collection of poems which republished the poems of *The Stone* and *Tristia* and contained only some twenty new poems (Ma, I, 93-116). This essay will concern itself with Mandelshtam's *The Stone* and *Tristia,* both published in their final form in 1923.

The Stone (Kamen'), which went through three editions (1913, 1916 and 1923), began with poems of 1908 when Mandelshtam was a bare seventeen years old. It expressed a profound sense of his poetic being that was not only to motivate the writing of his major poetry, but which also seemed to be touched by a poetic foreknowledge of his doom as a poet in a collective totalitarian society that was only a few years away.

The image of the desolateness of a stone lying somewhere, solid yet motionless, was a fitting metaphor for Mandelshtam's sense of aloneness and abandonment. His very first poem wtitten in 1908 suggested as much, leaving us with the cautious and muffled sound (zvuk glukhoy) of a fruit falling amid

---

226 See Nathan A. Scott, Jr., "The Broken Center: A Definition of the Crisis of Values in Modern Literature," in Rollo May, ed., *Symbolism in Religion and Literature* (New York, 1961), pp. 178-202, here p. 185.

227 Rainer Maria Rilke, *Die Aufzeichnungen des Malte Laurids Brigge* (Frankfurt am Main, 1979), p. 43, my tr.

228 See Nadezhda Mandelshtam, *Vospominaniya* (New York, 1970), and also her *Vtoraya kniga* (Paris, 1978).

229 Nils Åke Nilsson, "Osip Mandel'štam and His Poetry," in *Major Soviet Writers*, Edited by Edward J. Brown, *op. cit.,* pp. 164 -77, here p. 177. For corroboration see Ma, I, 149-270.

the incessant melody of a deep forest silence (Ma, I, 3). Thus the first note was struck imbuing his poems with a prophetic sense of personal isolation:

> Na stekla vechnosti uzhe leglo
> Moe dykhanie, moe teplo
> (Ma, I, 6)
> (My breath, my warmth/ Has already settled on the lenses of eternity.)

And he prayed that his lips might acquire and keep that pristine muteness that was there in the beginning (Ma, I, 9), a muteness that was expressed by one of the most beautiful and haunting images in the collection:

> I tishinu pereplyvaet
> Polnochnykh ptits nezvuchnyy khor.
> (Ma, I, 9)
> (And across the silence passes/ An inaudible choir of midnight birds.)

But with this muteness also came his terror of emptiness, a sickly and strange emptiness, he was prepared to carry as his poetic burden (Ma, I, 10), as sad as a "wounded grey bird" that had stopped singing (Ma, I, 12). In his world of poetry his personal identity was useless (Ma, I, 15), for his poetry was like God's name, or like a huge bird that had flown out of his breast leaving its empty cage behind (Ma, I, 18). And while eternity was ticking away in the stone clock marking the passage of time, all he could do as a poet was to live out his terror of emptiness as a personal sacrificial offering to eternity (Ma, I, 19-20).

Mandelshtam's linking his consciousness of God and eternity to his poetry, his cosmic sense and connectedness to the universe –

> Ya khochu pouzhinat', i zvezdy
> Zolotye v temnom koshel'ke!
> (Ma, I, 21)
> (I want to have dinner, and golden stars/ Are in my dark purse!)

allowed him to dream – in an analogy with the Cathedral of Notre Dame – that he too, one day, would be able to create poetry out of that evil weight of stone that terrified him and weighed him down (Ma, I, 24), and make the universe his home (Ma, I, 48).

Tristia

Tristia continued Mandelshtam's sense of being in a mute universe (Ma, I, 58, 60, 63, 64) and, once again, his poetic vocation took him out into the terrifying spaces of the universe:

> Na strashnoy vysote zemnye sny goryat,
> Zelenaya zvezda mertsaet.
> (Ma, I, 71)
> (My earthly dreams burn at a terrifying height,/ The green star flickers.)

A feeling of doom brought on by the green star would not let go of him (Ma, I, 72), even though the sacred isles were in the wind and the healing lungwort gave joyous hope to the wasps (Ma, I, 75). Muteness still flooded his consciousness:

> No ya zabyl, chto ya khochu skazat',
> (Ma, I, 81)
> (But I've forgotten what I want to say,)

And then, a sudden breakthrough in a poem of November, 1920, one of the most beautiful poems of the collection:

> Voz'mi na radost' iz moikh ladoney
> Nemnoga solntsa i nemnoga meda,
> (Ma, I, 84)
> (Take for your joy out of my hands/ A bit of sun and a bit of honey,)

The poem was a high point, a celebration of his wild creativity and love in a world of gathering terror. Other poems took up this feeling of personal doom as a poet in the real world of Soviet Russian communism. Indeed, in one poem, he equated the "dark velvet of the Soviet night" to a "global emptiness" (Ma, I, 85) and wrote:

> Chto zh, gasi, pozhaluy, nashi svechi
> V chernom barkhate vsemirnoy pustoty,
> (Ma, I, 86)
> (Well, what of it, extinguish, if you like, our candles/ In the dark velvet of global emptiness,).[230]

---

230 See also Clarence Brown, *Mandelshtam* (Cambridge *et al.,* 1973).

Poems and Poetic Fragments from the 1930s

Even if Mandelshtam had not written his anti-Stalin poem of November, 1933 (Ma, I, 202), trying to counter it later with a seemingly more adulatory longer poem on Stalin in January of 1937,[231] there can be no doubt that he was a marked man in the collective, totalitarian society of his time.

The theme of loneliness in his poetry would have been enough to make him into an undesirable anti-revolutionary presence. He caught this sense of personal doom in a two-line fragment of a poem of 1931:

> Zamolchi! Ni o chem, nikogda, nikomu –
> Tam v pozharishche vremya poet ...
> (Ma, I, 170)
> (Keep quiet! Not a word about anything, ever, to anyone –/ There, in the huge conflagration, I can hear time singing ...)

In the spring of 1935, in yet another remnant of four lines, he reminded the regime that it had not been able as yet to stop him from writing poetry:

> Gub shevelyashchikhsya otnyat' vy ne mogli.
> (Ma, I, 214)
> (You could not stop my lips from moving.)

In a very poignant fragment of a poem of February, 1937, he expressed his tragic situation as a poet in these words:

> Uzhe ne ya poyu, – poet moe dykhan'e –
> I v gornykh nozhnakh slukh i golova glukha.
> (Ma, I, 250)
> (It is no longer I who sings, – it is my breath that sings –/ I've left my hearing in a mountain scabbard, and my head is deaf.)

In a poem of May, 1931, dedicated to Akhmatova, he asked her to preserve his poetry:

> Sokhrani moyu rech' navsegda za privkus neschast'ya i dyma,
> Za smolu krugovogo terpen'ya, za sovestnyy degot' truda.
> Tak voda v novgorodskikh kolodtsakh dolzhna byt' cherna i sladima,
> Chtoby v ney k Rozhdestvu otrazilas' sem'yu plavnikami zvezda.
> (Ma, I, 167)
> (Guard my speech forever for its after-taste of misfortune and smoke,/ For the resinous patience required, and the awkward tar of labour involved./ It is thus that the water of the

---

231 See Osip Mandelshtam, *Sobranie sochineniy,* supplement volume IV, Edited by Gleb Struve, Nikita Struve and Boris Filippov (Paris, 1981), pp. 23-26.

Novgorod wells has to be both dark and manageable,/ So that by Christmas time it might reflect the star with the seven fins.)

The Noise of Time

In a sense *The Noise of Time* (Shum vremeni, Ma, II, 43-125), prose reminiscences published in 1925, was, like his poetry, an expression of Mandelshtam's estrangement from the world he found himself in. The title itself suggested an indistinctness about this world, as if the poet had removed himself to a point where the sounds of life had merged into a distant hum, blurring the outlines of the life around him. Thus he could write: "I would not like to talk about myself, but only to shadow our age, to track the noise and the germination of time." (Ma, II, 99)

This social alienation was also suggested by Mandelshtam's identification – especially in "Feodosia", the latter part of *The Noise of Time* – with the tragic lives of people caught up in the revolutionary upheaval, be it of 1905 or 1917, with human beings whose lives seemed meaningless in historical time. One such victim was "Sergey Ivanych" (Ma, II, 79-82) for whom the poet wrote a moving epitaph:

> If Sergey Ivanych had turned into a pure logarithm for calculating the speed of stars or into a function of space, I would not have been surprised: he had no choice but to leave this life, he was so much like a Chimera. (Ma, II, 82)

At another point he likened post-revolutionary Russia to a time of plague (Ma, II, 118) and observed that it was "better to be a bird than a human being," (Ma, ii, 117).

Mandelshtam was always afraid to be left alone. Luckily, he still had family and friends, perhaps the closest being his wife Nadezhda Mandelshtam and poets like Akhmatova and Tsvetaeva who valued his poetry greatly. Indeed Tsvetaeva, who for some as yet unaccountable reason had torn up Mandelshtam's *The Noise of Time* in disgust in 1926 (Ma, II, 551), wrote a loving psychological portrait of him in emigration, in the spring of 1931, defending him – and herself – from the émigré poet Georgy Ivanov's untrustworthy memoirs (see Ma, III, 306-44).

Her portrait of Mandelshtam, "with his feeling of great anguish and melancholy" (s ego vysokoy toskoy, Ma, III, 342), has left us with a moving recollection of a man and a poet whose strange and neurotic ways and pitiable unbalanced and restless life could only have contributed to his sense of utter loneliness. Mandelshtam's last refuge was his poetry, but, as fate would have it, even that refuge was to become increasingly uncertain.

Epilogue

J. B. Priestley, in his wonderful book *Literature and Western Man* (1960), had this to say about the 20th century:

> The modern age shows us how helpless the individual is when he is at the mercy of his unconscious drives and, at the same time, is beginning to lose individuality because he is in the power of huge political and social collectives. It is an age of deepening inner despair and of appalling catastrophes ...[232]

The twelve Russian poets in this collection of essays proved to be no exception to this devastating experience. The totalitarian nightmare left its tragic mark on their lives whether they were inner émigrés living in Soviet Russia or exiles living abroad. For the inner émigrés the enemy was always the Soviet regime and the consequences for being out of tune with the political ideology of the day varied for each poet. Mayakovsky and Esenin committed suicide; Gumilev and Mandelshtam were killed; Blok stopped writing; Akhmatova and Pasternak were persecuted to the end of their days. And though the exiles lived in a freer world, the consequences of exile were equally tragic: Tsvetaeva and Poplavsky committed suicide; Khodasevich stopped writing; and Brodsky's poetic inspiration was undermined and, possibly, Vyacheslav Ivanov's as well.

Another major contributing cause to their creative dilemmas, whether they were in Russia or outside, was a profound sense of rootlessness and loneliness. In Soviet Russia they were not allowed to speak. In the West they could finally speak but, more often than not, they had communication difficulties with their Russian émigré audience for political reasons, and even when this was not the case, they were not immune to a haunting sense of linguistic and cultural disconnection. A more existential cause of their undoing in both East and West, and varying from individual to individual, was their living in abject poverty – Brodsky was more fortunate towards the end of his life – and under enormous emotional stress, and suffering from poor physical and emotional health.

Indeed, these poets, like other European writers and poets, lived the grotesque traumas of the 20th century. In his fascinating study *The Grotesque in Art and Literature* (1957), Wolfgang Kayser observed that the grotesque tended to appear during times of turmoil and upheaval when reality was

---

232 J. B. Priestley, *Literature and Western Man* (New York, 1960), p. 443.

distorted, personality destroyed and the historical order fragmented. In this sense, Kafka's work, for example, was an apt description of life in the shadow of the holocaust, and the grotesque a sign of an unpredictable world of horror:

> We are so strongly affected [he wrote] and terrified because it is our world which ceases to be reliable, and we feel that we would be unable to live in this changed world. The grotesque instills fear of life rather than fear of death. Structurally, it presupposes that the categories which apply to our world view become inapplicable.[233]

Beyond the desperate anguish that these poets expressed, they thus also gave witness to the "evil that men do." In this they were kindred spirits to other European writers and poets like Wolfgang Borchert, Böll, Grass, Celan and Camus, who also experienced the totalitarian impact on human beings at close range. We should treasure them not only for their creative achievement, but even more for the human price they paid for remaining our spiritual guides through a very, very dark age.

Lawrence Langer, writing of Jakov Lind, an Austrian Jewish writer who survived the German Holocaust – yet another manifestation of totalitarianism at work – spoke of Lind's focus on the "metamorphosis in human nature that resulted from the experience of the Holocaust," and of the consequent loss of "human identity."[234] What Langer said of Lind's fiction is in essence also true for the experience of twentieth-century Russian poets living out the consequences of Soviet communism:

> Existence askew is the hallmark of his fiction; his art is dedicated to a deliberate distortion of reality, as if the fun-house mirrors that warp the human figure in their illusory world of glass had somehow escaped the confines of the amusement park to reflect an authentic universe of grotesque shapes that insist on being accepted as "normal" images of our time, in the absence of anything else to compare them with. His theme is a world gone so mad that insanity, now the only measure of experience, somehow seems sane; yet behind the imaginative lunacy of his novels and tales – and he never permits us to forget this – looms the historical deracination that inspired it.[235]

Let us hope that the twenty-first century will be kinder to us.

---

233 Wolfgang Kayser, *The Grotesque in Art and Literature,* Translated from the German by Ulrich Weisstein (New York-Toronto, 1966), pp. 184-85.

234 Lawrence L. Langer, "Blessed are the Lunatics," in his *The Holocaust and the Literary Imagination* (New Haven and London, 1977), pp. 205-49, here pp. 224, 247 respectively.

235 *Ibid.,* p. 205.

A Cultural Perspective –
Nineteenth-Century Russian Literature
as a Mirror of Society

Introduction

Great works of literature and poetry have always been and will remain a historical, social, cultural and psychological mirror of what Northrop Frye called the "Mythology" of an age.[236] As Lionel Trilling put it in 1945: "What marks the artist is his power to shape the material of pain we all have."[237]

With respect to Russian literary development, it was nineteenth-century literature in particular – and the underground fiction during the Soviet period – that caught the humane concerns of a divided nation. Old Russia between the 10th century A. D. and the beginning of the 18th century when Peter the Great began to Europeanize and modernize the country was, as Dmitry Likhachev has pointed out, a static and repetitive religious culture.[238] As such, the focus fell on otherworldly spiritual concerns rather than on the worldly experience of an increasingly brutal and despotic existence. In the 18th century, when Russia was confronted by the European Enlightenment, there was – with a few notable exceptions (Kantemir, Radishchev) – a similar dearth of social reflection in literature. Russian writers spent more time eulogizing Russian despotism and imitating European literary models than on the inhumanity of Russian serfdom. To be fair, eighteenth-century Russian literature had begun to be influenced by the moral and humane concerns of the European Enlightenment – liberty and the rights of man – but for the Russians this was still more of an intellectual preoccupation primarily among its intelligentsia, rather than an existential, social commitment.

It was only in the 19th century, when Russia experienced an extraordinary literary Renaissance, that literature began to reflect the more profound social and cultural issues of a nation doomed to despotic rule and still in the grip of

---

236 Northrop Frye, *The Modern Century. The Whidden Lectures 1967* (London *et al.,* 1969), p. 105. See also*The Educated Imagination. The Massey Lectures – Second Series* (Toronto, 1971), p. 52.

237 Lionel Trilling, "Art and Neurosis," in his *The Liberal Imagination. Essays on Literature and Society* (New York, 1953), pp. 159-78, here p. 173.

238 Dmitry Likhachev, "V chem sut' razlichiy mezhdu drevney i novoy russkoy literaturoy," *Voprosy Literatury,* No. 5 (1965), pp. 170-86.

serfdom (until 1861). As to Russia's modernist age (1890-1917 and beyond), irrespective of its poetic achievements, its emphasis on the whole fell on an illusionary aesthetics, not on social reality.

With the coming of the Soviet period (1917-91), the gap between social reality and the obligatory socialist realist political writing widened irreparably, until the lifelessness of artistic expression could at best only be taken perhaps as a metaphor for the cultural and social stagnation of the Russian people. Only the officially proscribed and persecuted underground writing tried to carry on the literary tradition left by the 19th century.

1. An Art Divided

Major nineteenth-century Russian fiction, under the impact of the Enlightenment and of European Romanticism, consistently mirrored a split in social and cultural consciousness in the duality of its thematic structure. Pushkin, Gogol, Turgenev, Dostoevsky, Leo Tolstoy and Chekhov, one and all, each in their own way, reflected in metaphorical terms the existential frictions of Russian life triggered by the perennial conflict between humaneness and civilized existence on the one hand, and the disfiguring impact of Russian tyranny and inhumanity on the other.

Pushkin's Little Tragedies

Given the fact that nineteenth-century Russia was an oppressive society, its literature, by virtue of being practically the only voice left for expressing social and cultural concerns – another voice was the revolutionary underground – became by necessity an even more acute mirror of society, reflecting the split consciousness of its culture.

Pushkin's poetic work, in its *thematic* structure, was one such record of the split consciousness of Russian culture. This had already been apparent in his longer *Southern Poems* (1820-24) where the romantic "Byronic" hero fleeing society in search of freedom found that his real enemy lurked closer to home, in his inner self which willful, self-centred and emotionally and spiritually bankrupt, lost all capacity for experiencing freedom and love. Pushkin's greatest longer poem, *The Bronze Horseman* (1833), defined this inner split in more relevant historical and social terms, by connecting it clearly to Pushkin's own and impossible double allegiance to Russian autocracy and Revolution.

This tragic conflict in Pushkin's inner self was most powerfully expressed in his four *Little Tragedies* which had been conceived for the most part in 1826, but were written down in the autumn of 1830 on his family estate of Boldino, where an outbreak of cholera held him captive for some three months.

The *Little Tragedies* expressed the rift in Russian consciousness thematically by juxtaposing conscience and self. The conflict between them suggested that conscience could not be violated without dire spiritual consequences to the self, irrespective of personal status, personal gifts or personal passions. As the literary historian Pavel Sakulin quite correctly discerned,[239] Pushkin's conscience – like the intelligentsia's conscience – was troubled, in his particular case with respect to Radishchev's revolutionariness and especially after the Decembrist uprising of 1825 which, for personal reasons – some of Pushkin's friends were hanged or exiled to Siberia – threw a long shadow over his poetic work.

Thus in *The Avaricious Knight* (Skupoy rytsar'),[240] the knight's wealth acquired through usury could not shield him from an intrusive conscience that gave him no rest. The baron's monologue in his vaulted cellar filled with glistening gold, sounded the central theme of the tragedy:

> Who knows how much of bitter self-denial,
> What rebel passions tamed, what pain, what gloom,
> What days of care and sleepless nights, my wealth
> Has cost me? Yet my son will say, no doubt,
> My heart with hoary moss was overgrown,
> That I have no longings, never felt
> The silent voice of conscience in my life –
> Yes, conscience, that sharp-toothed beast that scrapes
> About the heart, that fierce intruding guest,
> That wearisome companion, that creditor
> Most brutish, worst of witches at whose call
> The moon grows dark, *the tombs move restlessly*
> *And vomit forth their dead* upon the night! (K, 17, my italics)

In his second little tragedy *Mozart and Salieri,* Salieri's poisoning of Mozart was perhaps ultimately Pushkin's own recognition that his compromise with Tsar Nicholas I, and his "betrayal" in this sense of the Decembrists,[241] had

---

239 See Sakulin, *Pushkin iRadishchev, op. cit.*

240 I have used Eugene M. Kayden's excellent translation of the little tragedies in the Yellow Springs Ohio edition of 1965. Further page references to this edition will be given in the text as K.

241 See Anatole G. Mazour, *The First Russian Revolution of 1825. The Decembrist Movement, its Origins, Development and Significance* (Stanford, 1963); for Pushkin see D. S. Mirsky, *Pushkin* (New York, 1963).

poisoned his own poetic gift and genius. Once again, conscience came to Mozart-Pushkin in the shape of a man in black. As Mozart confessed to Salieri:

> That shape in black disturbs my rest by day
> And night. I see his presence everywhere
> Around me like a shadow. Even now
> I seem to feel him at our table, right
> Between us here. (K, 36)

The Stone Guest (Kamennyy gost') exploited the Don Juan theme. In Pushkin's handling of the legend, Don Juan too, like the baron and like Salieri-Mozart, was pursued by his conscience for having killed Doña Anna's husband in a duel. He needed forgiveness and absolution at her hands in order to regain his humanity, but atonement was ultimately out of reach for him. In his own words about himself to Doña Anna, Don Juan-Pushkin revealed his troubled conscience:

> I'm sure he's often been described to you
> As scoundrel, monster, rogue. O Doña Anna,
> There is perhaps some truth in hearsay tales.
> Perhaps a heavy weight of evil lies
> Upon my conscience. True, for long I've been
> The willing slave of lust. But since I first
> Saw you, it seems I have been born again,
> And loving you, I am in love with virtue.
> And now in humility I kneel at last
> Before all excellence on trembling knees. (K, 78)

In his first and deceptively playful longer poem *Ruslan and Lyudmilla* (1817-20), Pushkin, under cover of a fairytale, had already attacked Russian tyranny and autocracy in the figure of *Chernomor* (Black Plague), the evil magician who tried to keep the beautiful Lyudmilla prisoner. In his last little tragedy, *The Feast during the Plague* (Pir vo vremya chumy), the poet, personified by the Chairman, was – like Lyudmilla and Pushkin – surrounded and held captive by the Plague. And again, the man in dark, this time in the figure of a priest, tried to bring balm to the Chairman's burdened conscience amid the desperate carousing. But the Chairman rejected his help, saying to the priest that he had come too late to save his soul:

> *Chairman*
> Why do you come
> To trouble me? My place is here today.
> *Here I am held by dreadful memories,*
> Despair, the knowledge of my lawless ways,

By fear and horror of the deathly void
That meets me when I come into my house.
My place is here: I like their revelry,
Their riot, drinking – God forgive me – and
The wanton love of fallen simple creatures.
My mother's soul can summon me no more.
Too late I hear your voice; too late your help,
Too late your message of salvation calls
Unto my soul. Depart in peace, old man,
And cursed be anyone who follows you.
(K, 95, my italics)

Gogol's *The Overcoat*

Belinsky's outraged letter to Gogol in the summer of 1847 came in response to Gogol's just published *Selected Passages from Correspondence with Friends* which had been written in defense of Russian Church and State. For Belinsky, who considered Gogol to be a member of the Russian Western-oriented intelligentsia, especially after the publication in 1842 of the first part of his remarkable satirical novel *Dead Souls,* the *Selected Passages* came both as a shock and as an unforgivable offence by a writer who had given promise of taking on the Russian Establishment.

As for Gogol, after his initial praise of *Dead Souls,* he suddenly changed course and, obsessed as he was with evil in the world and with his own desperate need for salvation, he took his novel to be an expression of his demonic imagination. Consequently, after its publication, he worked for the last ten years of his life on its second part, trying in vain to stifle his creativity by working against the natural flow of his creative imagination which was satirical, grotesque and demonic.

His famous story *The Overcoat* published in 1842, just before his change of heart, may already have caught the gathering inner conflict by giving voice to the two opposing sides of his artistic temperament: the compassionate, the humane side of his art, on the one hand, and the dehumanizing, cruel and tyrannical side on the other. It is not difficult to see how the Russian ex-perience of humanism and despotism found its reflection in the story, whose nihilism far outstripped its humane intent.

On the humane side, one of the story's most moving moments was the downtrodden hero's death conveyed in Gogol's own narrative voice:

And St. Petersburg carried on without Akaky, as though he had never lived there. A human being just disappeared and left no trace, a human being whom no one ever dreamed of protecting, who was not dear to anyone, whom no one thought of taking interest in, who did not attract the attention even of a naturalist who never fails to stick a pin through an ordinary fly to examine it under the microscope.[242]

And yet, almost at the very beginning of the story, it was Akaky who was likened to a fly. At his place of work, where this lowly civil servant copied documents, we read:

Not only did the caretakers not get up from their seats when he passed by, but they did not even vouchsafe a glance at him, just as if a common fly had flown through the waiting room. (M, 235)

And Gogol, the naturalist, did not fail to stick pin after pin into this poor fly. *The Overcoat* brimmed over with Gogol's relentless ridicule and mockery of Akaky: he made fun of his name, of his speech, and put him into laughable situations. He underlined his lifeless existence in which, apart from the pleasure he received from copying documents and from his far too brief possession of his new overcoat, there seemed to be no joys in his life. Away from work, he lived in close to total isolation, venturing out only to see his tailor, Petrovich, his only purpose in life seeming to be to scrape enough money together for his new winter coat. He was blind to the outside world, did not taste or enjoy the food he ate, did not step out and had no friends. Clearly, Akaky was meant to be not a man, but the caricature of a man.

Akaky's tailor Petrovich, who was a number of times likened to the devil (M, 242, 247, 248), had a snuff-box. This snuff-box, where a general's face on the lid had been pushed in by a finger and then taped over (M, 243-44) was, metaphorically speaking, typical of Gogol's faceless and lifeless universe. And in describing Akaky's future overcoat as "a dear wife of his" (M, 249), Gogol, in effect, replaced a human being by an object.

Akaky's complaint to the "Very Important Person" about the theft of his new overcoat highlighted Gogol's cruel treatment of Akaky when the latter said that he had been robbed "in a most shameless fashion" (M, 262; the original here has the much more appropriate "in an inhuman manner: bezchelovechnym obrazom). Akaky's outcry suggested that the real thief in the story was Gogol himself who had mercilessly robbed Akaky of almost all traits of his humanity until only a few objects remained to mark his pitiful end:

Neither his room nor his belongings were put under seal, in the first place, he had no heirs, and in the second there was precious little inheritance he left behind, comprising as it did all

---

242 I have used David Magarshak's translation (with his introduction) of *The Overcoat and Other Tales of Good and Evil* (New York, 1965), pp. 265-66. Further page references to this edition will be given in the text as M.

in all a bundle of quills, a quire of white Government paper, three pairs of socks, a few buttons that had come off his trousers, and the *capote* ... (M, 265)

We might finish this critique of Gogol's story by suggesting a comparison between Gogol's tale and Herman Melville's "Bartleby, the Scrivener" (1853), in order to bring out the difference between a truly *compassionate* portrayal of the "little man" and one that is found wanting.[243]

Turgenev's *Hamlet and Don Quixote*

For Turgenev, love was an all-encompassing force and a life without love was totally meaningless. As he put it to Ivan Minitsky, a doctor and friend, in 1853:

> ... without passionate love and belief, irony is rubbish and criticism worse than all invective. If one were to analyze the poetry of evil embodied in the figure of Satan, we would find even there infinite love as its foundation.[244]

And love, as he wrote to the married and famous opera singer Pauline Viardot-Garcia in 1848 – who was to remain his femme fatale for the rest of his life, and because of whom he spent some twenty-four years abroad in France and in Germany – love was "... a reddish little spark in the sombre and mute ocean of Eternity, it is the only moment that belongs to us ..." (T, XII, 66).

But in his famous speech *Hamlet and Don Quixote* (Gamlet i Don Kikhot, T, XI, 168-87), which he gave in January of 1860, Russian society seemed to offer little fertile ground for such a love, nor for the idealism and humaneness of a Don Quixote (T, XI, 170, 182, 185). In its stead Turgenev found the nihilism of Hamlet to be much more typical of Russian society (T, XI, 169), with his analytical, egotistic and self-obsessed nature (T, XI, 177, 178, 172), his "oppressive and intolerant" attitude (T, XI, 183), and his inability to believe in anything or to love anyone (T, XI, 172, 173, 176). He was in fact a forerunner of the nihilist Bazarov in what was probably Turgenev's best novel, *Fathers and Children* (Ottsy i deti, 1862). Hamlet's cynicism, his contempt for the mass of humanity and his disbelief in the existence of Truth made him incapable of either humanitarian concerns or of any kind of social and humane vision (T, XI, 176, 178, 174, 175). Hamlet's particular tragedy – which turned out also to be Bazarov's – was, in Turgenev's view, that

---

243 For Gogol see Vladimir Nabokov's highly entertaining *Nikolay Gogol* (Norfolk, Conn., 1944).

244 See Ivan Turgenev, *Sobranie sochineniy* (12 vols.; Moscow, 1953-58), XII, 158, my tr. Further pagereferences to this edition will be given in the text as T. The translations are mine.

"thought and will had become separated" in him (T,XI, 179), destroying the wholeness of his personality.

In retrospect, we can see that Hamlet and Bazarov were kindred spirits. We find the same arrogance in Bazarov, the same denial of love and humanity, the abuse of everything and everyone, the same insolence, this time raised to delusions of grandeur, all of which in Turgenev's eyes defined him as a nihilist.[245] His intellectual conceit and his pride prevented him from any real *emotional* involvement with others, especially women (*Fathers*, pp. 86, 76, 79, 82-83). "With wide open eyes he stared vindictively into the darkness" (*Fathers*, p. 96). But when he fell in love with Odintsova, he realized that he was like everyone else, that he could not live up to his own assumed sense of superiority (*Fathers*, pp. 73-82) and that he was not cut out for that "bitter, rough, lonely existence" of the superman (*Fathers*, p. 148). Consequently he lost his will for life, his intellectual motivation for living which, ultimately, brought him to what was in effect a suicide (*Fathers*, pp. 141, 150, 153, 156). And he confessed as much to Odintsova:

> But I think I have been moving too long in a sphere which is not my own. Flying fish can hold out for a time in the air, but soon they must splash back into the water (*Fathers*, p. 147)

The young radical critic Dmitry Pisarev wrote at the time that the Bazarovism of the novel presented a "true, deeply felt picture of contemporary life" (*Fathers*, p. 209) and in this he concurred with Turgenev's view that it was Hamlet and not Don Quixote who was the more typical of Russian society.

Turgenev's *Hamlet and Don Quixote* turned out to be a barometer of the spiritual climate of mid-nineteenth-century Russia. It had in fact been written concurrently with his major novels between 1857 and 1860, *Rudin, A Nest of Gentlefolk* and *On the Eve*. During these three years he had tried desperately to create a *good man,* a Don Quixote from among his useless and superfluous male protagonists whose emotional inadequacy prevented them from committing themselves to the women who loved them but who could not overcome the emotional impasse. And so, though there were good women in his novels, in a country where the Bazarovs predominated, it is hardly surprising that Turgenev's socially conscious fiction could not find or create even one humane man with whom he could have countered the nihilist currents in the air and that despotic quality of Russian life that left such a deep rift in nineteenth-century Russian fiction.

---

245 See Ivan Turgenev, *Fathers and Sons,* edited and translated by Ralph E. Matlaw, A Norton Critical Edition (New York, 1966), p. 41. Further page references to this edition will be given in the text as *Fathers*).

Dostoevsky's *Notes from Underground*

The central and traumatic experience of Dostoevsky's life was being sentenced in 1849, first to be executed by firing squad, but then, on a whim of Nicholas I, being condemned to ten years of prison and exile for his perhaps innocent participation in the Petrashevsky revolutionary circle.

His *Notes from Underground* (Zapiski iz podpol'ya, 1864),[246] which were to shape all his future novels, presented a painful record of the impact of his prison sentence and of Russian despotism on his consciousness. In the third section of part one of the *Notes,* this traumatic experience was clearly expressed in the metaphor of the mouse that stood for the Underground man and for Dostoevsky. From the outset, the Underground man, who considered himself to be a man of "heightened consciousness" felt that he was actually a mouse and not a man at all:[247]

> Let's take a look now at this mouse in action. Let's suppose, for example, that it has also been mistreated ... and also longs to avenge itself. ... And there, in its loathsome, stinking underground hole, our mouse, insulted, crushed, destroyed by ridicule, immediately settles into cold, venomous, and, worst of all, lifelong malice. For forty years on end it will recall its humiliation.[248]

In his vengeful state the Underground man went on to reject the Crystal Palace and all that this World Exhibition in London stood for: reason, civilized consciousness, morality and goodness. Furthermore, he had worked out a philosophy of life for himself which would allow him to revenge himself on humanity. Thus *his* freedom was based on his arbitrary whims to inflict pain and suffering (D, V, 113, 115, 117, 119) – was he emulating the tsar? – and his pleasure in experiencing another's pain or humiliation became a measure of his willful sense of freedom (D, V, 102, 105, 106, 107). In the same breath he admitted that he was, in effect, a sick and vicious man (D, V, 99).

It seems, however, that his vindictive will was paralyzed because of the spiritual and intellectual vacuum of his subconscious Underground which undermined any action he might undertake. Proof of this spiritual paralysis came in his own admission that he did not really believe anything he had said in the first part of the *Notes* (D, V, 121) which, in turn, was also reflected in

---

246 See F. M. Dostoevsky, *Polnoe sobranie sochineniy v tridtsati tomakh* (vols. 1-29; Leningrad, 1972-86), V, 99-179. Further page references to this edition will be given in the text as D. The translations are mine.

247 See Fyodor Dostoevsky, *Notes from Underground,* Translated by Mirra Ginsburg, With an Introductionby Donald Fanger (Toronto *et al.,* 1981), pp. 9, 10 respectively.

248 *Ibid.,* pp. 10-11.

his railing against everything that was "'wonderful and noble'" (D, V, 109; Dostoevsky's ironic quotation marks).

The Underground man's cruel treatmen of the young prostitute Liza in the second part of the *Notes*, his planned intent to humiliate her and make a mockery of her (D, V, 173, 155), brought out his sadistic, compulsive self-will into the open and exemplified his philosophy of life. His only justi-fication in the reader's mind was that he, the Underground man, could not help being what he was, because his experience of Russian despotism had disfigured his soul irremediably. In his own words:

> For without power and without tyrannizing over somebody I cannot live; ... They won't let me. ... I cannot be ... kind! ... First of all, I couldn't even love anyone anymore because, I repeat, for me to love meant to tyrannize and to excel morally. All my life I've not been able to imagine any other love. (D, V, 175-76)

Lev Shestov, philosopher and literary critic, was very much aware of the dichotomy in Dostoevsky's being, when he said of the *Notes* that they ex-pressed Dostoevsky's bankrupt idealism:

> The wonderful and the lofty in quotation marks is not my invention. I found it in the *Notes from Underground*. In the *Notes* all "ideals" are presented in this way. Schiller, humaneness, Nekrasov's poetry, the Crystal Palace, everything that had ever filled Dostoevsky's soul with tenderness and exaltation, is now covered in a hail of the most venomous and the most personalized sarcasm. The ideals and the tenderness expressed for them evoke in him a feeling of disgust and horror. And it isn't that he questions the possibility of realizing ideals. He doesn't even think of it, he doesn't want to. In fact, it would be all the worse, if the magnanimous dreams of his youth should ever come true. And if ever the ideal of human happiness on earth should be realized, Dostoevsky anathematizes it ahead of time. I shall speak directly: no one had ever dared before Dostoevsky to express such thoughts, be it with corresponding notes. For such thoughts to spring up in a human mind, there had to be a great despair, and there had to be a superhuman impertinence to bring them before the people.[249]

Leo Tolstoy's *The Death of Ivan Ilych*

Tolstoy's *The Death of Ivan Ilych* (1886) was written at a time in his life when he was going through a spiritual crisis during which he set himself up against the Russian State and Church, against the nobility to which he him-self belonged. It was a stage in his life when he found fault with his own major works (*War and Peace, Anna Karenina),* had serious reservations about other major writers (Cervantes, Shakespeare, Molière, Pushkin, Gogol and Maupassant among others), was against the acquisition of social status

---

249 L. Shestov, *Dostoevsky i Nitshe (Filosofiya Tragedii)* (St. Petersburg, 1903), pp. 55-56, my tr.

and wealth, was hostile to women in particular – in short, like some kindred spirit to the Underground man, Tolstoy fumed at the Crystal Palace and the European society that had brought it forth. But unlike Dostoevsky's Underground man, he was still capable of ideals, in his particular case it was the idealization of the Russian peasant and of morally instructive art.

As a result, his didactic novella, showing the familiar rift in Russian nineteenth-century consciousness, contrasted the upper, educated society infected with all its social and materialistic ambitions, its superficial pretensions and concerns, with the healthy, simple life of the Russian peasant who alone could and would revitalize Russian society.

The story of the examining magistrate Ilych's life was intended as a morality tale: an insignificant minor accident of falling from a ladder while hanging curtains, led to Ilych's eventual death. In time, the unpredictable unfolding of this event made Ilych realize that life could not simply be bound and demarcated by social status, profession or by any kind of planning. And his fast approaching death made him also aware that he had lived a meaningless life.

This awareness, but also the fear of death, began to make him more sensitive to his human and social environment. Slowly, he opened himself up to another human being, the peasant Gerasim, whose compassion for his suffering struck Ilych with all its moral force. It convinced him that he had not lived his life as he ought to have lived it.

Ivan Ilych's spiritual journey was finally resolved for him at the very moment of his death, when he suddenly *felt* compassion for his little son and his wife, when his pain did not matter as much any more and when, just as suddenly, his fear of death had vanished: "There was no fear because there was no death. ... In place of death there was light."[250]

It was thus that Ivan Ilych celebrated his spiritual rebirth.

Chekhov's *Man in a Case*

Chekhov's mature stories written between 1886 and 1902 seem to derive their power more from a life-denying than a life-affirming poetic vision. And even though Chekhov – along with Pushkin – is perhaps the most humane among nineteenth-century major Russian writers, there was an *oppressive* energy in his fiction which undermined his characters' ability to feel and to

---

250 See Leo Tolstoy, *The Death of Ivan Ilich and Other Stories,* Translated by Aylmer Maud and J. D. Duff, With an Afterword by David Magarshak (New York and Scarborough, Ontario, 1960), pp.95-156, here pp. 155-56.

communicate with others.[251] This hermetic state of being has been called "futlyarnost'", based on Chekhov's story "The Man in a Case" (Chelovek v futlyare, 1898), a state that Karl Kramer described as "the failure of feeling."[252]

"The Man in a Case", Belikov, – yet another fictional representation of Russian despotism, – was a parody of a man who was unable to break out of his shell and become a living part of his society. The contrast between Belikov who tyrannized the people of his town over some fifteen years and the fun-loving Varen'ka, set up the tension in the story. Where Varen'ka was full of movement, loved to dance, laugh and sing and ride a bicycle, Belikov prevented the townspeople from mailing letters, reading books, playing cards, making new acquaintances, helping the poor or even speaking in a loud voice. After being made the laughing stock of the town, – we are reminded of Pushkin making a laughing stock of Black Plague in *Ruslan and Lyudmilla* – Belikov died. And death seemed the only desirable state for him. In the narrator's words:

> Now, when he lay in his coffin, he had a gentle expression of face, pleasant, even joyous, as if he were glad that he had finally been put in a case out of which he would never ever get out. Yes, he had reached his ideal.[253]

And Chekhov was aware of this darker side of his imagination which, he knew, he shared with all the other major Russian writers of his time. To the journalist and publisher A. S. Suvorin in a letter of 1892, he pointed to a disease or sickness in himself – he did not mean his tuberculosis – and in the writers who were his contemporaries: "In our souls there is a gaping emptiness" (*Pis'ma*, V, 134) he wrote, and he went on to say:

> Yes, I am intelligent enough at least not to hide my sickness from myself and not to lie to myself about it and to cover up my emptiness within with others' rags, such as the ideas of the sixties etc. ... It is not I who is to blame for my disease and its cure is not up to me, for this disease, one has to suppose, has its own good aims that are concealed from us and which has been sent down upon us not without reason. (*Pis'ma*, V, 134)

---

251 See "The Sick Self in Chekhov's Prose," in my *On the Dark Side of Russian Literature, op. cit.,* pp.183-97.

252 Karl D. Kramer, *The Chameleon and the Dream. The Image of Reality in Čekhov's Stories* (The Hague-Paris, 1970), p. 70.

253 See A. P. Chekhov, *Polnoe sobranie sochineniy i pisem v tridtsati tomakh* (30 vols.; Moscow, 1974-83) *Sochineniya*, X, 52. Further references to this edition will be given in the text. The translations are mine.

2. A Mind Divided

The European Enlightenment

An art divided reflected a society divided. From the very beginnings of Russian civilization a millennium ago, Russia's remarkable medieval iconology, as for example expressed in the famous icon *The Virgin of Vladimir* painted in the first half of the 12th century A. D. and in later icons,[254] pitted its compassionate spirituality against a growing oppressive and despotic age, at first Mongol, then tsarist.

With the emergence of a modern Russia in the 18th century, this inner clash between the ideal and the real was intensified by the cultural impact of the European Enlightenment on Russian writers, poets and thinkers whose moral and intellectual allegiance to the humanist ideals of the Enlightenment[255] clashed with their national and political allegiance to despotic rule and an inhuman social reality at home. Antiokh Kantemir's social satires (1729-44) and Alexander Radischev's *A Journey from Petersburg to Moscow* (published anonymously in 1790) with its indictment of Russian autocracy and serfdom, give us a good idea of the spiritual and moral turbulence caused by the European Enlightenment among the Russian intelligentsia. The Enlightenment also stirred up Russian national consciousness and forced, at least the educated layers of Russian society, to define their Russian identity.[256]

European Romanticism

In the 19th century the cultural confrontation with Europe became intensified under the impact of European Romanticism which provided the Russian intelligentsia with additional ways and means for supporting their allegiance to either Europe or Russia.

Thus, for the Westernizer Vissarion Belinsky, one of Russia's foremost idealist literary critics (1834-48) following in the footsteps of Schiller's *Über naive und sentimentalische Dichtung* (On Naive and Sentimental Poetry, 1795-96),[257] the romanticization of the poet as a social reformer allowed

---

254 See M. V. Alpatov, *Drevnerusskaya Ikonopis'. Early Russian Icon Painting* (Moscow, 1974), Plate 1, but see also plates 63 and 82.

255 See, for instance, Peter Gay, *The Party of Humanity. Essays in the French Enlightenment* (New York, 1964) and Ernst Cassirer, *The Philosophy of the Enlightenment* (Princeton, N. J. 1951).

256 See Hans Rogger, *National Consciousness in Eighteenth Century Russia* (Cambridge, Mass., 1960)

257 See C. V. Ponomareff, "Configurations of Poetic Vision: Belinskij as an Idealist-Critic," *The Slavicand East European Journal,* Vol. XIV, No. 2 (Summer, 1970), pp. 145-59.

Belinsky under cover of literary criticism to promote humanist ideals in Russia. For a Slavophile like Ivan Kireevsky or Nikolay Karamzin, on the other hand, the romanticization of the past enabled them to idealize an imagined pre-Petrine world whose spirituality could be set against Western European rationalism and materialism.[258]

But there was also a darker side to romanticism in its innate nihilism and hostility to life. Heinrich Heine, looking back on German romanticism in 1836, singled out its inhumane core[259] and, more recently, Mario Praz drew attention to the sadistic undercurrents of European romanticism.[260] Nikolay Mikhaylovsky's essay in 1882 on Dostoevsky's cruel talent was as applicable to Gogol as it was to other major nineteenth-century Russian writers.[261]

The Russians were very receptive to the darker, nihilist vibrations of European romanticism, and it may very well be, as the religious philosopher Nikolay Berdyaev has suggested, that their receptiveness to it might have been preconditioned by their own experience of a chronic political oppression which in time had "disfigured the soul of the [Russian] intelligentsia."[262] Perhaps Crane Brinton's idea of an "inverted idealism"[263] (in reference to Machiavelli), an idealism turned cynical because of disillusionment, is also relevant to the Russian historical experience.

European romanticism also brought with it, for Russians as well as Europeans generally, the devastating impact of romantic philosophy which undermined all faith in any meaningful continuity of traditional societal structures. Karl Marx's well-meaning social destructiveness was one of the first blows in the 19th century against the cohesiveness of European society. His utopian fantasy of a classless society was no substitute for the huge blow that he struck at the social structure of Europe. Darwin's sombre universe based on unpredictable chance alone left no possibility for any kind of meaningful continuity in human existence either. And Nietzsche's sheer joy

---

258 See Ivan Vasil'evich Kireevsky, "On the Nature of European Culture and its Relation to the Cultureof Russia," and Nikolay Mikhaylovich Karamzin, "Love of Country and National Pride," in MarcRaeff, ed., *Russian Intellectual History. An Anthology,op. cit.,* pp. 174-207, 106-12 respectively.

259 Heinrich Heine, "Die romantische Schule," in *Werke und Briefe,* Vol. 5 (Berlin, 1961), pp. 121, 123.

260 Mario Praz, *The Romantic Agony* (2nd ed.; London and New York, 1970). See also Isaiah Berlin, *TheRoots of Romanticism,* Edited by Henry Hardy (Princeton, N. J., 1999), pp. 56, 81-82, 87, 112, 116-17.

261 See my *On the Dark Side of Russian Literature, op. cit.*

262 Nikolay Berdyaev, "Filosofskaya istina i intelligentskaya pravda," in *Vekhi. Sbornik statey o russkoy intelligentsii* (Rpt. of the 2nd Moscow 1909 ed.; Frankfurt am Main, 1967), p. 22.

263 Crane Brinton, *The Shaping of the Modern Mind* (New York, 1953), p. 103.

in his intellectual and moral destructiveness delivered the final blow to any meaningful spiritual perspective.

This spiritual crisis showed itself in the desperate longing for faith that haunted Russians and Europeans alike in the 19th century. Leo Tolstoy himself confessed in 1883 to his own nihilism as a state of the soul that was *"void of all faith"*[264] (Tolstoy's italics). Such a sweeping and negative spiritual self-appraisal is surprising in a man who, be it in his own unconformable way, was socially active in promoting humane goals. In a sense this reminds one of the "gaping emptiness" that Chekhov found in himself and his contemporaries. Both Russian and European writers and poets suffered from what Dmitry Merezhkovsky, writing about Russian literature in 1892, called a "mystical longing" in the 19th century, an "unquenchable thirst for God," the "need to believe" countered by the realization that it was no longer possible to believe.[265]

At such a time of spiritual crisis, the romanticization of the national self to the point of experiencing delusions of grandeur had, no doubt, a compensatory function for the Russian intelligentsia. In this romantic process the intelligentsia practiced, perhaps unconsciously or half-consciously, what psychoanalytical experience has described as *projection*:

> To get rid of an objectionable object or impulse by removing it from the body in the way feces are eliminated is a frequent fantasy. In paranoia, the disease in which projection reaches greatest height, this fantasy achieves its climax in persecutory delusions *in which the persecutor outside the patient represents the sensations he feels in his bowels.* In general, the organism prefers to feel dangers as threats from without rather than from within because certain mechanisms of protection against overly intense stimuli can be set in motion against external stimuli only. ... Paranoid patients, whose function of reality testing is severely distorted, produce the most extreme projective misinterpretation of reality. *Neurotic patients do the same thing to a lesser degree by misunderstanding the actual reality in the sense of their unconscious needs.*[266] (My italics)

I had found this a very useful quotation for one of my essays on Nietzsche,[267] but it has just as much relevance to the Russian historical and cultural experience. In fact, another helpful analogy in this context is Isaiah Berlin's

---

264 See Henry Gifford, ed., *Leo Tolstoy. A Critical Anthology* (Harmondsworth, 1971), p. 57. For the original see L. N. Tolstoy, "V chem moya vera," in *Polnoe sobranie sochineniy* (Moscow, 1957), XXIII, 304.

265 See D. S. Merezhkovsky, "O prichinakh upadka i o novykh techeniyakh sovremennoy russkoy literatury," in *Izbrannye stat'i. Simvolizm, Gogol, Lermontov, op. cit.,* pp. 245, 296, 244-45 respectively. See also H. G. Schenk, *The Mind of the European Romantics. An Essay in Cultural History,* With a Preface by Isaiah Berlin (Oxford *et al.,* 1979), pp. 47-77.

266 See Otto Fenichel, *The Psychoanalytical Theory of Neurosis* (New York, 1945), p. 147.

267 See Ponomareff, "Nietzsche: Self as History in the *Genealogy of Morals,*" in his *The Spiritual Geography of Modern Writing, op. cit.,* pp. 33-49.

suggestion with respect to the Germans that the devastating impact of the Thirty Years War in the 17th century triggered a "huge national inferiority complex," and that this "wounded national sensibility" and "dreadful national humiliation" was "the root of the [German] romantic movement."[268]

All this implies that traumatized and humiliated nations will seek out ways to romanticize and idealize their historical experience in order to counter and overcome their inner emotional disturbance. And so, in the 19th century, the Russians projected their ailing self onto the West, making the latter sick and feeble, doomed by its materialistic values, as opposed to a Russia brimming with spiritual health and vigour, its uniqueness full of future promise.[269] Gogol expressed this national self-idealization when he finished part one of his *Dead Souls* with an evocation of a horse-drawn troika that symbolized Russia's unique destiny among the family of nations:

> Is it not like that that you, too, Russia are speeding along like a spirited *troika* that nothing can overtake? The road is like a cloud of smoke under you, the bridges thunder, and everything falls back and is left far behind. The spectator stops dead, struck dumb by the divine miracle: is it not a flash of lightning thrown down by heaven? What is the meaning of this terrifying motion? And what mysterious force is hidden in these horses the like of which the world has never seen? Oh horses, horses – what horses! Are whirlwinds hidden in your manes? ... the *troika* rushes on full of divine inspiration. Russia, where are you flying to? ... the air is torn asunder, it thunders and is transformed into wind; everything on earth is flying past, and looking askance, other nations and states draw aside and make way for her.[270]

European Romanticism may also have quite naturally appealed to the Russians with its concept of art as therapy, already contained, for example, in Belinsky's aesthetics. One might have thought that this aspect of romantic thinking would have held a special attraction for an intelligentsia whose art and mind, marked as they were by inner division and discord, were in dire need of healing. It is of course possible that the expression of such inner conflict was already part of a healing process at work. In actual fact, however, the themes of nineteenth-century Russian literature were much more focussed on the expression of this inner ailment than on the cure. At best, the metaphorical language of this literature spoke only of how to *protect* the chronic disorder in the Russian spirit from the onslaughts of a hostile outside world.

---

268 Isaiah Berlin, *The Roots of Romanticism, op. cit.,* pp. 35, 38 respectively.

269 See, for instance, James H. Billington, *The Icon and the Axe. An Interpretive History of Russian Culture* (New York, 1967), pp. 314-58.

270 See Nikolay Gogol, *Dead Souls,* Translated with an introduction by David Magarshak (Harmondsworth, 1975), p. 259. See also *The Mind of Modern Russia. Historical and Political Thought of Russia's Great Age,* edited by Hans Kohn (New York, 1962).

Thus, in Gogol's story, the overcoat as protection against the bitter winter cold was, metaphorically speaking, an expression of the Russian social and cultural self pitted against a hostile outside world. Turgenev's Bazarov and Dostoevsky's Underground man, each in their own way, used their *intellect* as a defense against the outside world. The most extreme case of self-protection could be seen in Tolstoy's and Chekhov's stories where the ultimate refuge of the self lay in death. Only Pushkin – and Chekhov in a more implicit manner – countered the protective mechanism of the Russian soul with an *explicit* call to conscience.

3. The Aftermath

The writer Vasily Grossman, in his memorable critique of Russian civilization, blamed – like Berdyaev before him – both Russian despotism *and* the Russian intelligentsia for Russia's spiritual losses over time: "The peculiarities of the Russian soul," he wrote, "are born not of freedom, for the Russian soul is a thousand-year-old slave."[271] Berdyaev was even more explicit:

> Our ailing soul and chronic autocracy have disfigured the soul of the intelligentsia, have enslaved it not only outwardly but also inwardly. ... But [the] intelligentsia is also itself to blame: the atheistic character of its consciousness is the fault of its will, the intelligentsia has itself chosen the path of the worship of man and has thereby disfigured its soul, and killed its instinct for truth. ... We shall liberate ourselves from external oppression only when we shall have liberated ourselves from inner slavery.[272]

But it was perhaps too hasty to attribute guilt to the Russian intelligentsia when, as we have seen, it was more a question of historical, social and cultural forces at work on the Russian consciousness. Nineteenth-century Russian literature pointed repeatedly to the tragic break in the Russian soul, a break that was created by historical circumstance in medieval time and then fostered by the incompatibility between domestic tyranny and the humanist ideals of the Enlightenment on the one hand, and the divisive and often aggravating influences of European romanticism on the other.

Given the historical and social conditions in Russia, it is to its credit that the Russian intelligentsia even tried to realize humane goals. Already in medieval times, at the beginning of Russian civilization, the Russian soul had pitted its compassionate spirituality and humanity against Mongol and tsarist oppression. In the 18th century, under the influence of the European

---

271 Vas. Grossman, *Vse techet ...* [Everything is in Flux ..., published posthumously in the West in 1970] (Frankfurt am Main, 1974), p. 175, my tr.

272 See Berdyaev, in *Vekhi, op. cit.,* p. 22, my tr.

Enlightenment, it transformed this religious impulse into a moral and secular force in order at the least to mitigate the despotic power of Russian tsars and empresses. Isaiah Berlin has pointed to the religious character of the Russian intelligentsia by calling it a "secular priesthood,"[273] and Berdyaev, too, thought of it as "a monastic order or sect, with its own very intolerant ethics," expressing a "Russian religiousness turned inside out."[274] In the 19th and 20th centuries the Russian intelligentsia continued its spiritual and moral struggle against Russian autocracy and later, after the Revolution of 1917, against the communist regime.

There is, however, an almost paradoxical side to this account of the intelligentsia's struggle against Russian tyranny. Berdyaev was one of the first to point to this incongruity in the make-up of the Russian intelligentsia. He did so by suggesting that it was the nineteenth-century Russian intelligentsia, notwithstanding its humanist intentions, who prepared the ground – or, perhaps, *we* would say, *could not help but prepare* the ground – for the Soviet Russian totalitarianism of the 20th century. Berdyaev's view of Leo Tolstoy was an instructive case in point:

> Positively, Tolstoy was opposed to communism; he did not accept violence; he was the enemy of all government and rejected the technique and rational organization of life; he believed in the divine basis of nature and life; he preached love not hate. But negatively he was a forerunner of communism; he rejected the past, the traditions of history, the old culture, Church and State; he rejected every economic and social inequality; he fulminated against the privileged ruling classes; he had no love for the cultured *élite*. In Russian *narodnichestvo* [populism] of the 'seventies no small part was played by "the conscience-stricken noble."[275]

And, casting a wider net, he wrote in 1937:

> Totalitarianism, the demand for wholeness of faith as the basis of the kingdom, fits in with the deep religious and social instincts of the people. The Soviet communist realm has in its spiritual structure a great likeness to the Muscovite Orthodox Tsardom. The same feeling of suffocation is in it.[276]

---

273 Isaiah Berlin, "The Birth of the Russian Intelligentsia," in his *Russian Thinkers,* Edited by Henry Hardyand Aileen Kelly, With an Introduction by Aileen Kelly (Harmondsworth, 1978), pp. 114-35, here p. 117. See also Marc Raeff, *Origins of the Russian Intelligentsia. The Eighteenth-Century Nobility* (New York, 1966).

274 Nicolas Berdyaev, *The Origin of Russian Communism,* Translated from the Russian by R. M. French (Ann Arbor and Toronto, 1962), pp. 19, 35 respectively.

275 *Ibid.,* p. 86.

276 *Ibid.,* p. 143. See also Herbert J. Muller, "'Holy Russia,' Byzantine and Marxist," in his *The Uses of the Past. Profiles of Former Societies* (New York, 1957), pp. 288-322, esp. pp. 298-99.

It is therefore not surprising if there was a real continuity in the spiritual temper of pre- and post-revolutionary Russia. Thus, during the Soviet period (1917-91), there was a return to the nineteenth-century populism in the communist Party's idealization of the proletariat, coupled with a renewal of the myth of Russia's glorious destiny in the utopian vision of the social and cultural potential of the Revolution of 1917 to produce a new world of freedom and equality for all.

But this vision of a – now secularized and officially atheist – paradise on earth was doomed from the start. For one, the Revolution of 1917 ultimately isolated Russia from Europe, as she had already once been isolated before the reign of Peter the Great. And though the Russian communist Party made the two European social philosophers Marx and Engels into its ideological founding fathers, there was nothing of the Marxian humanist spirit in the Marxist totalitarian doctrine of Lenin and Stalin and their followers. Needless to say, the Soviet idealization of the proletariat only sharpened social divisions to the point where, in the end, only Russian-type extermination camps could resolve the issue.

At the present time, thirteen years after the fall of the Soviet Russian communist state, it is not yet clear which way Russia will turn next, nor whether the political changes after 1991 will help turn Russian society into a more humane place to live.

Twentieth-Century Soviet Russian Underground Fiction.
A Nation's Conscience

Introduction

As mentioned in the foregoing essay, in the Soviet period which stretched from the Revolution of 1917 to the fall of Soviet communism in 1991, it was Russian underground fiction which carried on the nineteenth-century struggle against Russian despotism now turning into a full-blown Soviet totalitarianism.

The Russian revolution of 1917, like most revolutions in their initial stages, had been full of humane promise: a new Soviet man would supersede the old Adam; corruption, greed and exploitation would cease, and men and women would be free to follow their own creative ends in a world where freedom and social equality would become the mark of a classless, atheist, society in the not too distant future, creating its own paradise on earth.

This idealization of revolutionary Soviet reality was to bear bitter fruit in real Soviet Russian life, bringing with it a holocaust of death and destruction to tens of millions of Soviet people caught in Stalin's concentration camps. Alexander Solzhenitsyn (1918-) who experienced the Stalinist terror in the camps firsthand, who in his literary work, of which *One Day in the Life of Ivan Denisovich* (1962), *Cancer Ward* (1968) and his three-volume *The Gulag Archipelago* (1973-75) were the most notable, became one of the most courageous voices in the dissident moral protest of the 1960s, had this to say in his Nobel Lecture of 1972 on the tragic consequences of the Soviet totalitarian state:

> But woe to the nation whose literature is cut off by the interposition of force. That is not simply a violation of "freedom of the press"; it is stopping up the nation's heart, carving out the nation's memory. The nation loses its memory; it loses its spiritual unity – and, despite their supposedly common language, fellow countrymen suddenly cease understanding each other. Speechless generations are born and die, having recounted nothing of themselves either to their own times or to their descendants. That such masters as Akhmatova and Zamyatin were buried behind four walls for their whole lives and condemned even to the grave to create in silence, without hearing one reverberation of what they wrote, is not only their own personal misfortune but a tragedy for the whole nation –[277]

---

277 Alexander Solzhenitsyn, *Nobel Lecture,* Translated from the Russian by F. D. Reeve (New York, 1972), pp. 19-20.

Like Solzhenitsyn, the writers we will consider in this essay, risked their lives under Stalin and later went on to create major works of twentieth-century Russian underground fiction that were not condoned by the Soviet regime. In so doing, they did in fact as best they could bring back and give voice to a nation's cultural memory, repair the break in historical and spiritual continuity triggered by the Revolution of 1917, and pit the voice of conscience and humanity against the Stalinist holocaust.

4. Evgeny Zamyatin (1884-1937)

Zamyatin's family belonged to the intelligentsia. His father was an Orthodox priest and his mother a pianist. In his student years he joined the Bolshevik Party and was imprisoned and exiled in 1905. He returned, however, to graduate from the St. Petersburg Polytechnic Institute in 1908 as a naval engineer and became a member of its faculty.

From then on he divided his life between writing and shipbuilding. Once more imprisoned and exiled in 1911, he was amnestied in 1913. In 1916 he was sent to England to supervise the construction of icebreakers for Russia. He welcomed the Bolshevik revolution of 1917 and was soon involved in the cultural life of the new Russia. But already in a very short time, like so many other Russian writers and poets, he became disillusioned with the Bolshevik regime.

The 1920s, when compared to the terror that began after Stalin's takeover of power in 1928, seemed like a liberal period which still allowed a certain degree of literary competition between state-supported proletarian writers and writers who were or who, like Zamyatin, became fellow travellers and were increasingly critical of the Party's conservatism and political interference in art and literature. This interference grew in proportion as the Soviet state established its hold on the country.[278]

By the end of the 1920s, the creative freedom of politically non-aligned writers was severely curbed by the communist Party. Zamyatin was no exception, especially after the rejection of his novel *We* for publication in Russia and its appearance abroad in English translation in 1924. By the end of the 1920s he was no longer allowed to publish anything at all, and was forced into silence.

In 1931 he wrote a very courageous and outspoken letter to Stalin, asking for permission to go abroad. With Maxim Gorky's help, permission was granted, a very rare event in those days. Zamyatin and his wife left the Soviet

---

278 See, for example, Robert A. Maguire, *Red Virgin Soil. Soviet Literature in the 1920's* (Princeton, 1968).

Union in 1932. A year later he settled in Paris where he lived until his death in 1937.

Two Essays[279]

As early as 1921, in his essay "I am Afraid", Zamyatin cast doubt on the Marxist revolutionary myth and on the creative potential of the Revolution to promote a cultural environment in which art and literature would flourish. For this he blamed the conservatism of the Bolshevik Party that pretended to be revolutionary. In his words –

> ... true literature can exist only where it is created, not by diligent and trustworthy officials, but by madmen, hermits, heretics, dreamers, rebels and skeptics. (Gins, 57)

Describing the Soviet communist state as a "new brand of Catholicism," he foresaw the coming political regimentation of art:

> I am afraid [he wrote] that we shall have no genuine literature until we cure ourselves of this new brand of Catholicism, which is as fearful as the old of every heretical word. And if this sickness is incurable, then I am afraid that the only future possible to Russian literature is its past. (Gins, 58)

Zamyatin took issue with the growing political Marxist control of art and literature in another essay of 1923 entitled "On Literature, Revolution, Entropy and Other Matters". His main concern here was that the political triumph of the Revolution of 1917 signalled the "entropy of human thought" (Gins, 108) and the end of creative freedom in literature and other fields of endeavour. Consequently, Zamyatin spoke up in defense of a literature that was allowed to express the flux of modern life, with all its energy and complexity, in a style that would do justice to modern reality, a style more akin to the unpredictable and fantastic subatomic world of the scientists. His message was that in the absence of such freedom to write, forcing art and literature into a rigid ideological groove could only kill the creative instinct.

---

279 See *A Soviet Heretic: Essays by Yevgeny Zamyatin,* Edited and Translated by Mirra Ginsburg (Chicago and London, 1970). Further references to this edition will be given in the text as Gins. For the original source, see Evgeny Zamyatin, *Litsa,* introduced by Mikhail Koryakov, Afterword by Vladimir Bondarenko (New York, 1967).

We[280]

Zamyatin's anti-utopian novel *We,* with its prophetic critique of the Soviet state, was ahead of its time: finished in 1921, it anticipated the coming of the Stalinist and Nazi totalitarian regimes by a decade. In the literary context, we know that it influenced George Orwell's *Nineteen Eighty-Four* (1949),[281] nor could Aldous Huxley in his *Brave New World* (1932) or, for that matter, even Arthur Koestler in his *Darkness at Noon* (1940), not have been aware of *We*'s existence.

Though Zamyatin welcomed the Revolution of 1917, it is interesting to note that as early as 1918, in his longer story *Islanders,* and a few years later, in his play *The Fires of St. Dominic* (1922), there were already unmistakable echoes of *We.* But *We* as a critique of a Soviet civilization to come was also influenced by Dostoevsky's work, as David Richards has pointed out.[282] This is especially true if one thinks of Dostoevsky's *The Legend of the Grand Inquisitor* (a chapter out of his novel *The Brothers Karamazov,* 1879-80) which, like his novel *The Devils* (1872), had warned against the coming of twentieth-century totalitarianism.

In Zamyatin's glassed-in totalitarian United State of the future, set in the 26th century A.D., much had been achieved in the subjugation of the human spirit. The citizens of the State had lost their identity and were known only as numbers. Their days and nights, their sexual lives were regulated. An almost total social and political unanimity had been enforced in which the citizens had given up their individual freedom for the regulated happiness of all. A spaceship was being built to carry the State's philosophy to other planets. The past had almost been completely eradicated, except for the old museum, the "Ancient House", whose remnants of a primitive age were meant to highlight the achievements of the State. The whole population was under surveillance, and a ruthless secret police tortured those numbers who showed any signs of protest. Letters were opened and the guardians of happiness eavesdropped on its subjects, even along city streets. Those found guilty of any opposition to the State were executed in public under the Well-Doer's bell on the Day of Unanimity.

One area, however, that the State could not yet control fully, was the *emotional* life of its citizens. Love especially was seen as a "most dangerous

---

280 See Evgeny Zamyatin, *My,* Introduction by Evgeny Zhiglevich, Afterword by Vladimir Bondarenko (New York, 1967). Further references to this edition will be given in the text as Z. The translations are mine.

281 See Gleb Struve, *Russian Literature under Lenin and Stalin 1917-1953* (Norman, Oklahoma, 1971), p. 50. Further references to this edition will be given in the text as Struve.

282 See D. J. Richards, *Zamyatin. A Soviet Heretic* (New York, 1962).

illness" (Z, 65), and with it the "incurable" soul (Z, 78), and individual consciousness (Z, 111). All theses aspects of human life were dangerous to the State because they were part of a subliminal and unpredictable process (Z, 118).

Hence, the engineer D-503's love for I-330 was dangerous, all the more since she was involved in a plot to gain control of the spaceship he was in the process of constructing for the State. In this sense, D-503's underground diary was also the account of a tragic love story. To counter the emotional life of its subjects, the State ultimately devised a plan for a final operation that would remove the imagination (Z, 153). In the end, D-503 chose to undergo the operation, betrayed I-330 (Z, 196) and watched unperturbed as she was being tortured right in front of his eyes.

But even after a millennium of human tyranny, cracks began to appear in the United State, which proved that there was no such thing as a final revolution. For one, there were still numbers inside the Wall sufficiently aware of their humanity to try and get away from being caught for the operation (Z, 162). O-90, carrying D-503's child, managed to escape to the outside (Z, 172). There had, for that matter, always been sexual relations between women inside the Wall and the Mephis outside (Z, 140) who lived surrounded by nature and who had preserved their emotional life (Z, 141). There were now thousands of rebels and conspirators on both sides of the Wall (Z, 124, 148), and parts of the Wall had actually been blown up and destroyed (Z, 132, 134), so that birds had begun to appear inside the Wall (Z, 187, 190). An armed uprising had begun (Z, 177, 188) in which a "significant number" of citizens had turned against the State (Z, 200). The United State was falling apart and perishing (Z, 197). Human nature would not be subdued.

Ultimately, Zamyatin's purpose in writing *We* was to warn his contemporaries of what he perceived as a growing tyranny under the Soviet communist state. And D-503, writer and engineer, Zamyatin's double in the distant future, did in fact address Zamyatin's contemporaries:

> I believe – you'll understand, how difficult it is for me to write, no author in all the history of mankind has ever found it so difficult to write. Some writers wrote for their contemporaries, others for their descendants, but no one has ever written for their savage and distant ancestors, kindred creatures. (Z, 23-24)

And later in the novel he came back to the same thought:

> I am looking through my Notes and see that I've again forgotten that I'm writing not for myself, but for you, unknown ones, whom I love and pity – for you who are dragging yourselves along in the mists of antiquity. (Z, 117)

It is all to easy for us, who have lived through the 20th century, to recognize as fact what Zamyatin only imagined. His novel will remain a remarkable prophecy of Soviet Russian totalitarianism.

2. Mikhail Bulgakov (1891-1940)

Bulgakov's grandfather was a Gogol scholar, his father a professor of religion at the Kiev Theological Academy. Mikhail was the eldest of seven children, four sisters and two brothers. He had a very happy childhood, due in no small measure to his mother, Varvara Pokrovskaya, an extraordinary woman with a dedicated sense for family life.

Though Bulgakov graduated with distinction as a medical doctor in 1916, he pretty well abandoned his medical practice in 1920 and devoted himself to writing stories, novels and plays. By the end of 1920, his two brothers Nikolay and Ivan left Russia for good and, by way of the Balkans, eventually settled in Paris.

Bulgakov's writing career in the twenties resembled Zamyatin's. His novel *The White Guard* (1924), a sympathetic portrayal of the Whites, was first published in a two-volume edition in Paris between 1927 and 1929. His novella *Heart of a Dog* (1925), a satire of the Soviet proletariat, was also published in the West, in Frankfurt and Paris (1968, 1969). And though most of his plays of the twenties – except *Flight* (1927), perhaps his best, never performed in his lifetime in the Soviet Union – saw performances on the Soviet stage, none of them were published at home and had to await publication abroad.

As early as 1921 and later, Bulgakov had tried and failed to get an exit visa to Paris to join members of his family. By the end of the twenties, in the summer of 1929, when all his work was banned, he wrote a letter to Stalin, again asking for permission to leave the Soviet Union. His request was refused. But in April of 1930, in a telephone conversation, when Stalin gave him the choice to leave for abroad, Bulgakov declined.[283] He would remain in Moscow to the end of his days.

Stalin did, however, help him get established as a playwright with the Moscow Art Theatre, which he left in 1936 to become a librettist for the Bolshoi Opera Theatre. During his collaboration with the Moscow Art Theatre, he was able to see his dramatizations of Gogol, Molière and Pushkin

---

283 See A. Colin Wright, *Mikhail Bulgakov: Life and Interpretations* (Toronto-Buffalo-London, 1978), p. 146. Further references to this edition will be given in the text as W. See also J. A. E. Curtis, *Manuscripts Don't Burn. Mikhail Bulgakov. A Life in Letters and Diaries* (Woodstock, New York, 1992).

performed on stage. For the Bolshoi Opera he wrote the libretto for Don Quixote.

Though, as in Pasternak's case, Stalin kept a benign eye on Bulgakov (W, 252), it was clear that his theatrical productions were meant to keep him from writing his stories and novels. But time was running out for Bulgakov. Like his father before him, he too fell victim to nephrosclerosis. Knowing exactly how long he had left to live, he devoted all his energies to finishing his greatest work, *The Master and Margarita,* by the spring of 1939. It was a novel that he had thought about and worked on for some twelve years. He was now totally blind and died in March of 1940.

The Master and Margarita

Bulgakov's novel *The Master and Margarita* had to wait a quarter of a century after its author's death before it was published abroad in its complete version in 1967, and in the Soviet Union in 1989, just before the fall of the Soviet empire.

Viewed structurally, it was a complex novel, as Ellendea Proffer pointed out in 1973.[284] It was, of course, also a very moving love story. But the novel's main thrust was the moral confrontation between good and evil, between spiritual and temporal power. The confrontation was played out in two distant historical times: Jesus in Jerusalem, two thousand years ago, against Pilate, the Roman procurator of Judea and the high priest Caiaphas; and the devil Woland in Bulgakov's Moscow of the thirties against Stalin's totalitarian regime.

It should be mentioned at the outset that Woland, with all the devilry at his command, functioned as a *benign and humane* force in Moscow, not as an antagonist but as an emissary of Jesus. In this sense he was very much like Mephistopheles in Goethe's *Faust.* For, when asked by Faust who he was, he replied:

Ein Teil von jener Kraft,
Die stets das Böse will und stets das Gute schafft.[285]
(I am a part of that force,/ That always wants to do evil and yet always does good.)

284 Ellendea Proffer, "The Master and Margarita," in *Major Soviet Writers. Essays in Criticism, op. cit.*pp. 388-411.
285 Johann Wolfgang von Goethe, *Faust. Der Tragödie erster und zweiter Teil – Urfaust,* edited and commentary by Hans Jürgen Meinerts (Hamburg, n. d.), p. 55.

In the biblical sense, the novel expressed Jesus's exhortation to his disciples on the insubstantiality of worldly gain and power as over against spiritual riches: "For what is a man profited, if he shall gain the whole world, and lose his own soul? or what shall a man give in exchange for his soul?" (Matthew, 16:26).

Bulgakov used the metaphor of a gathering storm and the darkness it brought with it to Jerusalem and Moscow to suggest the transitoriness of worldly empires. Thus, at the beginning of chapter 25 we read:

> The mists that came from the Mediterranean Sea blotted out the city that Pilate so detested. The suspension bridges connecting the temple with the grim fortress of Antonia vanished, the murk descended from the sky and drowned the winged gods above the hippodrome, the crenelated Hasmonaean palace, the bazaars, the caravanserais, the alleyways, the pools. ... Jerusalem, the great city, vanished as though it had never been.[286]

And later, the end of chapter 29, now in Moscow, echoed the above:

> The thunderstorm that Woland had predicted was already gathering on the horizon. A black cloud was rising in the west; first half and then all of the sun was blotted out. The wind on the terrace freshened. Soon it was quite dark. The cloud from the west enveloped the vast city. Bridges and buildings were all swallowed up. Everything vanished as though it had never been. (MG, 360)

The spiritual would always triumph. Hence the master's novel could not be destroyed, even when it had been burned by its author. Woland proved as much when he showed the master his manuscript in its entirety, adding that "Manuscripts don't burn." (MG, 286).

As if to confirm the truth of Woland's statement, the spiritual did indeed triumph when Bulgakov's *The Master and Margarita* surfaced out of the depths of the Stalinist era into the light of day a quarter of a century later.

3. The Gathering Spiritual Storm

In the quarter century or so that it took Bulgakov's novel to surface in the West, novels and poems began to be written both above and below ground, which ranged from moral protest to outright political and cultural dissidence. Though this creative momentum increased, especially after Stalin's death in the spring of 1953 and the de-Stalinization process begun in 1956, dissident

---

286 I have used Mikhail Bulgakov, *The Master and Margarita,* Translated from the Russian by Michael Glenny (New York and Evanston, 1967), p. 297. Further references to this edition will be given in the text as MG.

literature in the 1960s still brought with it forced-labour camp sentences and enforced stays in psychiatric wards for its authors.

But even before the rise of the dissident movement in the 1960s, there had been literary critiques of Soviet totalitarianism. Foremost among them was Boris Pasternak's (1890-1960) novel *Doctor Zhivago* – one of the most spiritual novels to come out of the Soviet Union – first published in Russian in Milan, Italy in 1957, and then in English translation in London, in 1958, which attacked the credibility of the Bolshevik revolution of 1917 and its Stalinist aftermath. The novel received the Nobel Prize in 1958, but Pasternak, threatened with forced emigration to the West, rejected the Prize and died two years later, literally hounded to death by the Soviet communist press.

There were, of course, noteworthy ripples of protest above ground.There was Ilya Ehrenburg's (1891-1967) *The Thaw* (1954) signalling the end of the Stalinist Terror; Then came Vladimir Dudintsev's (1918-98) *Not by Bread Alone* (1956); and then two of Evgeny Evtushenko's (1933-) longer poems, "Baby Yar" (1961) and "The Heirs of Stalin" (1962). Both were an attack on the Soviet regime, with their implicit indictment of Soviet atrocities and concentration camps. The latter anti-Stalin poem especially, was a more direct expression of the fear that the spirit of Stalinism would – as it did – continue to persist in Russia.

A greater moral impact, however, was made by the flood of dissident writing in the *Samizdat* underground press of the 1960s, much of it eventually published in the West. I have already referred to Solzhenitsyn's (1918-) trailblazing literary works exposing the inhumanity of Soviet concentration camps. In this connection, one should also mention Varlam Shalamov's (1907-82) *Kolyma Tales* begun after 1953 which described his grim and appalling experiences in the forced-labour camps of north-eastern Siberia. They were first published in full in London in 1978, and in the Soviet Union in 1989.[287]

There were other notable dissident works of the 1960s as well. Andrey Sinyavsky's (1925-97) essay *On Socialist Realism,* published abroad in 1960, was a trenchant critique of Soviet culture, and his *Fantastic Stories* (1963), first published in France in 1961, were an equally potent satire of Soviet life. Sinyavsky, a literary critic in his own right, who had written under the pseudonym of Abram Tertz, was tracked down and imprisoned in 1965, released in 1971, and allowed to emigrate to France in 1973 where he became a professor of Russian at the Sorbonne. Then came Georgy Vladimov's (1931-) *Faithful Ruslan* , the story of a Soviet concentration camp guard dog,

---

287 See Varlam Shalamov, *Kolyma Tales,* Translated from the Russian by John Glad (Harmondsworth, 1994), especially John Glad's Foreword, pp. ix-xix.

published in the West in 1964. Anatoly Kuznetsov (1929-) defected to the West in 1969 and published the uncensored version of his *Baby Yar* in 1971. Among many others there was also the "socialist realist" Chingiz Aitmatov's (1928-) *The White Steamship* (1970), with its poignant critique of the inhumanity of the Soviet State, a haunting novel that was actually published in the Soviet Union.

Last, but not least, was the powerful impact on the spiritually starved Soviet Russian audience of its bards and minstrels whose anti-Soviet songs were officially proscribed: Bulat Okudzhava (1924-97), Vladimir Vysotsky (1938-80), and Alexander Galich (1919-77) who was allowed to emigrate to Paris in 1974.[288]

Enough has been said to suggest the growing moral and spiritual impact of Russian, mostly underground, writing and the high personal price these writers paid for their profound sense of humane outrage.

4. Lidiya Chukovskaya (1907-96)

Lidiya Chukovskaya was born in St. Petersburg but spent part of her childhood (1912-17) in Kuokkala, Finland where her parents' home was often visited by writers and poets, among them Vladimir Mayakovsky, Nikolay Gumilev and Anna Akhmatova. Later, in St. Petersburg , other well-known writers and poets like Alexander Blok, Osip Mandelshtam, Maxim Gorky, Vladislav Khodasevich, Evgeny Zamyatin and others came to visit. This tells us something about her remarkable father, Korney Chukovsky (1882-1969) who, though of lower class origin and self-taught, was able to attract some of the most outstanding literary figures of the time. He made a name for himself as an editor, a literary critic, a translator of American and English fiction and especially as the author of a book on the speech and psychology of children *From Two to Five* (1928) which was published both at home and abroad. In 1962 he received an Honorary D. Litt. degree from Oxford University.

---

288 Useful references are the *Handbook of Russian Literature,op. cit;* Leon Trotsky, *Literature and Revolution,* Translated by Rose Strunsky (Ann Arbor, 1960); Max Eastman, *Artists in Uniform. A Study of Literature and Bureaucratism* (New York, 1972); Deming Brown, *Soviet Russian Literature since Stalin, op. cit.*); Gleb Struve, *Russian Literature under Lenin and Stalin, 1917-1953,op. cit.*; Yu. Mal'tsev, *Vol'naya russkaya literatura 1955-1975* (Frankfurt am Main, 1976); *Major Soviet Writers. Essays in Criticism,* Edited by Edward J. Brown, *op. cit.* But see also N. N. Shneidman, *Soviet Literature in the 1970s: Artistic Diversity and Ideological Conformity* (Toronto-Buffalo-London, 1979), and also his *Soviet Literature in the 1980s: Decade of Transition* (Buffalo-London, 1989), for the officially sanctioned Soviet Russian literature.

Chukovskaya was very close to her father whose love of literature she inherited and who watched over her and remained an important literary and moral influence for her throughout his long life. She too became a literary scholar and, in the 1930s, an editor of children's books. The incentive for writing fiction came after the arrest of her second husband – she married him in 1934 – Matvey Bronshtein (1906-38) in the summer of 1937 during Stalin's Great Purge (1936-38). He was executed early next year. Bronshtein was an exceptional man, one of those increasingly rare academicians in the Soviet period who was an internationally respected theoretical physicist but equally at home with English, French and Greek literatures. No doubt, in the paranoid atmosphere of Stalin's Russia, his international scientific connections, as for example with Niels Bohr, were enough to incriminate him. Chukovskaya received the details of his death only in 1957, after his rehabilitation.

It was this traumatic experience which propelled Chukovskaya into writing fiction about the Stalin Terror and its impact on the Soviet people. She wrote her first novel *The Deserted House* between 1939 and 1940. If this book with its indictment of the Stalin regime had been discovered, she would surely have ended up in a concentration camp or worse. Instead, friends kept the manuscript safe for her for many years until it began to circulate in the *Samizdat* press before being published abroad in Russian in New York in 1966. It was published in Leningrad only in 1988. Chukovskaya left it in its original form in order not to undercut her eyewitness account. Her second novel *Going Under,* written between 1949 – the year that marked Stalin's anti-Semitic drive intended to unleash a second Great Purge – and 1957, was published in New York in 1972. Its first publication in the Soviet Union only came in 1989, shortly before the collapse of the Soviet State. Both novels were translated into many languages. Chukovskaya also wrote two volumes on her conversations with her friend, the poet Anna Akhmatova, which were published in Paris in 1976 and 1980. The Soviet Russian edition came out in Leningrad in 1989.

But Chukovskaya also showed her moral courage and her commitment to literature in her open letters during the 1960s in defense of Russian writers, poets and scientists. For example, she wrote on behalf of the imprisoned poet Joseph Brodsky and later, in 1969, in defense of Solzhenitsyn, and of the nuclear physicist and human-rights advocate Andrey Sakharov in 1973, who had held her second husband in such high esteem. She also wrote an open letter to the Nobel laureate Mikhail Sholokhov in 1966 taking him to task for his denunciation of the writers Andrey Sinyavsky and Yuli Daniel. She had always enjoyed some protection while her father was still alive, but when she let Solzhenitsyn write part of his *Gulag Archipelago* in her father's dacha in

Peredelkino, she was expelled from the Soviet Writers Union in 1974 and began to be hounded and persecuted in her public as well as in her private life by the official organs of the Soviet State.From then on she could only publish in the underground press or abroad.

In the West she was made a member of the French Pen-Club in 1980 which awarded her its first Freedom Prize for her books on Akhmatova. She re-entered the literary public sphere only in the spring of 1987 at an official evening devoted to Pasternak. Between 1987 and 1992 all her works were published in Russia. In 1990 she received the First Sakharov Prize for her moral courage. Though she was going blind and suffered from tuberculosis and from a serious heart ailment, she worked with her daughter Elena (1931-) editing and publishing her father's journals.[289]

Throughout her life she remained an intrepid fighter against the machinations of the Soviet State, continued to defend individual and creative freedom and, above all, the truth. She was, and she remains, one of the most humane Russian writers of the 20th century.

Going Under

In Chukovskaya's *Going Under* (Spusk pod vodu: The Descent Under-water),[290] the woman narrator, haunted by the disappearance of her husband in the Great Purge of the 1930s, comes to a health resort for Soviet writers in Finland in 1949 to find solace from the pain left by her husband's end. In a sense, it is an equivalent of what post-World War II West-German writers and critics used to call a "Vergangenheitsbewältigung", the overcoming of past trauma.

As in her first novel – which reminds one of Akhmatova's longer poem *Requiem* written berween 1935 and 1940 – *Going Under* also deals with the terror, fear and suffering spread by Stalin's rule. The narrator, who is in fact writing the novel, has come for a twenty-six-day stay at this rest home. The novel she works on is one of the two links she has to life and to healing herself. The other is her daughter Katyusha.

This typical Soviet health resort referred to as a *Dom tvorchestva,* a House for creative work, is anything but that, for it is actually a place for those writers who have sold out to the regime, who have lost their artistic

---

289 See Annette Julius, *Lidija Čukovskaja. Leben und Werk,* in the Series *Papers and Texts in Slavic Studies 60,* edited by Wolfgang Kasack (Munich, 1995), pp. 14- 45.

290 See Lidiya Chukovskaya, *Spusk pod vodu* (New York, 1972). Further references to this edition will be given in the text as Ch. The translations are mine.

integrity and are now rewarded for it by the Soviet State with social privileges and material advantages.

In this context the novel becomes a *moral* indictment of all those Soviet writers who have compromised their art. What makes *Going Under* psychologically more interesting, however, is its focus not on writers without conscience but on those who were basically still *decent* people but acted out of self-preservation and fear.

Such a writer is Bilibin whom the narrator meets here and befriends. Bilibin, a former concentration camp prisoner now released, is also writing a book about his experiences. But, as it turns out, his book is a total whitewash of the system, and the narrator confronts him, calls him a "coward" and a "false witness", and asks him why he had not found it in him just to "keep silent" instead? (Ch, 120, 121). Ultimately, however, she realizes that life is too complex to be reduced to one common denominator and that her judgement of Bilibin has been too severe. She is overcome by what she should have said to him instead:

> "Put your hat on, or you'll catch cold," I wanted to say, as I had that other time. "Stay a bit, don't hurry, let the pain subside," I wanted to say, as I had done so often during our walks. "Forgive me!" I wanted to say. "I had no right to judge you, I, whom dogs never pounced on, I, who had never seen a wooden identification tag on the foot of a corpse ... Forgive me! You don't want to go back to timber felling or to the mines for a second time! Your story is your powerless shield, your unreliable defense ... Forgive me! You've already had one heart attack – illness is expensive and you need an income. And what else can you do as an invalid to make money, except write, even if what you write is made up of cliché falsehoods ... Forgive me! I had no right to demand the truth from you; after all, I'm healthy, and even then, I've been silent. I was not beaten unmercifully nights during interrogations. And when you were being beaten, I kept silent. So what right do I have to judge you now? Forgive me my damned cruelty, forgive me!" (Ch, 125)

At the end of her stay, as she is leaving, there is a kind of reconciliation between them (Ch, 131).

Central for Chukovskaya and her novel was the existential problem of how to free oneself creatively from the Stalinist nightmare. In *Going Under* breath and breathing became metaphors for creativity (Ch, 64) which in effect was an allusion to the poet Alexander Blok who died in 1921 due, according to his own admission, to the lack of creative air with which to breathe. Consequently, her stay at this health resort was an attempt "to learn how to breathe again." (Ch, 78)

It was in this creative sense that the metaphorical descent underwater, as a place where one could write freely and unafraid, became such a spiritually crucial undertaking in the novel. It was, first of all, a refuge from Stalin's police state (Ch, 32), a haven from fear where one's soul was safe from outside intrusions (Ch, 35). It was also a space that could provide one with a "happy clarity of vision" (Ch, 39). It was a silent world (Ch, 55), – free from the barrage of propaganda – in which one could work and write for long stretches of time (Ch, 63), a place where one could attempt to understand and make sense of the inner lives of the citizens of a totalitarian State (Ch, 129). And – in yet another allusion, this time to Pasternak's survival during the Stalin era – it was an underwater realm which was akin to a safe-conduct (Ch, 81), safe from the bestial world above where Nazis burned mothers and their children to death (Ch, 77) or where Stalinists were responsible for the plight of a mother standing in line with a dead infant in her arms, afraid to lose her place in a queue waiting to find out any news about her imprisoned husband (Ch, 95). The underwater world was, finally, an environment where one could find back to one's inner self and initiate a possible spiritually healing process.

Chukovskaya's *Going Under* reminds me of Wolfgang Borchert's (1921-47) play *The Man Outside* (Draußen vor der Tür, 1947),[291] in the sense that there too a catastrophic time was reflected in images of water. But Chukovskaya's watery realm seems to have a greater potential for spiritual renewal than Borchert's. In any case, as J. E. Cirlot has pointed out, the symbolism of water as "an expression of the vital potential of the psyche, of the struggles of the psychic depths to find a way of formulating a clear message comprehensible to the consciousness,"[292] always brings with it the possibility of spiritual rebirth, be it out of the midst of historical and social upheaval.

5. Venedikt Erofeev (1938-90)

Erofeev was born in Zapolyar'e, the polar region of the Kola Peninsula, which he saw from his childhood on to his mid-teens turn into a place dotted with concentration camps. His father was a womanizer who left the family when Erofeev was born. His father was later arrested in 1946 for some anti-Stalin remarks and only released in 1954, by which time labour-camp prisoners were being amnestied. In the meantime, his mother had left the children and Erofeev ended up in a children's home. She would later return to her family in 1953.

---

291 See the essay "Wolfgang Borchert (1921-1947): Nightmares of Primordial Sea," in my *The Silenced Vision. An Essay in Modern European Fiction* (Frankfurt am Main/Bern/Las Vegas, 1979), pp. 13-25.

292 See J. E. Cirlot, *A Dictionary of Symbols, op. cit.* p. 346.

Erofeev remembered the children's home as a violent nightmare. With his mother's return, when he was in his 8th grade, he came back home again and finished his last two years of education in a regular school. He graduated with a gold medal and was accepted by the Philological Department of Moscow State University in 1955. He was, however, expelled in 1957 after only three semesters for not attending lectures and seminars and probably also for his anti-authoritarian attitude. From March 1957 he lived a loose life and became a jack-of-all-trades until he was able to enrol in 1960 in the Vladimir Pedagogical Institute which actually gave him a special stipend. But here too he was expelled in 1962, it seems both for his religious views but also for being involved in a student confrontation with the administration. During his time at the Institute his friendships also tended to be with dissident young writers and artists.

He married a student at the Institute, Valentina Semakova, and though they would soon separate, she bore him a son in 1966. By this time he was working for the telephone company laying telephone cables and repairing telephone lines, a job that he held until 1974. He was very close to his son who lived with his mother, and would often travel to Myshlino, near Petushki, to see him. It was Erofeev's second wife, Galina Erofeeva, who looked after his well-being in his last years and who preserved his manuscripts and notebooks, just as his sister Tamara had kept his letters from 1955-88.

In the mid-eighties, Erofeev was diagnosed with throat cancer and operated on. He was invited to come to Paris for further treatment, but the Soviet authorities would not let him out. He saw the birth of a grand-daughter in 1988. Three years after his death, Galina Erofeeva committed suicide.

In spite of his incomplete formal education, Erofeev was extremely well-read, especially in history and literature. His favorite poets were the symbolists and acmeists, and he was influenced by Gogol and Dostoevsky among others. He read both Latin and German and the bible was his life-long companion. He was a profoundly religious man and in 1987 he converted to Catholicism, rejecting Russian Orthodoxy as totalitarian in spirit. There is little doubt that his tragic life and his heavy drinking contributed to his death, but his friends maintained that he drank in order to be able to write.[293]

---

293 This biographical material is based on his "Kratkaya avtobiografiya" (1980) and on the interview with Leonid Prudovsky "Sumasshedshim mozhno byt' v lyuboe vremya," in *Venedikt Erofeev. Zapiski psikhopata,* edited by V. Murav'ev (Moscow, 2000), pp. 423-24 and pp. 425-43 respectively. See also Karen Ryan-Hayes' introduction to *Venedikt Erofeef's Moscow-Petushki. Critical Perspectives* edited by her (Bern *et al.,* 1997), pp. 2-5.

Moscow-Petushki[294]

Erofeev's novel *Moscow-Petushki* (or Moscow to the End of the Line) is a major work of 20th-century Russian literature. It was, obviously, an outburst of pent-up inspiration, written between the 17th of January and the beginning of March of 1970, but it was also, in the final analysis, an outburst of pain and trauma caused by the totalitarian experience of Soviet life. It made its rounds in the *Samizdat* press and was first published in Russian in Israel in 1973, and then in Paris in 1977. It appeared in French translation in 1973, in English translation in 1980 and 1981, and was translated into German, Polish and Italian. An incomplete version of the novel appeared in 1989 in Russia, shortly before its author's death. It was finally published in full in Russia only in 1995, a quarter of a century after its initial completion.

There is no doubt that Erofeev's novel is a complex piece of work capable of a variety of interpretations.[295] Ultimately, however, it is the spiritual journey of its central character Venichka (VE, 126) – who bears the author's first name – to Petushki, a paradise and spiritual destination (VE, 37, 38, 47, 131), irrespective of its geographical location at the end of the Moscow line, or the nightmarish, hallucinatory pilgrimage to it (VE, 144-46), or the dream landscape of the novel (VE, 126) seen through the drunken consciousness of Venichka. Though the latter never reaches paradise, his journey through the spiritual darkness of his Soviet Russian world is always bent on reaching the light (VE, 128-29). That is also why, in the final pages of the novel, there is an explicit analogy of Venichka's life to Christ's Golgotha (VE, 156-59).

As a spiritual journey, the novel is an indictment of the Revolution of 1917 which has given rise to the spiritual emptiness of Moscow, the centre of the Soviet Russian godless empire (VE, 156). The four thugs who kill Venichka in front of the Kremlin wall by driving an awl into his throat represent the inhuman Soviet regime (VE, 160), bent on eradicating anything spiritual. The angels who laugh at him and his undoing have nothing in common with the Sacred, for *God is silent* (VE, 21, 159, my italics), and are therefore clearly on the regime's side.

Venichka, in his failure to "revolutionize the heart and raise the spiritual level so as to be able to acquire the eternal moral categories" (VE, 122), rejects the Soviet world he lives in (VE, 150). At the same time, however, he attempts to be the conscience of his sorrowful nation (VE, 40, 68). He tries to understand himself and his contemporaries (VE, 95, 35, 153), he is full of

---

294 I have used Venedikt Erofeev, *Moskva-Petushki* (Paris, 1981). Further references to this second editionof his work will be given in the text as VE. The translations are mine.

295 See, for instance, *Venedikt Erofeev's Moscow-Petushki. Critical Perspectives,* edited by Ryan-Hayes, *op. cit.*

compassion for suffering humanity (VE, 92), and is overcome by sadness and grief (VE, 82). In the final analysis, his journey is an attempt to counter the spiritual and cultural despair of a totalitarian age (VE, 78-79).

In this context, the obsessive drinking is but a metaphor for the *spiritual yearning* of the author's double (VE, 11-12,20-21, 39, 62, 67. His closeness to God (VE, 27, 61), his suffering in the shadow of Christ's Golgotha (VE, 35), reminds one of the spiritual thirst of the 19th and 20th centuries. Venichka's never having seen the Kremlin wall until the very end of the novel, is also suggestive of his spiritual quest (VE, 34).

True to his spiritual consciousness and his Christ-like awareness of human suffering, the book ends with these words:

> I did not know that there could be such pain in the world, and I twisted and writhed in agony, ... *And from that time on, I have not regained consciousness, and never will.* (VE, 160, my italics)

This curious end suggests that Venichka's end in front of the Kremlin wall is not an actual but a *symbolic* death in a godless land, and that he will persist in his spiritual quest.

6. Thoughts in the Wake of Erofeev's Moscow-Petushki

Erofeev's spiritual journey in search of God in his *Moscow-Petushki*, – as well as 20th-century Russian underground literature's quest – has something of Boccaccio's profound spiritual despair in his introduction to *The Decameron* over the seeming absence of God during the dreadful outbreak of the Black Death. In a more modern context, Erofeev's novel reminds one also of Malcolm Lowry's *Under the Volcano* (1947) with which it shares the same existential despair and derangement of a drunken consciousness in the wake of profound trauma. Both novels express the modern suffering conscience,[296] with its indictment of twentieth-century inhumanity and the global anguish and destruction that it unleashed.

The "absolute" and "desperate isolation of consciousness" which Stephen Spender in his introduction to *Under the Volcano*[297] found in the novel's central character, the British Consul, as a symptom of the utter inner devastation of a human being, is a perceptive comment on the spiritual state of

---

296 See Ponomareff, "Malcolm Lowry's *Under the Volcano: The Suffering Conscience,*" in his *In the Shadow of the Holocaust & Other Essays, op. cit.,* pp. 122-27.

297 Malcolm Lowry, *Under the Volcano,* With an Introduction by Stephen Spender (New York, 1971), p. xxi.

twentieth-century war-torn and holocaust Russia and Europe generally. It was Alexander Pushkin, in a poem of 1833, who was one of the first to express the fear of losing his mind as a consequence of living under the despotic thumb of Nicholas I.[298] By the time of the Soviet totalitarian state a century later, the reality of human derangement had become an almost daily occurrence nation-wide. The dissident poet Natalya Gorbanevskaya (1936-), who was herself for a brief period of time forcibly confined to a psychiatric asylum in 1968, but allowed to emigrate in 1975, likened the Soviet Union to a madhouse in a poem of 1966.[299] In the 1990 interview Erofeev gave to Leonid Prudovsky, he remembered that even as a six-year-old he had already internalized the insanity of the times which, as we know now, could pick its next victim at random. "You can be insane at any time," Erofeev said but, when pressed by the interviewer, softened the claim by suggesting that he had only pretended to be mad.[300] Certainly, in his novel *Moscow-Petushki,* the overpowering atmosphere of a world gone berserk, was no mask.

298 A. S. Pushkin, *Sochineniya* (3 vols.; Moscow, 1955), I, 328-29.

299 See N. Gorbanevskaya, *Angel derevyannyy* (Ann Arbor, 1982), p. 86.

300 Venedikt Erofeev, *Zapiski psikhopata, op. cit.,* p. 427, my tr.